BETWEEN

➤ **THE** ◀

PIPES

||||||||||||||||||||||||||||||||||||||||||||||

A REVEALING LOOK AT HOCKEY'S LEGENDARY GOALIES

||||||||||||||||||||||||||||||||||||||||||||||

RANDI DRUZIN

BETWEEN

►THE◄

PIPES

GREYSTONE BOOKS
Vancouver/Berkeley

Greystone Books Ltd.
www.greystonebooks.com

Cataloguing data available from Library and Archives Canada
ISBN 978-1-77100-014-7 (pbk.)
ISBN 978-1-77100-015-4 (epub)

Editing by Shirarose Wilensky
Copy editing by Peter Norman
Cover and text design by Jessica Sullivan
Cover photograph by iStockphoto.com
Interior photographs: Hockey Hall of Fame
Printed and bound in Canada by Friesens
Distributed in the U.S. by Publishers Group West

We gratefully acknowledge the financial support of the Canada Council for the Arts, the British Columbia Arts Council, the Province of British Columbia through the Book Publishing Tax Credit and the Government of Canada through the Canada Book Fund for our publishing activities.

Greystone Books is committed to reducing the consumption of old-growth forests in the books it publishes. This book is one step toward that goal.

796.962
D

To my mother, my rock

► CONTENTS ◄

Author's Note *ix*
Foreword by Roy MacGregor *x*

AUTHOR'S NOTE

THE INFORMATION in *Between the Pipes* is gleaned from a myriad of sources. Some of the quotes are taken from books, newspapers, magazines, websites, television and radio broadcasts and DVDs. You will find full source citations for these quotes in the endnotes. Other quotes are taken from interviews conducted by me or, in some cases, by one of my researchers. There are no citations for those quotes. Also, there are no citations in most of the cases in which a person gives a public address, most often at a news conference. Those events are covered by dozens of media outlets and, in many instances, covered live.

Statistical information is included for each goalie. It is worth noting that a goalie's overall rank is determined not by numbers alone but by how he stacks up against other goalies. For example, Ed Belfour recorded 76 shutouts in his career. That is the seventh-best total overall. However, three goalies tied for the sixth-best total (81). As a result, eight goalies had more shutouts than Belfour, and he is ranked ninth overall.

FOREWORD
ROY MACGREGOR

IT WAS THE summer of 1998, a time so long ago that sports was still not a 24-hour-a-day seven-day-a-week treadmill race to see who could get out the most insignificant minutiae first and, preferably, in less than 140 characters. It was in the dying days of storytelling—something that sports journalism had always excelled in. The next-best thing to playing the games was reading about them, and the best sportswriters were—and still are today, but to a diminished extent—as entertaining as the best players in whatever sport they happened to cover.

Ken Whyte was named editor-in-chief of a brand-new national newspaper, and owner Conrad Black handed him a sheaf of blank checks and carte blanche—not exactly the same thing—to bring the *National Post* to fruition in a matter of months. He was told simply to go after the best.

"Who's the best sportswriter in the country?" he asked me over lunch one day.

"Cam Cole," I replied.

"Same as I think," he said and promptly went out and hired Cam Cole, then the star columnist for the *Edmonton Journal*.

Whyte nailed the superstars—columnists like Cole and Christie Blatchford, editors like Martin Newland and David Walmsley from Great Britain, Stephen Meurice and, as sports editor, Graham Parley—but he also gave those editors latitude to bring on young writers and editors who were not well known then but have, in the years since, often risen to the very top of their trade.

The sports department took on a young woman named Randi Druzin. She worked as a copy editor, but she also wanted to write.

Cam Cole and I would often be talking in sports with the likes of terrific young talent like Sean Fitz-Gerald and Chris Jones, both wonderful writers, and this young woman would hold her own, especially on hockey. Turned out she had even played—talking her parents into letting her drop out of figure skating and sign up for a girl's team, where she was, by far, the youngest player on the roster. She knew the game.

Since those early years, Randi has moved on to write and produce for CBC and Global News, but the "hockey writer" inside her would not let her be until she turned, once again, to telling the sorts of stories that first turned heads at the *National Post*.

She decided to write a book about goaltenders a few years ago, to look at hockey's most interesting position and, all too often, the game's most interesting characters. She chose well, from the happy-go-lucky Bernie Parent and Martin Brodeur to the stressed and angry Terry Sawchuk. Ken Dryden, who is to goaltending what Socrates is to philosophy, politely told her he would only grant a long interview if she could prove to him she actually understood the position and its great demands. She got her interview, all right, and brings great insight into one of the game's all-time greatest.

This is a storyteller's book, and as such it is also a reader's book. You don't have to be a goaltender to enjoy it; you just have to be a reader who loves words, loves sports and appreciates the sorts of insights that will never be found in 140 characters or less.

ROY MACGREGOR

300

1

THE TORTURED SOUL
TERRY SAWCHUK

> "I don't think Terry enjoyed his successes.
> That's what happens when you're depressed; you don't
> have the capacity to enjoy what you've accomplished.
> I just never saw that joy in him."
>
> Former Toronto Maple Leafs
> teammate **RON ELLIS**

NEAR THE END of the 1965–66 season, Terry Sawchuk appeared on the cover of *Life* magazine to promote a story called "Hockey Goalies: Their Bludgeoned Faces and Bodies." In the photo, scars criss-cross his face like train tracks across the Great Plains. Looking into the distance, Sawchuk appears to be scowling at someone—perhaps the photographer's assistant—and sending a message to readers. With a curled lip, he seems to be saying, "Go to hell!"

Considered one of the best goalies ever to strap on the pads, Sawchuk was as unpleasant off the ice as he was brilliant on it. Haunted by personal demons and plagued by endless health problems, he was sullen and moody. Thanks to his ornery nature, often worsened by alcohol, he alienated his loved ones, his teammates and just about everyone else. In the end, he died much the way he lived—mad as a hornet.

TERRY SAWCHUK grew up in a working-class neighborhood of Winnipeg, Manitoba, wedged between the Red River and the Canadian Pacific Railway tracks. His father, Louis, who had fled poverty in Ukraine, was known for his toughness. According to legend, he once settled an argument with a former Canadian boxing champion by knocking him out with a single punch. Louis didn't earn much money as a tinsmith, but it was enough to support his wife, Anne, and their five children.

Sawchuk was born in December 1929, the third of four sons. No sooner had he learned to walk than he was spending winter days racing across a backyard rink, chasing a piece of frozen horse dung that served as a puck. Encouraged by his older brother Mitch, he became a goaltender. Mitch, a goalie himself, taught his kid brother the importance of staying balanced and keeping his eye on the puck at all times.

In addition to sharing a passion for hockey, the brothers shared a bed in their modest family home. The arrangement served a dual purpose—it saved space in cramped quarters, and the body heat it generated kept them from waking up as frozen as the horse dung so central to their lives.

Mitch died of a heart attack when he was just 17. His death devastated family members, none more than the brother who had been his constant companion. Louis and Anne, who had lost another son to scarlet fever when Terry was a baby, were too grief-stricken to comfort their remaining children. Left to cope with the pain on his own, Terry cried himself to sleep most nights and descended into a darkness from which he never fully emerged.

Yet his passion for sports continued. On his way to church one Sunday, Sawchuk came across a group of boys playing rugby. Instead of sitting in a pew for the next few hours, he spent that time exchanging bone-crushing blows with his new friends. He emerged from one pileup with a throbbing pain in his right elbow but didn't tell his parents for fear of being punished. The pain subsided over time, but the broken arm didn't heal properly.

It ended up two inches shorter than his left arm and had limited range of motion. It troubled him for the rest of his life.

Sawchuk was a big, chubby kid when he started playing organized hockey, but his prodigious talent was evident right away. It caught the attention of Bob Kinnear, a midget-hockey coach and scout for the Detroit Red Wings. At his urging, the Red Wings invited Sawchuk to Detroit for an evaluation in 1944. The teenager impressed the Red Wings, and they kept an eye on him in the following months.

He was playing for the Junior A Winnipeg Monarchs in the 1945–46 season when the Chicago Blackhawks[1] came calling. That prompted Detroit to spring into action. Kinnear visited the Sawchuk family home and convinced Terry's parents to put his career in the Red Wings' hands.

The young goalie, who had dropped out of school to take a job as a sheet metal worker, soon headed to Galt, Ontario, (now part of Cambridge) to play for the Galt Red Wings of the Ontario Hockey Association. On his own for the first time, Sawchuk lived at a local rooming house.

The team joined the International Hockey League for the 1947–48 season and became the Windsor Spitfires. Sawchuk started in net but didn't stay long. Detroit, desperate to add an elite goalie to the mix, signed him to a professional contract. With the ink drying on the paper, a Red Wings executive handed the teenager a check for $2,000, the equivalent of $19,000 in 2013. For the tinsmith's son, it was a king's ransom.

The Red Wings sent him to the Omaha Knights of the United States Hockey League. He played in 54 games that season, winning 30 of them. He notched four shutouts and led the league with a 3.21 goals-against average. To absolutely no one's surprise, he was named the league's top rookie.

Of course, the season wasn't without its dark periods. On his 18th birthday, he took a stick to the face during a goalmouth scramble, and it cut his right eye. With the dexterity of a winemaker plucking a grape from a vine, a surgeon removed the goalie's eye from its socket, stitched it up, popped it back in and sent him home wearing an eye patch. Much to everyone's relief, Sawchuk didn't lose any vision and returned to the ice two weeks later.

Sawchuk headed east for the 1948–49 season, when he was promoted to the Indianapolis Capitols of the American Hockey League (AHL). He had another stellar season. He played in 67 games, collecting two shutouts and a 3.06 goals-against average. Sawchuk was named the AHL's best rookie.

In Indianapolis, Sawchuk refined his unique style. In the set position, he bent his knees in a crouch so low that his chin was almost resting on his goalie pads. It was an unorthodox stance—goalies stood straight up in those days—but it allowed Sawchuk to maintain balance in various positions and to make quick lateral movements. Nestled behind his pads like an eagle in its nest, Sawchuk peered out at the ice and tracked the puck with relative ease—even as shots from the point and goalmouth traffic became more common. Effective though it was, the stance took a toll on his back; by the end of his career, Sawchuk walked with a permanent stoop and suffered from swayback, which prevented him from sleeping for more than two hours at a time.

NHL

1949-50

The 1949–50 season started off well for him, and then got better. In January, the Detroit Red Wings called him up to replace veteran Harry Lumley, who had suffered an ankle injury. In Sawchuk's NHL debut, the Red Wings lost 4–3 to the Boston Bruins, thanks in part to Detroit's defense corps, which accidentally put two pucks past their own goalie. Still, Sawchuk played well despite his nerves and stayed in net for the next six games. He gave up an average of just two goals a game and posted his first NHL shutout. When Lumley returned to good health, Sawchuk returned to Indianapolis. On the day the Red Wings won their first Stanley Cup in almost a decade, Sawchuk was gone—but not forgotten.

1950-51

Heading into the 1950–51 season, the Red Wings had some of the best young guns in the league: Gordie Howe, Ted Lindsay, Alex Delvecchio, Marcel Pronovost and Red Kelly. Jack Adams, the Red Wings general manager, put his faith in Sawchuk and sent Lumley to the Chicago Blackhawks.

Sawchuk didn't place as much emphasis on covering angles as other goalies. Instead, he relied on lightning-quick reflexes to keep the puck out of the net. In his first season as a starter in Detroit, his acrobatics and explosive movements blew the fedoras off heads in the press box.

"How good is he?" Montreal *Gazette* columnist Dink Carroll wrote, pounding on the keys of his Underwood after one game. "That question was thoroughly discussed after the game in the Leland, which is the hockey hotel in Detroit, and consensus was that he is very, very good. Indeed, [*Montreal Daily Star* columnist] Baz O'Meara, who has seen a lot of puck-stoppers come and go, pronounced him the greatest young goalkeeper he had ever seen."

(Incidentally, O'Meara was known for dubbing Maurice Richard the "Rocket," but he couldn't take credit for Sawchuk's nickname. The goalie's teammates, showing a woeful lack of imagination, called him the "Uke" in reference to his Ukrainian background.)

"Young Mr. Sawchuk is good, all right," Carroll continued breathlessly. "He is big, fast and rarely loses sight of the puck, which is quite a feat in the type of hockey they are playing today." Regaining his composure, Carroll noted Sawchuk might "run into trouble with rebounds because he tended to get his foot behind his stick on low shots and kick the puck straight out in front of him."[2]

Of course, Sawchuk didn't run into trouble. He led all goalies in wins (44) and shutouts (11)—and had the best goals-against average (1.99) among starters. He won the Calder Memorial Trophy as the NHL's top rookie and finished just one goal shy of the Vezina Trophy, which was then awarded to the goalie on the team allowing the fewest number of goals in the regular season. (Since the 1981–82 season, it has been awarded solely on merit.)

Sawchuk and the "Production Line" of Howe, Lindsay and Sid Abel led Detroit to the top of the regular-season standings, with 101 points. Montreal (65 points) defeated Detroit in a six-game semifinal, but the Wings continued to soar.

Just as Sawchuk's prodigious talent was evident from the outset of his NHL career, so was his temper. After being heckled during a game in New York, Sawchuk confronted his tormenter and they exchanged words that would redden the cheeks of a long-haul trucker. A week later, Sawchuk received a summons charging assault. Philip Vetrano, the manager of a grocery store in Brooklyn, claimed the goalie had hit him with his stick. Sawchuk said he had merely waved his hand at Vetrano. A magistrate dismissed the charge four months later.

Cranky and contemptuous, Sawchuk seemed to regard life as something to be endured not embraced. Yet, in some respects, he approached it like a Roman senator at a bacchanalian feast. He smoked cigarettes, drank beer and ate to excess.

1951-52

When Sawchuk, who stood a shade under six feet, showed up for the start of the 1951–52 season weighing 220 pounds, Adams ordered him to lose weight. Sawchuk lost about 40 pounds—and people around him swore he grew surlier with each passing ounce. For the rest of his career, he remained under 200 pounds and as irritable as a baby with diaper rash.

Detroit (100 points) finished at the top of standings again, and Sawchuk played a big part in the team's success. Again, he led all goalies in wins (44) and shutouts (12). He also finished with a 1.90 goals-against average, the best record among starters. He won his first Vezina Trophy.

Sawchuk hoisted another trophy that season too. The Red Wings swept the Toronto Maple Leafs (74 points) in the semifinal then did the same to the Montreal Canadiens (78 points) in the final to win the Stanley Cup. Sawchuk was brilliant, notching four shutouts in eight games and allowing just five goals. He finished the playoffs with a remarkable 0.67 goals-against average.

His performance in the second game against the Leafs was a showstopper. He foiled Leafs captain Ted "Teeder" Kennedy several times. Then, with Detroit protecting a 1–0 lead in the third period, Toronto forwards Max Bentley and Sid Smith burst into the Red Wings zone on a two-on-one. Convinced that Bentley would try to score, Sawchuk moved toward him. But Bentley slid a pass across to Smith, who was in the open. Smith fired a shot at the net and was about to raise his hands in victory when Sawchuk somehow kicked the puck away. At the end of the game, the goalie celebrated his second straight shutout.

Columnist Milt Dunnell recounted Sawchuk's third-period heroics. "His best saves were against Sid Smith," Dunnell wrote in the *Toronto Daily Star*. "On one of the tries, Sid camped on Terry's toecaps when he accepted a pass from Bentley. A little later, Sawchuk did a version of the buck and wing to get his brogan in front of a shot that Smith fired from close quarters." (A "buck and wing" is a tap dance and a "brogan" is an ankle-high leather shoe. How Sawchuk could have done the former while wearing the latter is anyone's guess.)

According to Dunnell, the only way Toronto could have been as strong in net as Detroit is if the Leafs had played two goalies at once. "[Leafs general manager Conn] Smythe was right when he put our estimable citizen, Mr. Walter Broda, back in the Leafs net. The only mistake he made was that he didn't leave

Al Rollins in with him," Dunnell wrote. "With two men in goal, we'd have been about even-steven with the Red Wings, who have four arms and four legs in their cage—all owned by the same guy. His name is Terrance Gordon Sawchuk."

Before signing out, Dunnell added a tidbit about Detroit fans. "There were indications that Leafs are not the only ones who have suffered frustration at Olympia. Detroit fans apparently came armed for a repetition of Tuesday night's brawling among the players," he wrote. "When the hey-rubes didn't happen, the customers had to jettison their ammunition. Hence, four dead fish, an orange and a grapefruit came down from the stands in the final two minutes. Maxie Bentley made a beautiful play on the grapefruit, backhanding it into the second tier."[3]

That summer, Sawchuk underwent one of three surgeries to remove dozens of bone chips from the elbow he had injured as a boy. He displayed 20 of them in a jar on his mantel.

1952-53

Sawchuk needed medical attention again midway through the 1952–53 season, when Delvecchio unleashed a shot in practice that fractured the goalie's foot. Sawchuk was forced to miss six games. His replacement was a hot young goalie named Glenn Hall. Sawchuk's stomach was in knots watching Hall's exploits— he helped the Red Wings win four games during his stint, posting an impressive 1.67 goals-against average—and he feared Hall's arrival would lead to his departure, just as his own arrival three years before had hastened Lumley's departure. Much to Sawchuk's relief, Hall was sent packing and Sawchuk reclaimed his place between the posts.

Fractured foot notwithstanding, Sawchuk barely missed a step. He helped the Red Wings finish first in the regular season with 90 points, posting the most wins (32) and the best goals-against average (1.90) among starters. The Boston Bruins (69 points) eliminated the Red Wings in a six-game semifinal, but Detroit's star netminder won the Vezina Trophy again.

IN WINNIPEG that summer, he checked into a hospital complaining of nausea and a stomach ache. He was diagnosed with appendicitis and went under the knife soon after. (Curiously, he chose not to display his appendix in a jar on his mantel.) When a newspaper ran a photo of a nurse taking care of him during his hospital stay, Sawchuk sent it to Patricia Morey, a teenager he had met a few months before in the Detroit area. Overcome by jealousy, Morey agreed to marry him.

Sawchuk was sullen and withdrawn from the outset of their union, and his behavior only grew more troublesome. Patricia later complained about her husband's heavy drinking, philandering and abuse, both verbal and physical. Incredibly, the marriage lasted 16 years, and the couple had seven children together.

1953-54

Domestic life didn't slow down Sawchuk. In the 1953-54 season, he had more wins (35) than any other NHL goalie. Thanks in part to his exploits, the Red Wings finished first in the regular season, with 88 points, dispatched the Leafs (78 points) in five games in the semifinal, and then squared off against the Canadiens (81 points) in the final. The series went down to the wire.

The Red Wings clinched victory when Tony Leswick, the smallest player on either team, scored in overtime of Game 7. Standing at the top of the face-off circle, the five-foot-seven winger—known as "Mighty Mouse"—took a shot that somehow found its way through a maze of players into the Canadiens net. The record crowd at the Olympia erupted, and the Stanley Cup was awarded to the Red Wings for the third time in five seasons.

Despite Leswick's contribution to the 2-1 victory, much of the credit belonged to Sawchuk, who withstood a blistering attack by Montreal's forwards late in the game. One reporter noted that "the Detroit netminder virtually held off the Frenchmen by himself in a one-sided third period."[4]

The same reporter later recounted Sawchuk's antics off the ice. He laid eyes on Sawchuk for the first time in 1953, when the

MEETING ONLEY

▶   ◀

HOCKEY BOOKS are bursting at the bindings with accounts of Sawchuk's combative behavior, but there is some evidence that points to a kinder, gentler goalie.

Forty years before David Onley became the 28th lieutenant governor of Ontario, he was a Toronto teenager devoted to the Leafs. He was 16 years old when he scored tickets for a game in March 1967. From his wheelchair, he looked on as his beloved Buds got the better of the Chicago Blackhawks, and with thousands of other fans in Maple Leaf Gardens, he raised the roof when Sawchuk posted his 100th shutout in a 3–0 victory.

After the game, Onley rolled up to the dressing room, hoping to catch a glimpse of his heroes. When *Globe and Mail* reporter Dick Beddoes wheeled Onley inside, the man who would one day address crowds of thousands was speechless. "I was in the Leafs dressing room," he says. "I had reached the inner sanctum. No one got in there."

Beddoes introduced him to Sawchuk, who was in front of his stall, standing in a pile of damp goalie equipment. Onley braced for the worst. "Sawchuk was known as an irascible guy—and didn't need the mask on to be scary," he remembers. But the goalie surprised him. Sawchuk grabbed a stick from teammate Bob Pulford and handed it to the gobsmacked teenager. Elated, Onley got some autographs then left. "I was probably in there for five minutes, but it felt like half an hour," he recalls.

After Sawchuk's death, Beddoes wrote a story quoting one of the goalie's four daughters, who said she had few memories of her father and knew little apart from what she had read in the press. Onley wrote a letter to the *Globe and Mail*, sharing his story. He wanted the daughter to know that her father had been a warm and gracious man…if only for a fleeting moment.

goalie was going berserk, shouting obscenities and throwing his skates at another reporter.

When Sawchuk unfastened his goalie pads after the last game of the 1953–54 season, he was looking forward to a summer of rest and relaxation. But it was not to be. Driving home after a day on the links, Sawchuk swerved to avoid an oncoming car and slammed into a tree. He ended up in the hospital once again, this time with a collapsed lung. But in keeping with tradition, he bounced back.

1954-55

Sawchuk's stats were exceptional in the 1954–55 campaign, when he recorded far more wins (40) and shutouts (12) than any other goalie and won his third Vezina Trophy.

The Red Wings were unstoppable too. They soared past the Canadiens in the final weeks of the regular season to finish at the top of the standings, with 95 points. They swept the Leafs (70 points) in the semifinal then beat the Canadiens (93 points) in a seven-game final yet again, to win the Cup.

"Mighty Mouse" wasn't the hero this time. That honor went to Delvecchio, who scored twice in the 3–1 victory. It was sweet vindication for the "bad boy." He had been dropped to the second line earlier that season because of lackadaisical play.

Despite his stunning success that season, Sawchuk's demons began to take hold of his life. Whereas his teammates had once rolled their eyes at their grumpy goalie, they were now concerned about his well-being. His gaunt appearance early in the season led to speculation that his drinking had become a serious problem. After he allowed eight goals in a game against the Bruins in February, the Red Wings scratched his name from the roster. They told the public they wanted him to get some rest and relaxation, but in fact, they wanted him to get some help. They ordered him to undergo psychiatric and alcohol counselling. Sawchuk reportedly cursed at the psychiatrist and ordered him out of his room.[5]

Hall replaced Sawchuk once again and started in two games. Two years earlier, Sawchuk's fears about Hall had been unfounded; this time they weren't.

In June, just seven weeks after the Red Wings won the Cup, they traded their star goalie to the Boston Bruins in a record nine-player deal and chose Hall as their starter. Sawchuk was devastated. In fact, Patricia later said it was the darkest moment of his life.

1955-57

Sawchuk's performance in Boston was good but not great, and he failed to deliver the Bruins to the promised land. They finished fifth in the six-team league and missed the playoffs.

Boston media were not enamored with the Uke, who routinely ordered reporters to "get lost." They were often scathing in their criticism of him. The negative press made Sawchuk even more sullen. He couldn't turn to his family for support; his wife and kids had stayed behind in Michigan, leaving him alone in a sometimes hostile environment.

His situation went from bad to worse midway through his second season in Boston, when he was diagnosed with mononucleosis. Doctors told him he would be in hospital for up to two months. Sawchuk gave them a dismissive wave and returned to the ice after just two weeks. But his play was unspectacular. He was worn down by illness and injury. Just after the holidays, he announced he was quitting. Then, like the Ghost of Christmas Past, he disappeared.

When he didn't show up for practice, the Bruins suspended him. "If he's sick, we'd send him home to rest. But how do we know if he won't see us?" said the team's dumbfounded coach, Milt Schmidt. "If he is [sick] I'll be the first to apologize [for suspending him]."[6]

Sawchuk reappeared near his family home in Michigan, reaming reporters who had been critical of him—and even those who hadn't. "I'm not talking," he said, talking. "I've quit and I'm gonna stay quit. I'm mad. And I got news for you. I'm gonna sue four Boston papers for what they said about me."[7] When one reporter asked him if he was a "quitter," Sawchuk flew into a rage and threatened to punch him in the nose.[8]

Amid reports that he was just one blocked shot away from a nervous breakdown, Sawchuk missed the rest of the season. With the young Don Simmons in net, the Bruins, who finished third overall with 80 points, beat the Red Wings (88 points) in a five-game semifinal. But in the final they lost to the Canadiens (82 points) in as many games.

Sawchuk's marriage became even more troubled. Fed up with his bad behavior, Patricia filed for divorce. Sawchuk talked her out of it, and he asked the Bruins to trade him to the Red Wings, in part to be closer to his family.

The Red Wings sent forward Johnny Bucyk to Beantown— where he later contributed to the Big, Bad Bruins' success—and welcomed Sawchuk back to the fold. The Uke took over for Hall, who had been sent to Chicago after alienating Adams. "Terry is too good to stay out of the game," said Adams. "This is his home, this is where he got his start, this is where he belongs and we're very happy to have him back."[9]

1957-64

Sawchuk spent the next seven seasons in Detroit. The Red Wings were competitive for most of that span, but because of a series of bad trades, were not as good as they had been in the early 1950s. They went to the final three times, but they lost to the Blackhawks once (1961) and the Leafs twice (1963, 1964). In two of those seasons, they missed the playoffs entirely.

Sawchuk was solid during his second stint in Detroit but not dominant. Still, he had his moments. One weekend in January 1964, the Red Wings arrived in frigid Montreal to play the Canadiens. Sawchuk was hounded by reporters eager to know how he felt about being just one shutout away from an NHL record. Sawchuk, even more disagreeable than usual thanks to a wrenched back, had little to say. But his performance that Saturday left people speechless. He held off a blistering Montreal attack late in the game and turned aside 36 shots overall as the Red Wings beat the Canadiens 2–0. With that, Sawchuk recorded his 95th regular-season shutout and broke a record set by George Hainsworth, his childhood hero, in 1936.

After the game, Sawchuk assured media he hadn't thought much about the record during the heat of battle. Then he did the unexpected—he smiled a little. "I guess we'll have to start on the next 95," he told startled reporters.

No one was smiling in the Montreal dressing room. Less than two months earlier, members of the Le Bleu-Blanc-Rouge had looked on helplessly as Sawchuk's teammate Howe notched his 545th career goal to break a record set by Rocket Richard, the pride of French Canada.

Sawchuk had other surprises up his sleeve. He stepped on the ice to start the 1962–63 season wearing—insert collective gasp here—a mask. It was made of fiberglass and sat so close to his face it barely protected him. But Sawchuk had received about 400 stitches in his face at that point and, in recent years, had to contend with an onslaught from the likes of Bobby Hull, whose shot was clocked at 120 miles per hour. He reasoned that even feeble protection was better than none at all. Sawchuk said the mask boosted his confidence, and statistics bore that out. The "Phantom of the Olympia" allowed just 13 goals in the first 10 games of the season as the Red Wings went undefeated.

Proving that old habits die hard, Sawchuk spent time in hospital during his second stint in Detroit. When Leafs forward Bob Pulford skated over the goalie's left hand during a game in Toronto in January 1963, Sawchuk underwent a two-hour operation to repair lacerated tendons. His cast was removed a month later, and he returned to the ice after missing 17 games.

1964-66

Just as they had nine years before, the Red Wings abandoned Sawchuk in favor of a hot, young goalie—this time the upstart was Roger Crozier.

Left unprotected in the 1964 intra-league draft, Sawchuk was picked up by Leafs general manager and coach George "Punch" Imlach. (Imlach did not earn his nickname, as would seem likely given his pugnacious nature, by thumping players who crossed him. He got it as a senior-league player, when he was knocked down during a game, got up in a daze and took a swipe at a trainer who had come to his aid.) Sawchuk was none too pleased with the move, but Imlach was elated. He believed that Sawchuk and the veteran Johnny Bower, a star in his own right, would form a great goaltending duo. He was right.

In their first season as teammates, Bower, then 40 years old, recorded 13 wins and three shutouts in 34 games. He also posted a 2.38 goals-against average—the best in the league. Sawchuk, four years his junior, recorded 17 wins and one shutout in 36 games. He had a 2.56 goals-against average. The Leafs allowed fewer goals than any other team, so Sawchuk and Bower shared the Vezina Trophy—Sawchuk's fourth and Bower's second. (The NHL had been hesitant to set a precedent and give the award to two goalies, but Sawchuk and Bower had insisted on sharing the accolades and the cash prize.)

Despite their shared success, the goalies were polar opposites. Bower worked as hard in practice as he did in games, whereas Sawchuk had no interest in playing unless there was something at stake. "Bower would do everything he could to stop every puck," recalls teammate Ron Ellis. "Once, when he was in the middle of a drill, [Leafs captain] George Armstrong, who was standing off to the side, flipped a puck into the net. Bower got upset. He didn't like the puck getting past him, ever. But Sawchuk was different. During shooting drills, he would stand so close to the goal post, he would leave half the net empty. He didn't want pucks hitting him in practice."

Sawchuk had a simple explanation for his disinterest in drills. "Terry used to say to me, 'John, I'm paid to stop pucks in games, not in practice,'" recalls Bower. He remembers one practice in particular. "There was a stretch where I couldn't stop the puck," Bower says. "I asked Terry to give me some pointers. He watched me from the sidelines even though I would have preferred him standing beside me on the ice. Afterwards, he said, 'John you're doing fine.' I said, 'But Terry, I'm playing lousy!' He didn't really help me at all."

Quick with a firm handshake and a broad smile, Bower was as affable as Sawchuk was surly. "Johnny was very talkative and outgoing, whereas Terry would almost ignore you," recalls Ellis. "I don't think he enjoyed his successes. I never saw joy in him." After most road games, Toronto players would file into a local watering hole and, over a few pints of beer, compare bruises and share stories about their night in the trenches. But Sawchuk would keep his distance. "Once in a while he would come along to the bar," recalls Bower. "But he wouldn't join us at the table. He would sit on a stool by the bar, drinking on his own. I guess it was just his nature."

1966-67

Near the end of the 1966–67 season, Sawchuk posted his 100th shutout in a 3–0 win over the Chicago Blackhawks. "The first hundred are the hardest," he told reporters afterwards.

The Leafs ended the regular season third in the standings with 75 points and were paired up with the Blackhawks in the semifinal. The Blackhawks breathed a sigh of relief. They were a team of young guns that had just set the regular-season points record (94), and the Leafs were an "over-the-hill gang" that included aging stars such as Kelly and Tim Horton as well as two grizzled goalies. The Leafs, whose average age was 31, just shrugged and carried on.

Young Dave Keon led the Leafs attack, while Sawchuk and Bower formed a dynamic duo that gave the team a much-needed "kapow!" in net. Hull and the other Chicago snipers couldn't bring the veteran goalies to heel. Sawchuk's performance in Game 5 was one for the ages. Bower played the first period, but in the words of one reporter, he "was shakier than a bridegroom," so Sawchuk played the next two. The Blackhawks peppered him with shots, but not one crossed the goal line. The Leafs won 4-2.[10]

"There was no statistical justification for the Maple Leafs winning [that] game," wrote columnist Jim Coleman. "They were out-shot, 31-49. Sawchuk blocked 37 shots in the final 40 minutes and this Chicago fusillade included some genuine block-busters fired by Bobby Hull, Dennis Hull, Doug Mohns and Stan Mikita."[11]

"Terry just made up his mind that he was going to challenge [Bobby] Hull," Ellis, one of the few youngsters on that Leafs team, recalls. "You could just see it in his eyes. I don't know what went through his mind, because he didn't share it with you, but maybe he thought, 'This is my last chance to win the Cup.' He just took those blows. After the game, you could see welts on his body where the puck had hit him."

Sawchuk looked "pale and drawn" in the dressing room. He lit up a cigarette and fielded reporters' questions. "I don't remember a thing that went on out there," he said. When asked about being knocked off his feet by a shot from Hull, he grinned ever so slightly. "I guess maybe that's what woke me up." Blackhawks coach Billy Reay said it was the greatest game he had ever seen Sawchuk play.[12]

The Leafs went on to win the series in six games. They then headed into the final looking for redemption against the Habs (77 points), who had brushed them aside in the last two semifinals. Sawchuk started in the opening game in Montreal, but like the frat boy who stumbled into a Tupperware party, he soon wished he had stayed home. The Leafs allowed six goals and scored just two in that contest.

The Leafs won the next two games with Bower in net. He was set to start in the fourth game at home, but when he stretched a hamstring in the warm-up, Sawchuk stepped in. This outing was no better for the Uke than his previous one. The Leafs lost 6–2 again. With Bower unable even to tie the straps on his goalie pads, Imlach started Sawchuk in Game 5 in Montreal. He was masterful. The Leafs won the game 4–1 and headed home leading the series three games to two.

On May 2, Imlach told media he was so confident the Leafs would clinch the series that night, he hadn't booked accommodations in Montreal, where the teams would play a possible Game 7 a few days later. But that did little to calm the nerves of anxious Leafs fans. That night, people gathered around television sets in bars and living rooms across the country to watch the game. Those lucky enough to score tickets for the showdown streamed into Maple Leaf Gardens. The atmosphere was electric by game time, and the fans started chanting "Go Leafs Go!" as soon as the puck dropped.

Sawchuk gave them reason to cheer the entire game. He made 41 saves, many of which brought the crowd to its feet. The Leafs defied the odds by winning the game, the series and the Cup. (It was a great feat, which, as Montreal fans delight in reminding their counterparts in Toronto, the Leafs have not repeated since.) Soon after Armstrong hoisted the Cup, Toronto fans poured onto the streets to celebrate, and their heroes headed to the dressing room.

When reporters entered the room after the 3–1 victory, the players were guzzling champagne and beer and merrily conspiring to toss Imlach into the shower. All the players except Sawchuk, that is. Red Burnett of the *Toronto Daily Star* said the goalie "could have been a million miles away" as he sipped a soft drink in a corner. Sawchuk, normally a heavy drinker, explained that he "[didn't] like champagne or ale" and said he was "too tired to dance around." A few minutes later, he ducked out.[13]

Montreal goalie Lorne "Gump" Worsley had watched Sawchuk's exploits. "He was one of the great ones, but a strange man," Worsley later recalled. "There were days when he would meet you in the rink or on the street and talk for 30 minutes. The next time, he'd walk right past you without saying a word. He drove his own teammates nuts too because he was so eccentric. But maybe that's the mark of a good goaltender. We're not well, you know, or we wouldn't be playing the position."[14]

1967-70

The Leafs left the aging goalie unprotected in the 1967 expansion draft, when the league doubled in size, and he was the first player selected. The Los Angeles Kings—whose coach was Sawchuk's former teammate Kelly—hoped Sawchuk would serve as an anchor for a new, unskilled team. But he was well past his prime. The hard-living, battered and tormented goalie had a stormy stint in the Golden State. He would often give his teammates the cold shoulder, even walking out of a bar when one of them walked in. His relationship with local reporters was strained at best. On the ice, his play was mediocre. His goals-against average ballooned to 3.07. In Game 7 of the quarter-final against the Minnesota North Stars, he allowed five goals in eight minutes. The Kings lost 9–4, and the team's fans pelted Sawchuk with garbage.

Exasperated, the Kings traded him to the Red Wings for the 1968–69 season in exchange for a journeyman forward. In Detroit, where he had once been the toast of the town, Sawchuk was a third-string goalie on a hapless team. He played just 13 games that season, and the Red Wings missed the playoffs. To make matters worse, Patricia finally divorced him.

The Red Wings sent Sawchuk to the New York Rangers for the 1969–70 season. He played just eight games as a backup goalie for Ed Giacomin. Sawchuk played less than a minute of a game in the quarter-final against the Bruins—a series the Rangers ultimately lost—and it proved to be his last appearance in the NHL.

WITH HIS MARRIAGE over and his career just a step behind, Sawchuk was drinking more than ever in the spring of 1970. He and Rangers teammate Ron Stewart—who had also played with Sawchuk in Toronto—rented a summer home in Long Island, New York. While chatting at a pub one night, they downed more than a few pints. An argument over household expenses and cleaning duties started there and ended in the yard of their home. During a scuffle, Sawchuk tripped over a barbecue and smashed into Stewart's knee.

Sawchuk was taken to hospital, where doctors removed his gall bladder in one operation and, in two others, treated a lacerated liver. It was no use. He died when a blood clot traveled into a pulmonary artery. The man who had ascended to the top of the sports world sneering at contemporaries and shaking a clenched fist at the heavens ended up lying motionless on the basement floor of a morgue. He was 40 years old.

The news sent the sports world reeling. "The death of Terry Sawchuk is a tragic and shocking loss to hockey in general and the New York Rangers in particular," said Rangers general manager and coach Emile Francis. "His record speaks for itself. He was one of the great goalies of all time."

A criminal investigation was launched, but a Nassau County grand jury exonerated Stewart, ruling Sawchuk's death accidental. The decision echoed the words of Sawchuk himself, who, while hospitalized, took responsibility for the incident and called his injury a fluke. "There were rumors that Stewie kicked him," Bower recalls more than four decades later. "So I asked George [Armstrong] and he said, 'Don't believe that. Stewie would never do that. Did you ever see him in a fight when he played for us?' I said, 'No.' Then he said, 'Well, that's because he couldn't fight his way out of a paper bag. Sawchuk probably could have beat him in a fight.'"

Sawchuk was buried at a cemetery in Pontiac, Michigan, not far from the home he had shared with Patricia and their kids. Hundreds of people attended, including some of his former teammates. "We all felt sorry for Terry," says Bower. "He ruined his life … It was just a shame to see him go like that."

A year later, Sawchuk was elected to the Hockey Hall of Fame. He was one of a handful of NHL greats who had the three-year waiting period waived. He was also awarded the Lester Patrick Trophy for his contribution to hockey in the United States.

In March 1994, the Red Wings retired his number. Before an afternoon game at Joe Louis Arena—which had taken over from the Olympia as the Red Wings' home in 1979—a banner bearing his famous No. 1 was hoisted to the rafters.

Sawchuk has received other posthumous honors too. In 2001, his image was featured on a Canadian postage stamp, and he was the subject of a collection of poems released in 2008, *Night Work: The Sawchuk Poems*, by Randall Maggs.

Sawchuk's regular-season shutout record (103) was considered unassailable for years, but Martin Brodeur, born two years after Sawchuk died, broke the record on December 21, 2009. The next day, reporter Ken Campbell compared the goalies. Despite "interesting statistical parallels" between them, he said, the two men could not have been more different. Brodeur had a "calming personality," whereas Sawchuk "played most of his career as a chain-smoking nervous wreck who seemed bent on self-destruction. He was perceived as a moody, aloof cuss who seemed to be dogged by the dark clouds of insecurity." Sawchuk, the journalist concluded, was "one of the NHL's true tragic heroes."[15]

SAWCHUK · ALL-TIME RANKING*

REGULAR SEASON			PLAYOFFS		
GAMES	WINS	SO	GAMES	WINS	SO
971 [3rd]	447 [5th]	103 [2nd]	106 [15th]	54 [15th]	12 [9th]

* statistics as of July 2, 2013.

> NHL ALL-STAR TEAM **(1ST)**: 1950–51, 1951–52, 1952–53

> NHL ALL-STAR TEAM **(2ND)**: 1953–54, 1954–55, 1958–59, 1962–63

➤ 2 ◄

THE
TROOPER
GLENN HALL

> "Glenn Hall's 18 years as Mr. Goalie of the National
> Hockey League were an unremitting ordeal.
> Or so he always let on, anyway. If this was partly an act
> he came to enjoy, the portrayal of agony was altogether
> convincing. His suffering seemed genuine."
> Columnist **JIM PROUDFOOT**, in 1993[1]

AFTER DECADES OF blocking imaginary shots in his sleep
and heaving into a bucket, Glenn Hall was fed up. In the summer of 1966, he announced he was unfastening his pads and
hanging up his skates for good. "I'm just tired of hockey," he said.
"I have been meaning to retire since I was 15 years old."[2] Yet he
was back in the Chicago Blackhawks net just weeks later and
had one of his best seasons ever.

The intense pressure to perform pushed Hall to compete in
game after game, despite pulled ligaments, broken bones and
even fever. But he pressed on and, through 16 seasons as an NHL
starter, established himself as one of the most consistent and
most accomplished goalies in NHL history.

WHEN GLENN HALL was born in October 1931 in Humboldt, a
railroad town in central Saskatchewan, job prospects were bleak

and money was scarce. But Hall's childhood was far from dreary. When he wasn't in school, he was playing with his older brother, Doug, and the neighborhood boys.

Hall spent summer days on the baseball diamond. He shied away from playing catcher—which would seem a natural position for a future Hall of Fame goalie—because he didn't have a great throwing arm. But he had a knack for catching, so he headed to the outfield and tracked fly balls until his shirt was drenched in sweat.

On frigid winter days, he pulled a woolen Toronto Maple Leafs sweater over his head, grabbed his stick and ran outside. With his brother and their friends, he chased chunks of frozen horse dung around the frozen pond. Hall played forward early on, distinguishing himself as a great skater and a leader. But when his school team lost its goalie, he moved between the pipes. Hall never looked back. "If you played on a weaker team, well, there was lots of action around the net, and that's what I enjoyed about the game," he explained years later.

Not even in their most fanciful moments did the boys imagine playing professional hockey. Hall later admitted he "didn't think for a minute that hockey players [came] from little towns in Saskatchewan."[3] Still, his talent was undeniable, and he soon started playing competitively. He laced up for the Humboldt Indians of the Saskatchewan Junior Hockey League for two seasons (1947–48, 1948–49).

Hall attended a Detroit Red Wings evaluation camp on a lark and impressed team brass. They persuaded the teenager with the lightning reflexes to join their junior affiliate, the Windsor Spitfires of the Ontario Hockey Association. Hall hit the dusty road and arrived on the southern shore of the Detroit River in 1949. He stayed in Canada's automotive capital for two seasons (1949–50, 1950–51). With the Spitfires, he shifted his career into high gear and won the Red Tilson Trophy as the league's most outstanding player.

Hall returned to Humboldt in the summer of 1951 a conquering hero and became a man in demand among the local ladies. One of them, Pauline Patrick, caught his eye and would later become his wife. The nursing student wasn't the only person Hall won over. Detroit scouts were so impressed by his talent, the team promptly signed him. Hall played in the Red Wings farm system for the next two seasons, taking the ice for both the Edmonton Flyers of the Western Hockey League and the Indianapolis Capitols of the American Hockey League.

To this day, he has vivid memories of his time in Edmonton. He recalls gathering around a ping-pong table with friends at the local YMCA and, with the faint smell of chlorine in the air, taking turns hitting a small plastic ball back and forth. For Hall, it was an opportunity to socialize and a great way to improve his reflexes before training camp.

NHL

1952-55

Detroit called Hall up to be the backup goalie in the final of the 1952 playoffs, but he ended up watching from the sidelines as the formidable Gordie Howe led the Red Wings to a four-game sweep of the Montreal Canadiens, with help from Terry Sawchuk. Sawchuk won the Vezina Trophy—awarded to the goalie(s) on the team allowing the fewest goals—whereas Hall won the dubious distinction of having his name engraved on the Stanley Cup before ever playing in an NHL game.

Hall played six games for the Red Wings in the 1952-53 season after Sawchuk fractured a bone in his foot. He played well, but the club sent him packing, and he spent most of the next two seasons cooling his heels in Edmonton. Hall made two appearances with Detroit in the 1954-55 season, but with Sawchuk still winning games and accolades, Hall was forced to wait in the wings. He got a big break in June 1955, when Detroit, seeing star potential in Hall, sent Sawchuk to the Boston Bruins in a nine-player trade.

1955-57

Hall took center stage in the 1955–56 campaign and brought down the house. He played in all 70 games and recorded 12 shutouts, more than any other goalie in the league. He wasn't stellar in the final, when Montreal, which had finished first overall with 100 points, beat second-place Detroit (76 points) in five games, but he was awarded the Calder Memorial Trophy as the league's best rookie that season.

Hall's unorthodox technique set tongues wagging. He would routinely drop to the ice and, while keeping his knees together, splay his legs to cover the lower corners of the net. He would then spring back to his feet, prepared to move in any direction. With shots coming in faster than ever before, the so-called butterfly style was effective.

Still, purists were as horrified watching Hall play in 1955 as millions of parents were a year later, watching Elvis move his pelvis on *The Ed Sullivan Show*. In those days, singers and hockey goalies were expected to ply their trade standing ramrod straight. "They used to tell us to stand up and not drop to our knees. They also told us to keep our legs together. But that was absolutely stupid. In that case, you may as well have had a steel post positioned in front of the net," Hall says. He recalls that he used to get flak for his playing style, but he was insistent. "I used to say to them, 'If you want someone who plays differently than me, bring him in. Give my job to him.' But they never did, because I was stopping the puck."

Just as hockey fans were coming to terms with *le style papillon*, they had to digest some unsettling information: in the dressing room before each game, Hall would pull his chin toward his chest, bend over a bucket and splatter its walls with the contents of his stomach. "I started doing that in junior hockey. It wasn't peas and carrots I was throwing up. I would take a glass of water and throw it up," he says. "Actually, I was gagging more than throwing up." Hall sometimes vomited mid-game. "The game would begin. Then a couple of minutes into it, Glenn would signal to the referee," recalls retired sports broadcaster Dick Irvin Jr., who was the official scorer at the Montreal Forum then. "He would skate off the ice and head into the dressing room. Everybody knew what he was doing… nobody made a fuss about it. Glenn would come back out and the game would resume. What an awful way to make a living."[4]

You wouldn't catch Hall soaking in a hot bath on game days, listening to whale songs or ocean surf. He embraced the nervous tension that tied his stomach in knots. "A lot of guys like to remain calm, but that never worked for me," he explains six decades later. "For example, I tried whistling and humming on the ice to relax, but I didn't like the way I played." Hall used to insist if he didn't throw up, he wasn't doing all he could to play well. "I set the standard I wanted to play at, and anything less was not acceptable. Playing well is not an accident." Still, the ritual annoyed Pauline, who often chose not to prepare his meals. "How would you like to cook for a guy who's going to throw up what you just made in a matter of hours?" she once asked.[5]

> "I think Glenn was motivated by fear rather than joy. He was just fearful he would let in a goal. He was anxious all the time."
>
> *Former Chicago Blackhawks teammate*
> **DAVE DRYDEN**

HALL PLAYED every game of the 1956–57 season and notched more wins (38) than any of his peers. The Red Wings finished first overall, with 88 points, but lost to the Bruins (80 points) in the semifinal.

In the end, Hall spent about as much time in the Motor City in the 1950s as the Dodge La Femme—a car that was designed for women but that they avoided in droves. Detroit sent him to the Chicago Blackhawks in the summer of 1957, along with Ted Lindsay, a ferocious competitor whose no-holds-barred approach to the game led the NHL to introduce penalties for elbowing and kneeing. Lindsay had infuriated club management by trying to organize a players' union, and Hall was guilty by association. Nonetheless, the two men remained good friends, and almost a decade later, Hall named his youngest son Lindsay in honor of "Terrible Ted."

1957-60

In the late 1950s, structural changes in the steel industry and stockyards were putting blue-collar employees out of work in Chicago, and racial tension was escalating. But the arrival of two young men from rural Canada, one from Saskatchewan and the other from Ontario, offered a welcome distraction—at least for long-suffering hockey fans.

Hall walked into the dressing room under the stands in Chicago Stadium just ahead of a teenager from a dairy farm in Point Anne, Ontario. Broad, muscular and blond, Bobby Hull bore an uncanny resemblance to Aquaman and soon became a superhero in his own right. He had blinding speed and a shot so hard (120 miles per hour) it had goalies shaking in their skates. He notched 47 points in his first season, finishing second in voting for the Calder Trophy. The two stars soon started to gel with Stan Mikita, a skillful playmaker with a great scoring touch who had first donned a Blackhawks jersey in the 1958–59 season, and Pierre Pilote, a small but tenacious defenseman. The four men led Chicago's slow march up the standings.

In the 1958–59 campaign, the Blackhawks made the playoffs for the first time in six years. They lost to the Canadiens in the semifinal that season, and the next one, but Chicago fans were optimistic. They began flocking to Chicago Stadium on Madison Street and soon earned a reputation as the most boisterous in the league. Musician Al Melgard played tunes on the largest theater organ in North America, dramatically raising the decibel level in the arena. In fact, legend has it that when a riot broke out at a boxing match in the 1940s, Melgard pumped up the volume to such an extent that it shattered light bulbs and windows—and sent fans running from the building, clasping their hands to their ears. The cavernous arena, which held almost 19,000 people, seemed to pulsate during games, earning it the moniker "The Madhouse on Madison."

"I could block out all the noise," Hall later recalled with a laugh, "except for the one guy who kept yelling, 'Cold beer! Get your cold beer!'"[6]

The playing surface was more troublesome. It was 15 feet shorter than most other rinks, and the ice was the worst in the league. "We had terrible ice in Chicago," Hall later recalled. "They used to flood it with a hose, and any time you flooded with a hose it would chip out."[7]

1960-67

The Blackhawks finished third in the 1960–61 regular season, with 75 points, and squared off against the Canadiens (92 points) in the semifinal for the third straight year. With more stars than an Elton John Oscar party, Montreal had a formidable offense. But Chicago clinched the series in six games—and Hall didn't allow a single goal in the last two contests. The stands erupted when the final game ended, and the fans "filled the ice with hats, streamers and anything dispensable which happened to be within reach."[8]

Chicago took on Detroit (66 points) in the final. The "Golden Jet" scored two goals to lead the Blackhawks to a 3–2 victory in the first game. The teams duked it out in four more contests, and then headed to Detroit for Game 6 with the Blackhawks leading the series. With momentum on their side, the Blackhawks clipped the Red Wings 5–1 to win their first Stanley Cup since 1938. Ecstatic Chicago players mobbed their goalie at the final buzzer. When the hoopla died down, NHL president Clarence

||||||||||||||||||||||||||||||||||||||||||||||||||||||||||||||||||||||

MASKED MAN

BY THE mid-1960s, hockey fans had grown used to Hall's unorthodox playing style, his unusual rituals and his aversion to training camp. But they weren't prepared for what they saw one night in the 1968–69 season. Hall donned a mask for a game in New York and might have caused less of a stir if he had stepped onto the ice in Madison Square Garden wearing a nun's habit. Two minutes into the game, he berated a referee—perhaps hoping the mask would hide his identity—and was tossed out. He later said his fear of eye injuries is what led him to follow Jacques Plante's lead and cover his face.

||||||||||||||||||||||||||||||||||||||||||||||||||||||||||||||||||||||

Campbell presented the Stanley Cup to beaming Blackhawks captain Ed Litzenberger.

THE BLACKHAWKS continued to play well in the 1961–62 season, finishing third overall with 75 points. With Mikita leading the charge, they upset the Canadiens (98 points) in the semifinal. The Leafs (85 points) then beat the Blackhawks in a six-game final, but Hall and his teammates were unbowed.

Chicago remained one of the NHL's best teams in the next four years and went to the final again in the 1964–65 season. After upsetting the Red Wings (87 points) in the semifinal, the Blackhawks, who had finished third in the regular season with 76 points, pushed the Canadiens (83 points) the distance. The Habs wrapped up the series with a 4–0 victory in Game 7, but Chicago coach Billy Reay didn't fault his goaltender. "Hall should be awarded the Conn Smythe Trophy [as the playoffs' most valuable player] the way he played for us in this series," he said after the Canadiens had been awarded the Cup.[9]

Hall was one of the best goalies in hockey for the first six seasons of the 1960s. He was especially good in the 1962–63 season, when he led the league in wins (30) and had the best goals-against average (2.47) among starters. He and Montreal's star netminder, Jacques Plante, tied for the most shutouts (5). Hall edged out the Leafs' Johnny Bower that year to win his first Vezina Trophy. Chicago's celebrated goalie led the league in wins (34) the following season and again in the 1965–66 campaign (34). He also led the league in shutouts (6) in the 1960–61 season and the one after (9).

Hall's pre-game rituals were as consistent as his play. He continued to embrace his anxiety on game days and to alleviate the tension at the 11th hour by throwing up. The "Ghoulie" sometimes opted for another fail-safe method. He and a team trainer would square off in the dressing room, rear back on their haunches and then lunge at each other like two hungry bears fighting over a slice of salmon—or two professional wrestlers going to the mat. "Believe it or not, we started wrestling each other an hour or two before game time. Glenn would be Sweet Daddy Siki and I'd be Bulldog Brower, and we'd clear the dressing room and go at it hammer and tongs," former Blackhawks trainer Don "Sockeye" Uren later recalled. "Anybody who saw us in there thought we were nuts. We'd beat the heck out of each other, and after a while Glenn would call a halt and say he felt better and was ready to suit up."[10]

HALL SUFFERED pulled groins, bruised bones and countless other injuries. He sustained one of his worst injuries during a game in Toronto. With the clock winding down and the

Blackhawks ahead by two goals, Maple Leafs coach Punch Imlach pulled his goalie and sent out an extra attacker. Toronto forwards swarmed the Chicago net like angry bees. When Hall leapt up to stop one shot, the puck smashed him in the mouth. He left the ice with blood streaming down his face and was replaced by backup goalie Denis DeJordy. Hall emerged from the Blackhawks dressing room after the game, a Chicago win, with more than 20 stitches on his face and a gap in his mouth where a tooth had been. Near the end of his career, Hall estimated he had received more than 250 stitches in his head and face.

Although he spent much of his career wracked with nerves and nursing injuries, Hall kept returning to the net. In fact, he didn't miss a game in his first seven seasons as an NHL starter. His consistency became more celebrated as his streak continued, and he came to be known as "Mr. Goalie." "Facial injuries were just pain. They didn't restrict your movement. And you forgot about pain once you were in game conditions," he told *Sports Illustrated* years later. "I had a reaction to penicillin once after a trip to the dentist, and that almost ended the streak. And the flu would knock you down a little bit. But everyone played with the flu."[11]

The streak ended in November 1962, when Hall hurt his back bending over to adjust his equipment before practice. He started a game against the Bruins the next night anyway but left before the end of the first period. He was diagnosed with a strained ligament. "I guess the fact that I had that string going made me want to play against Boston just that much more… The doctor assured me that I couldn't do myself any harm physically by playing, and I felt good during the warm-up," Hall said. "I was able to take a comfortable stance in the net. But I couldn't move with the play when it crossed in front of the net—and a goalie who can't do that might as well be up in the stands."[12]

At that point, Hall had played 502 straight complete games, not including the playoffs. That record has not been broken, and most hockey experts believe it never will be. NHL teams now have two goalies on their rosters and rely on both. "Remember, goaltenders were expected to play in almost all games back then, and I never thought the streak was that remarkable," Hall says.[13]

IN THE SUMMER of 1965, Hall and his wife purchased a small grain farm in Stony Plain, a town 20 miles west of Edmonton. The Hall family—which by then included sons Patrick and Lindsay and daughters Leslie and Tammy—retreated there in the off-season. For the goalie, it was a welcome respite from the clamor of Chicago.

The property included a barn, and Hall frequently painted it—or so he claimed. "I avoided training camp whenever I could. I said I was painting the barn or something like that," he later admitted. "I never thought training camp was necessary—not for me. There's no learning at training camp. I didn't think I had to be there just so some other fellows could get in shape. So when I didn't report to training camp, and the phone would ring, and someone wanted to know where I was, I'd tell my wife, Pauline, 'Tell them I haven't finished painting the barn.'"[14]

"Years later, my wife and I visited him on the farm," says former teammate Terry Crisp. "I looked around and said, 'There's no barn here.' Then he said, 'Crispy, there it is.' He pointed to a little shed. I swear it was no more than 8 by 12 feet," Crisp recalls, laughing. "It had a wood-burning stove in the middle. He would go in there with a six-pack of beer and listen to a game on the radio."

There was another explanation for Hall's aversion to training camp: the Golden Jet and his brother, Dennis, who joined the Blackhawks in the mid-1960s. Both had shots that could blast a hole through a Sherman tank. "Why would any goalie report to camp on time in those days? Just to stand there facing shots from Bobby or Dennis Hull? Those guys would drive you crazy," Hall says.[15]

➤ THE ASCENDENCY ◄
OF "TONY O"

TONY ESPOSITO is remembered for his distinctive white contoured mask and for being the younger brother of Phil, one of the highest-scoring NHL players in history. But most of all, he's remembered for perfecting the butterfly style of goaltending introduced by Glenn Hall in the 1950s.

After playing 13 games for the Montreal Canadiens in the 1968–69 season, Esposito went to Chicago—and his NHL career took flight. Like Hall, he kept the puck out of the bottom of the net by dropping to his knees with his legs splayed to the sides, and he relied on a quick glove hand to defend the top of the net. His style confounded attackers, and one after another skated away from the Blackhawks net banging their sticks on the ice in frustration.

With "Tony O" in net and Bobby Hull and Stan Mikita on the attack, the Blackhawks soared to the top of the six-team East Division in the 1969–70 season. Esposito finished with the most wins (38) among NHL goaltenders and the most shutouts (15). He also posted the best goals-against average (2.17) among starters. He won the Calder Trophy and the Vezina Trophy.

Two years later, he garnered international attention for his role in the Summit Series. He stood his ground against many Soviet snipers, leading some observers to believe he played better in that legendary series than goaltending partner Ken Dryden.

By the time Esposito retired in 1984, he had won three Vezina Trophies. He had also been named to the NHL's first all-star team three times and its second all-star team twice.

To this day, he tips his hat to Hall. "A lot of Blackhawks fans today never got to see Glenn play and how great he was, but he was the one that started [the butterfly]," Esposito said in an interview in 2009. "He was up there with the best ever. I was lucky I didn't have to come directly after Glenn, or else I'd have had more pressure. We both were agile and had quickness, [but] he was the beginning of the change of goaltending style."[25]

||||||||||||||||||||||||||||||||||||||||||||||||||||||||||||||||||||||||

Although Blackhawks management indulged their star goalie, he gradually became less eager to play. Having battled nerves and injuries for more than two decades, he started to talk about calling it quits. He announced his retirement in 1966. "Without the usual fanfare or pleasing platitudes which go hand in hand with retirement, goaltender Glenn Hall bowed out of hockey Tuesday," the *Edmonton Journal* reported. The paper made reference to his "sleepless nights" and "upset stomachs" and quoted him as saying, "You've got to be stupid to play hockey." Hall changed his mind soon afterwards, possibly enticed by a pay raise, and returned to the Blackhawks net.[16]

THE 1966–67 campaign has been immortalized by long-suffering Leafs fans as their team's last triumphant season. But those not swept away by the current of loving tributes and retrospectives remember that the Blackhawks ran roughshod over their competition in the regular season. Led by Hall and Mikita, they finished atop the standings with 94 points, a whopping 17 points more than second-place Montreal. Splitting goaltending duties evenly, Hall and DeJordy shared the Vezina Trophy.

Still, when the underdog Leafs (75 points) sent the Blackhawks packing in the semifinal, Chicago executives decided it was time for a change. Confident in DeJordy, they left Hall unprotected in the expansion draft, when the league doubled in size. The 36-year-old goalie pondered retirement—again.

1967-71

The St. Louis Blues picked Hall up, hoping he would change his mind about hanging up his skates. Hall claimed he would report to their camp, but only if the money was right. He said he expected to get a letter from the club saying they were glad to have him. "Well, I'll just have to write them back," the goalie said, "and ask them, 'How glad?'"[17]

The Blues made him an offer he couldn't refuse—a salary of around $50,000. It was almost $35,000 less than baseball star Reggie Jackson earned that year, but it was more than Hall had earned in Chicago the previous year. He rewarded them with a solid season. The Blues finished third in the West Division and eighth overall with 70 points. They beat the Philadelphia Flyers (73 points) and the Minnesota North Stars (69 points) to advance to the Cup final against Montreal. The Habs (94 points) beat them in four games, but thanks to Hall's heroics, each contest was decided by just one goal. Hall was awarded the Conn Smythe Trophy—a rare feat for someone from the losing team.

But even amid the celebrations, he didn't lose sight of the tribulations of his job. "When you're a farmer you can miss a strip with the plow and nobody will get too excited," he said. "Now, in this game, when the puck slips behind you into the net, people get excited."[18] That same month, a reporter suggested that Hall "might even find himself getting to like the game," thanks to his high salary.[19]

That might have been a stretch, but he did return to St. Louis for the 1968–69 season. He shared goaltending duties with

Plante, who had come out of retirement to join the Blues. The veterans combined efforts to win the Vezina Trophy. Hall led the league in shutouts (8).

Red Berenson, a talented goal-scorer then in his eighth NHL season, helped lift the Blues to the top of their division and fourth overall, with 88 points. They beat the Flyers (61 points) and the Los Angeles Kings (58 points) before taking on the Canadiens (103 points) in the final for the second straight season. Once again, the Habs swept them aside in four games.

Hall earned his new teammates' respect for his exploits on the ice and his poise elsewhere. Crisp, who spent time in the NHL as a player and then as a coach, recalls a memorable incident. "We were all in the dressing room getting ready for practice. One brash kid was sitting in his stall yelling at the trainers, demanding some tape. Glenn, who was at the other end of the dressing room, walked up to the table in the middle of the room, picked up the tape and handed it to the kid. You could have heard a pin drop. That kid never had an outburst like that again. It just goes to show, you can teach a lesson without uttering a word."

"I was taking a correspondence course at the time, so I would read Shakespeare on road trips. Glenn would read an encyclopedia. He was just so curious about the world and everything else. I just idolized the guy." –DAVE DRYDEN

In the summer of 1969, Hall announced his retirement yet again. Still, Blues coach Scotty Bowman protected the goalie in the intra-league draft. Bowman said he hoped Hall would change his mind and vowed to "work on him" all summer. "Maybe a few months rest will be what he wants," Bowman speculated.[20] As it turned out, Bowman was right.

Hall returned to St. Louis and played 18 games in the 1969–70 season. The Blues placed first in their division and sixth overall with 86 points. They beat the North Stars (60 points) and the

Pittsburgh Penguins (64 points) before squaring off against the Bruins (99 points) in the final.

Hall's appearance in the fourth game of that series has been immortalized—but not for a reason he would have liked. Forty seconds into overtime, a whippersnapper named Bobby Orr passed the puck to Derek Sanderson behind the goal line. Somehow able to see through his shaggy brown hair, Sanderson passed the puck back to the rushing defenseman, who slipped it between Hall's legs to win the game, the series and the Bruins' first Stanley Cup in 29 years.

A photographer snapped a picture a split second later. It shows Orr, who had been tripped by a Blues defenseman, flying through the air with his stick raised in victory while a defeated Hall falls backwards, clasping the crossbar with his glove hand. It's one of the most famous images in sports history. "If I had royalties on that one [photograph], I'd never have to work again. I have fun with it, though. It doesn't bother me [that] they show it all the time," Hall said 16 years later. "I tell everyone that when Orr scores and gets hit, by the time he [came] down, I was in the dressing room and already half-showered."[21]

In the 1970–71 season, the Blues bowed out of the playoffs early, losing to the North Stars in the quarter-final. The Blues left Hall unprotected that summer, and no one picked up the 39-year-old goalie in the intra-league draft. He announced his retirement again. This time, it was for real.

RETIREMENT

Hall retired to his farm, and his oft-painted barn, in Stony Plain. But he couldn't give up hockey entirely. He coached his son's junior team for a while, and when the World Hockey Association was established in 1972, he took a job as assistant coach with the Alberta Oilers. Hall took the game as seriously as he had during his playing days; after one loss, Oilers coach Ray Kinasewich heard him retching in the bathroom. That job lasted less than a year.

The following year, Hall's name came up during a police inquiry into organized crime in Quebec. Former Montreal bookmaker Theodore Aboud told the inquiry he bet on some hockey games in the early 1960s after getting a tip that the Chicago Blackhawks goalie had bet against his own team. The hockey world shook with disbelief. Columnist Jim Coleman contacted former Blackhawks coach Rudy Pilous, who "screamed incredulously" when told of the accusation and "lay on the floor hooting and hollering in merriment." Coleman quoted Pilous as saying, "Glenn Hall wouldn't bet that Wednesday follows Tuesday. Glenn Hall and Bobby Hull were the two guys on our Chicago hockey team who didn't believe in spending money recklessly. Kidding aside, any suggestion that Glenn Hall ever bet on an NHL hockey game is just too bloody crazy for words."[22]

Hall denied the accusations. "The effect of those statements has been devastating as far as my family and I are concerned. There is no truth in them," he said. "My only hope is that people believe me when I say there is no truth in those statements."[23]

Hall need not have worried. The hubbub passed as quickly as the contents of his stomach on a game day—and he soldiered on, just as he always had.

In 1975, the St. Louis Blues hired him as goaltender consultant. A few times a year, he traveled to St. Louis to work with John Davidson, a goalie who later played for the New York Rangers then went on to become a well-known broadcaster.

Also that year, Hall was inducted into the Hockey Hall of Fame. Although he had spent most of his playing days with the Blackhawks, he chose to wear a Blues jersey for his official portrait. He admitted to having "a soft spot in [his] heart for the Blues. [Missouri is] a beautiful state. You get away, out in the country. I guess that's what I liked best."[24]

A few years later, the Colorado Rockies hired Hall to work with the team's goalies. When the club moved to New Jersey, Hall moved on. He joined the Calgary Flames and stayed with the team for more than 15 years.

IN CALGARY, he shaped an agile young goalie named Mike Vernon into one of the best netminders in the NHL. Vernon was a stand-up goalie but gradually adopted elements of the butterfly style. In 1986, Hall predicted Vernon would help the Flames win their first Stanley Cup—and that is exactly what happened, in 1989. Eighteen years after he retired, Hall's name was engraved on hockey's Holy Grail for the third time.

Also that season, the Blackhawks retired Hall's jersey (No. 1), along with that of Tony Esposito (No. 35). When Hall stepped onto the ice, the crowd gave him a standing ovation. Taking the microphone, he simply thanked the fans for "putting up" with him during his time with the Blackhawks. A banner with his name was then raised to the rafters of Chicago Stadium.

It was lowered almost six years later, in another pre-game ceremony. The historic arena was to be torn down, and the banners honoring Hall, Esposito, Hull and Mikita were to be moved across the street, to the United Center. Fans jammed the arena for the ceremony in April 1994. They whistled, stomped their feet and banged on the glass around the ice as the banners were lowered into the open arms of their heroes. The following year, the faithful looked on in tears as a wrecking ball smashed the historic arena to bits. Like an ambitious showgirl, the console of the famous organ hooked up with a wealthy businessman and headed to Vegas.

HALL EASED into retirement in subsequent years, spending most of his time tending to his farm, hunting and playing the occasional round of golf.

In 2005, the city of Humboldt erected a monument to his career, in Glenn Hall Park. An illustration of Hall is front and center on a black board with red trim. It's surrounded by photos of Hall in action. The park is located near Highway 5, now known as—you guessed it—Glenn Hall Drive.

In November 2005, Hall attended a game between the Calgary Flames and the San Jose Sharks. The contest marked the

NHL debut of his grandson, Grant Stevenson. Hall was delighted to see the winger score his first goal in the league. (Stevenson played 47 games for the Sharks that season, and then returned to the American Hockey League.)

Pauline passed away four years later. Hall now lives alone, puttering around his 153-acre property. He spends time in the garden and enjoys the company of his children and grandchildren.

The infamous red barn is just down the lane from his house. He doesn't paint it frequently these days, and he's not about to—that is, unless the Blackhawks suddenly demand he attend training camp. The prospect of playing makes him queasy—just as it always has. "There was always the fear that you weren't going to do well, even though you had done all the things you needed to do to play well," Hall says, looking back on his career. "You knew you were quick enough and smart enough and had researched the opposition, but there was still a fear you would not play well."

HALL · ALL-TIME RANKING*

REGULAR SEASON			PLAYOFFS		
GAMES	**WINS**	**SO**	**GAMES**	**WINS**	**SO**
906 [6th]	407 [8th]	84 [4th]	115 [12th]	49 [17th]	6 [23rd]

* statistics as of July 2, 2013.

> NHL ALL-STAR TEAM **(1ST)**: 1956-57, 1957-58, 1959-60, 1962-63, 1963-64, 1965-66
> NHL ALL-STAR TEAM **(2ND)**: 1955-56, 1960-61, 1961-62, 1966-67

3

||||||||||||||||||||||||||||||||||||||||||

THE
MAVERICK
JACQUES PLANTE

||||||||||||||||||||||||||||||||||||||||||

"One of the contributing factors to his innovative
style was his personality. Plante just didn't care what
others thought or did. He was a maverick."

Hockey historian **KEVIN SHEA**

MONTREAL CANADIENS goalie Jacques Plante would
stop booming shots with his limbs, his torso and even his head.
He would play with broken bones and with blood streaming
down his face. But he wouldn't stay at the Royal York Hotel.

"Since the atmosphere of the Royal York doesn't agree with
Plante's asthma, the goalie always stays at another hotel near
Maple Leaf Gardens when the Canadiens come to Toronto," a
wire service reported the day of a game in March 1963. "However, he comes down [to the Royal York] to eat steak with his
teammates, and also attends the club meetings on the morning
before a game."

Plante had missed practice the previous day, complaining of
an asthma attack. "I stayed around [the Royal York] too long,"
he explained, while watching his teammates put through their
paces at the Gardens. "When I went back to my own hotel, I
couldn't breathe."[1]

Fans, teammates and even his coach sneered at Plante's aversion to the landmark hotel, just as they derided his decision to wear a mask and ridiculed his passion for knitting. But Plante couldn't have cared less. He marched to a different drummer. Always.

JACQUES PLANTE entered the world in January 1929, in Mont-Carmel, a small community in eastern Quebec. He was the first of 11 children born to Palma and Xavier Plante. Soon after he was born, the family moved to Shawinigan Falls, on the Saint-Maurice River, where his father worked as a machinist.

Jacques took his first tentative steps on ice when he was four years old, holding a stick his father had carved from a tree root. For the next few winters, he chased a tennis ball around the ice. It proved to be challenging, and not just because he didn't have skates. Plante suffered from asthma. More than once, he buckled over, coughing and wheezing as his bronchial tubes narrowed. Hesitant to give up playing hockey, Plante made a practical decision—he became a goaltender.

He soon took to the ice wearing skates and makeshift pads— stuffed potato sacks reinforced with wood panels. He also wore a toque to protect his ears from frostbite and to prevent his head from assuming the properties of a frozen cabbage. Plante's mother made her son's first toque, and then he took over. After mastering the basic knit and purl stitches, he began making his own toques and undershirts. He continued knitting for the rest of his life, packing balls of yarn in his suitcase even when he could afford to buy outerwear.

PLANTE STARTED playing organized hockey as a student at L'école St-Maurice. On that fateful day, he was standing in the clubhouse with his back against a stove, watching the school team practice. When the goalie stormed off the ice after an argument with the coach, Plante dashed outside. The 12-year-old convinced the coach to let him lace up, even though he was five years younger than the other players. It was soon apparent that Plante could hold his own, and he became the team's starter. Within three years, he was playing in four different age groups and on an industrial league team. The factory team paid Plante 50 cents per game, on the condition that he didn't tell his teammates.

Plante soon started to receive job offers. A British team tried to recruit him, as did the Providence Reds of the American Hockey League (AHL). But Plante turned down those offers, opting to finish high school. He graduated in 1947 and started working as a clerk in a local factory. A few weeks later, the Quebec Citadelles of the Quebec Junior Hockey League made an offer he couldn't refuse. Plante donned the team jersey for the 1947–48 season and plied his trade against future NHL stars such as Jean Beliveau.

When Beliveau's Victoriaville Tigres played against the Citadelles, he came across an unusual sight. When the puck skidded into the Citadelles end, the team's lanky, toque-wearing goalie skated out of his crease and stopped it behind his net or passed it up ice to his defensemen. Plante reasoned that as long as he was in control of the puck, opponents couldn't shoot it at him. Plante's wandering ways rankled his coaches—traditionalists who believed a goalie's place was at home, between the pipes. But when his coaches scolded him, Plante just shrugged and continued to play as he saw fit. Such defiance might have cost a lesser goalie his job, but Plante was too valuable to the team. As agile as he was tactical, Plante stood head and shoulders above the competition from the start.

While playing with the Citadelles, Plante married Jacqueline Gagne. In the next five years the couple had two sons, Michel and Richard.

NHL teams soon came calling. Although Plante was a Francophone who had grown up in the hallowed glow of Les Glorieux, his sights were set on another team. He felt he had a better chance of becoming a starter with the New York Rangers than the Montreal Canadiens. The Habs had two top-notch goalies (Bill Durnan and Gerry McNeil), whereas the Rangers had just one (Chuck Rayner). But the Canadiens persevered and signed Plante after his second season with the Citadelles. They sent him to their farm team, the Montreal Royals of the Quebec Senior Hockey League.

In the summer of 1952, after his third season with the Royals, Plante underwent surgery to fix his left wrist. He had broken it on a playground slide years before, and it had never healed properly. He had trouble catching the puck with his glove hand. Aware that the problem diminished his career prospects, he went through with the surgery despite the risks. It was successful.

Midway through the 1952–53 season, the Canadiens sent him to the Buffalo Bisons of the AHL. Plante was a strong addition to a weak team. "Throughout the American Hockey League today everyone buzzed excitedly about the same subject—Buffalo's fabulous new goalie, Jacques Plante," a wire service reported after one game. "Plante, who had scored successive shutouts against Pittsburgh and Syracuse prior to last night's game with Cleveland, finally was scored upon midway through the third period after a shutout string which stretched to almost three full hours of goal tending, but he paced the Bisons to a 2–1 triumph anyway." Fans started calling Plante "Jake the Snake." He loved the adulation.[2]

NHL

1952-53

Durnan had retired at the end of the 1949–50 season and left McNeil the undisputed champion of the Canadiens crease. In January 1953, McNeil fractured his jaw. It was a bad break for him but not for Plante. When the Canadiens called the Bisons goalie, he picked up his belongings—including his knitting needles—and left the smokestacks of Buffalo behind.

He gave up just four goals in three games for the Canadiens, all of them victories. Plante's athleticism impressed the Habs head coach, but his appearance didn't. Dick Irvin Sr. felt the head of an NHL goalie was no place for a toque. He ordered Plante to play without one. The goalie resisted, but when his toques disappeared from the dressing room, he had no choice but to play *sans chapeau*.

Relegated to the sidelines during the playoffs, he watched Montreal, which had finished second overall in the six-team

> "Once I went up to him after the game and said, 'You were great Jacques, but you only had ten shots.' He said, with a heavy accent, 'You bastard, Bassgate!'"
>
> *Former New York Ranger*
> **ANDY BATHGATE**

league with 75 points, fall behind the Chicago Blackhawks (69 points) three games to two in the semifinal. With the clock winding down to the start of Game 6 in Chicago, the butterflies in McNeil's stomach became pterodactyls. A nervous wreck, he urged Irvin to replace him with Plante "for the good of the team." When Irvin informed Plante that he would be playing, the startled goalie responded, "What? Me?"[3]

In the dressing room before the game, Plante was so nervous that he had trouble tying his skate laces. Canadiens superstar Maurice "Rocket" Richard approached Plante and showed him his own hands. They were also shaking. Richard assured the 24-year-old goalie that he would calm down once the game started—and he was right. Plante made an excellent glove save early on and was solid for the rest of the game. The Habs bottled up the Blackhawks offense, scoring one goal in the first period and two in the second. Plante stopped 23 shots as the Canadiens won 3–0.[4]

Irvin considered putting McNeil back in net for Game 7, certain that the goalie had rebounded from "his little crack-up and nervousness." But during practice the day before the deciding game, Richard unleashed a shot that struck McNeil in the ankle and sent him back to the sidelines. When Plante was tapped to start, Blackhawks coach Sid Abel told reporters he felt confident. "Plante can't be better than McNeil." As it turned out, Plante stopped 32 shots and allowed just one goal as the Canadiens won the game 4–1, and a berth in the Stanley Cup final.[5]

(In its coverage of the game, a wire service managed to both compliment and insult Habs forward Eddie Mazur. It reported that he had scored two goals but described him as a "big, 23-year-old rookie with a beak nose.")[6]

Plante played in the first two games of the final against the Boston Bruins (69 points), notching a win and a loss. McNeil played in the next three games, all of which the Habs won. Forward Elmer Lach, one of the best playmakers in the league, blasted the puck into the Bruins net a minute into overtime of Game 5, giving the Habs a 1–0 win. Lights blinked, sirens wailed and the organ boomed as fans in the Forum celebrated the team's first Cup in seven years.

1953-55

In each of the next two seasons, Gordie Howe led the Detroit Red Wings past the Canadiens in the overall standings and in the Cup final, adding the sweet scent of success to that "new car smell" in the Motor City. Detroit's Terry Sawchuk was the top dog among NHL goaltenders.

For most of the 1953-54 season, McNeil tended the net in Montreal while Plante brought spectators to their feet in Buffalo. But when McNeil suffered another injury in February, Plante returned to the Habs. In 17 regular-season games, he recorded a 1.59 goals-against average. He played in eight of the Canadiens' 11 playoff games, posting a 1.88 goals-against average.

➤ PUTTING PEN TO PAPER ◄

HAVING STUDIED the game of hockey and the art of goaltending for years, Plante decided to share his observations with the public late in his career. He wrote a book called *Goaltending* in 1972. It offers goalies instruction on training regimes, equipment and styles of play. It also gives coaches advice on how to groom young netminders. To this day, many people regard it as the seminal book on playing between the pipes. Plante also wrote about hockey for several periodicals.

||||||||||||||||||||||||||||||||||||||||||||||||||||||||||||||||||||||||

By the fall of 1954, McNeil's nerves were shot. Just before the start of the regular season, he bid farewell to the Canadiens. He confessed to having "a nervous temperament" and said he wanted to "do something that involve[d] less worry." He mentioned that he had recently purchased a service station.[7]

Plante became the team's starter. The more he played, the more people talked about his unorthodox style. He continued to skate out of the crease—not just to play the puck but also to cut down shooters' angles by reducing the amount of open net available to them. His analytical approach to the game was legendary. He filled notebooks with his observations about the league's shooters and even its arenas.

Plante spent hours in his hotel room writing, knitting or answering fan mail. He was alone at those times—and at most other times. He didn't socialize with his teammates at all. Even on the team bus, when they played cards or shot the breeze, Plante sat on his own, several rows away. He believed friendships required more effort than they were worth and didn't hesitate to say so.

"Goalies will sometimes be a little different. Jacques liked to be by himself. That's just the way he was," says Beliveau, the Canadiens captain from 1961 to 1971. "You know, the other thing I noticed is that some goalies are tight with their money. I remember some of the players talking about Jacques being like that. I used to tell them, 'Just leave him alone. That's his business. He's getting the job done on the ice, so just let him be.'"

"Each of us would put two dollars in the pot to buy some drinks. If Jacques had just one drink, he would take back one of his dollars," recalls Dickie Moore, who played for the Habs for 12 seasons, starting in 1951. "But you know, I understood Jacques. He came from a working-class family, like myself. I understood what he was doing. He was saving as much money as he could for a rainy day."

1955-56

In the 1955–56 season it became clear the Canadiens were poised to push the Red Wings off their perch at the top of the NHL. Rocket Richard had a strong supporting cast. Beliveau, a strong skater who was nearly impossible to stop, and Bert Olmstead were among the league's top scorers, while Bernie "Boom Boom" Geoffrion's hard shots and aggressive play were giving goalies fits. Doug Harvey was patrolling the blue line with the diligence of an East German border guard—and Plante was excellent.

The Habs finished first overall (100 points) in the regular season. Plante notched more wins (42) than any other goaltender and posted the best goals-against average (1.88) among starters. He won his first Vezina Trophy, which was then awarded to the netminder(s) on the team allowing the fewest goals.

Montreal defeated New York (74 points) in the semifinal, and then took on the Red Wings (76 points) in the final. Plante was spectacular in Game 5, stopping Howe and his teammates time and again. Beliveau, Richard and Geoffrion each scored to give the Canadiens a 3–1 victory, and the Stanley Cup, in front of 14,000 screaming fans.

"At the risk of being monotonous, this recorder feels impelled to say once again that Jacques Plante disappointed critics who had nominated him as the humpty-dumpty of lord mayor's show," wrote columnist Milt Dunnell. "In the last two games, Plante stood off the Detroit shooters until the Montreal powerhouse started humming."[8]

1956-57

The Red Wings were formidable the following season when both Howe and Ted Lindsay went on point-scoring tears. Detroit finished first overall with 88 points, six more than second-place Montreal.

Plante's asthma acted up in November and forced him to miss eight games. But he managed to end the season with the best goals-against average (2.00) and the most shutouts (nine) in the NHL. He also won his second Vezina Trophy.

The Habs defeated the Rangers (66 points) in the semifinal, while the Bruins (80 points) managed to upset Detroit. Both series ended in five games.

Montreal battered Boston in the first three games of the final, out-scoring their rivals 10–3. The Bruins regained their footing to notch a 2–0 win in Game 4. The next game was a rough-and-tumble affair that included a slugfest between Olmstead and Fern Flaman. The Bruins defenseman won the fight, but his team lost the game, 5–1, and the series. At the end, the Bruins "congratulated their conquerors as crowds of spectators piled over the boards to the ice," a wire service reported. "The Cup was presented to captain Maurice (Rocket) Richard of the Canadiens by Cooper Smeaton, cup trustee."[9]

Plante said he couldn't afford to take a holiday because he was in the process of building a $40,000 house. Too bad, Dunnell concluded in the *Toronto Daily Star*: "Plante needs a vacation. He dropped close to 30 pounds during the season."[10]

1957-58

Injuries hampered the Canadiens in the 1957–58 regular season. But while established snipers such as Richard, Beliveau and Geoffrion spent time on the sidelines, other stars emerged. Henri Richard stepped out of his famous brother's shadow by notching the second-highest point total (80) in the NHL. (The five-foot-seven forward was nicknamed the "Pocket Rocket" because he was small enough to fit into the back pocket of his famous older brother, Maurice "Rocket" Richard.) Moore, a tenacious forward who rushed into the corners like a bull charging at a matador, won the league scoring title (84 points), even though he played some of it wearing a cast over a broken wrist. (Moore would go on to win another scoring title the following year.)

Plante endured more asthma-related problems and suffered a concussion. He missed 13 games but managed to lead all goalies in wins (34), shutouts (9) and goals-against average (2.11). He won his third Vezina Trophy.

After finishing first overall with 96 points, the Canadiens crushed the Red Wings (70 points) 8–1 in the first game of the playoffs and won the next three to complete a semifinal sweep. Rocket Richard was the star of the final game, silencing spectators in Olympia Stadium by scoring three goals in a 4–3 Habs win.

The Habs met the Bruins (69 points) in the final. The series was tied when the teams met for Game 3, in Boston. Plante came up with some big saves as the Richard brothers combined to score all the goals in Montreal's 3–0 win. It was Plante's only shutout of the 1958 playoffs.

The Canadiens won the series in six games. In the dressing room after the last game, a 5–3 win, the sudden release of pressure led Plante to break down. "I'm glad it's over," he said, his cheeks wet with tears. "It was a tough series. Tonight it was very tough. And I had an asthma attack earlier in the day."[11]

The next day, more than two thousand fans jammed into Montreal's Windsor Station to welcome home the Stanley Cup champions.

PLANTE, WHO had played in all 10 playoff games and posted the league's best goals-against average (1.94), had many die-hard fans—but his coach wasn't one of them. Hector "Toe" Blake, who had taken over from Irvin in 1955, was annoyed that Plante sat out so many games with bronchial problems, and he suspected the goalie's asthma was not as severe as he claimed. The two men mixed like pineapples and milk. Blake, a traditional "hockey man," cut a stern figure standing behind the bench in a fedora. He cast a wary eye at Plante, an aesthete who was proud of his cooking, sewing and knitting skills.

"Sometimes [Blake] would want Jacques to change something. That would lead to an argument," recalls Moore. "The rest of us would get upset when Jacques went against Blake because we considered [the coach] to be just like one of the players."

1958-59

The Rocket's red glare dimmed somewhat in the 1958–59 campaign, the 17th season of his NHL career. But Moore and Beliveau picked up the slack, finishing one-two in league scoring. Montreal finished first overall with 91 points. Plante had another solid season, leading NHL goalies with the most wins (38) and shutouts (nine) and the best goals-against average (2.16). He won his fourth Vezina Trophy.

The Habs met Chicago (69 points) in the semifinal. In Game 6, with the Habs enjoying the upper hand, the contest suddenly came to a halt. Frustrated Chicago fans tossed debris on the ice. Two plucky spectators leapt over the boards and swung at referee Red Storey, while supporters of each team came to blows behind the Montreal bench. Order was restored after 15 minutes, and Montreal went on to win the game, 5–4, and the series.

The Canadiens then faced the Toronto Maple Leafs (65 points). The Leafs had prevailed in the teams' previous final showdown, in 1951, but this series would be different. The Canadiens won it in five games and drank champagne from the Cup for the fourth straight year. Plante was in net for all 11 games and recorded a 2.33 goals-against average—the best among all goalies.

1959-60

Montreal continued its domination the following season. Of the 20 top scorers in the NHL, 6 played for the Canadiens. Beliveau led his teammates with 74 points, and Harvey was solid on the blue line after a disappointing 1958–59 season. Plante won more games (40) than any other goalie and had the best goals-against average (2.54) among starters. He won his fifth Vezina Trophy.

The Habs ended the regular season at the top of the standings with 92 points and beat Chicago (69 points) in the semifinal for the second straight year. It wasn't even close this time; the Canadiens swept the Blackhawks aside in four games, with Plante recording shutouts in the last two contests.

The Habs won their fifth consecutive championship, beating the Leafs (79 points) in four straight games in the final. The Rocket hoisted the Holy Grail for the last time. He retired a few months later.

ALTHOUGH THE HABS didn't lose a single playoff game, that season is best remembered for another reason. Even the most casual hockey fan is familiar with the events of November 1, 1959.

On that Sunday night, the Canadiens and Rangers squared off in New York. Early in the first period, Rangers star Andy Bathgate fired a shot that hit Plante in the face. The goalie headed to the dressing room with blood streaming down his face. A Rangers doctor used sutures to close the cut on his nose and upper lip, but Plante, who had received hundreds of stitches in previous years and had broken his nose and his cheekbones several times, refused to return to the ice unless he could wear the fiberglass mask he had been sporting in practice for three years.

Blake balked at first. In his opinion, a goalie who didn't fear for his life was a complacent goalie. Besides, wearing a mask was about as manly as wearing nylon stockings. But Blake relented when faced with the prospect of replacing his elite goaltender with a Madison Square Garden maintenance worker or middle-aged usher. (NHL teams didn't have backup goalies at the time. Home teams were expected to supply emergency replacements as needed.) Blake agreed to let Plante wear the mask on the condition that the goalie discard it when the cut healed. Plante agreed and returned to the ice with his face covered.

All 15,925 spectators did a double take when Plante took up his position between the pipes wearing "a plastic, flesh-colored mask with slits for his eyes and mouth."[12]

"Only a day late for Halloween, the mask made its appearance in the National Hockey League and both goalie Jacques Plante, who wore it, and Coach Toe Blake, who once hated it, think it might be around to stay," reported a wire service.[13]

"It's the coming thing in the game," Blake said, appearing more receptive to the mask than his actions indicated. "The time will come when they'll have an even better mask than Plante's and it'll be standard equipment for goalies."[14]

"I'll tell you this—I'm much less cautious about mixing into a goal-mouth melee when I wear the mask," Plante said. "And if they'll let me wear it all the time, I can play until I'm 45."[15]

The Canadiens won the game 3–1. In subsequent weeks, the masked man led his team to a 10-game winning streak. He gave up just 13 goals in his first 11 games with the mask, silencing Blake and others who claimed it impaired his vision. In March,

Plante started a game in Detroit without his mask. The Red Wings shut out the Canadiens, 3–0. Plante put the mask back on for the next game and never took it off—except, rumor has it, to eat, drink and sleep.

Suddenly presented with an alternative to reconstructive facial surgery, other goalies followed suit—and in a matter of years, more goalies than not were wearing masks.

"I don't go out with other players. Why should I, if I have nothing to say?"[26]

JACQUES PLANTE

More than 50 years later, Bathgate remembers that historic game vividly. He recalls that Plante checked him early on, sending him crashing into the boards. "A teammate helped me up, and I went to the dressing room. I should have gotten stitches, but I didn't. I figured I had to get back on the ice, or I would become gun-shy," Bathgate says. "My head was clear when I went back on. I got the puck, skated down the wing and shot it at Plante, hoping to hit him in the cheek. I thought, 'I'll give him a little boo-boo to let him know there are ways of getting even.' I wanted to let him know that if you play around, you will get hurt too. He left the ice to get stitched up and returned wearing that mask. All of us on the bench thought, 'What the hell is this? You big chicken!'"

1960-61

The Canadiens' offensive might was still awe-inspiring in the 1960–61 season. Montreal was the top-scoring team for the eighth straight campaign, with Geoffrion and Beliveau leading the pack. But for the first time in six seasons, the team didn't allow the fewest goals in the NHL. Plante began suffering from intense pain in his left knee because of an earlier injury and ended up playing in just 40 NHL games that season. (He joined the Montreal Royals for eight games.) Charlie Hodge took his place in the Habs net.

The Canadiens finished the season first with 92 points, and then squared off against Chicago in the semifinal yet again. After spending decades waiting in the wings, the Blackhawks had taken center stage and recorded the most regular-season points (75) in the team's history. Chicago boasted a nucleus of elite players, including defenseman Pierre Pilote, goalie Glenn Hall and Bobby Hull, who was fast, strong and boasted a booming shot.

The third game of the series turned out to be one for the ages. Murray Balfour scored in the third overtime period to win the game for the Blackhawks and put them ahead in the series. Convinced a Chicago player had been in the crease when the goal had been scored, Plante and a few of his teammates skated after referee Dalton McArthur as he headed to the bench, imploring him to reconsider. McArthur was leaning over the boards, talking to the scorekeeper, when Blake charged across the ice and took a swing at him, making contact with the stunned official's neck and shoulder. Two Habs players grabbed their coach and escorted him, kicking and screaming, to the Montreal dressing room. "McArthur had been giving us trouble all season, and what I did was touched off by something that has been building up for a long time," Blake explained. "I knew I was doing wrong, but I couldn't help myself."[16]

The league fined Blake $2,000 but didn't suspend him because, in the words of President Clarence Campbell, "there was nothing vicious about the attack and no injury was sustained."[17]

The Blackhawks were leading the series three games to two when the puck dropped for Game 6 in Chicago nine days later. Riding a wave of adulation from more than 16,000 boisterous spectators, the Blackhawks overwhelmed the Canadiens. Chicago posted a 3–0 win to clinch the series. When the game ended, elated fans threw hats, papers and other objects onto the ice. One imaginative soul contributed a skull—origin unknown.

It rolled toward Plante, who swept it into his net. Twelve days later, the Blackhawks dispatched the Red Wings to win their first Cup since 1938.

1961-62

The Canadiens finished first in the standings (98 points) for the fifth straight season, even without the services of Harvey, who had been traded in the off-season, and Beliveau, who missed 27 games with an injury.

Bouncing back from summer knee surgery, Plante played in all 70 regular-season games. He also won more games (42) than any other goaltender in the NHL and had the best goals-against average (2.37) among starters. He won the Vezina Trophy again and became just the fourth goaltender in history to win the Hart Memorial Trophy, awarded to the player most valuable to his team. But Plante's goals-against average ballooned to 3.17 in the playoffs as the Canadiens lost to the Blackhawks (75 points) in a six-game semifinal.

1962-65

Before a practice in Chicago Stadium in January 1963, Plante told his teammates that the crossbars of the nets there were lower than required by NHL regulations. Beliveau still remembers that moment. "We asked him how he knew that. He said, 'When I take up my position in front of the net here, my body makes contact with the crossbar. In other arenas it doesn't.' We didn't believe him. But after practice, we measured the height of the crossbar—and it turned out that Jacques was right."

When word spread, the goalie informed reporters that the nets in New York and Boston were also too low. "Jacques Plante, Montreal Canadiens goalie who has changed the techniques of his job with his wandering habits and mask, now wants to change the size of the nets in Detroit, Toronto and Montreal," wrote one indignant reporter. "Plante said that in New York,

Boston and Chicago the crossbar is two or three inches lower...
[He] figures the extra couple of inches in the Montreal net could
cost him the Vezina, which he has already won six times."

General managers insisted Plante was wrong, but the mea-
suring tape proved otherwise. The crossbars of nets in the cities
Plante named were raised to meet league standards.

Plante sat out much of that
season, complaining of asthma-
related problems. His relationship with Blake worsened, and
after the Canadiens bowed out
of the opening round of the
playoffs again, this time to the
Leafs, it broke down completely.

IN JUNE 1963, two months after
bowing out in the first round of
the playoffs, Canadiens traded
Plante to the New York Rangers
as part of a seven-player deal. He
heard the news from a reporter.
"Just like that," Plante said. "I'm
traded to New York. It was like
telling me a friend had died."[18]

Plante headed to Manhattan,
leaving a team that had won
five Stanley Cups in the past
decade for one that had made
the playoffs just four times in
that span. Rival goalie Gump Worsley, who was traveling in the
opposition direction, said he felt like he had been released from
prison. New York finished fifth in each of the next two seasons,
missing the playoffs altogether. Plante's only distinction was
allowing more goals (220) than any of his peers in the 1963–64

> "In a game against Toronto,
> Dave Keon broke in on net, and
> Jacques moved to one side,
> anticipating Keon would go that
> way. But Keon went the other
> way and scored on Jacques. The
> next day, Toe Blake talked to
> Jacques, cautioning him against
> over-anticipating. Plante
> stormed out of the dressing
> room and said he wouldn't play
> that night... Of course, he did
> end up playing that night. But
> he didn't take to criticism well."
>
> *Former Montreal Canadiens teammate*
> **ERNIE WAKELY**

season. The Rangers sent him to the minors in March 1965, attributing the decision to Plante's bad right knee. The goalie played 17 games with the AHL's Baltimore Clippers. When knee surgery proved successful in May, fans expected him to return to New York. Instead, he quit.

Rangers general manager Emile Francis made the announcement at a press conference at the Queen Elizabeth Hotel in Montreal, and then Plante spoke. "I thought about retiring several times last winter when I was hurt and wasn't playing much. But I decided to quit only about a week ago," he said. "I have been away from my wife and family an awful long time during my hockey career. My two boys, Michel, 14, and Richard, 10, are growing up and I believe it's time to spend more time with them." He said his decision had nothing to do with his health. "I feel fine, and maybe I could play another four or five years."

He was 36.

1965-68

Six months later, Plante played for the Montreal Junior Canadiens in a game against a touring Russian national team. On December 11, he told a broadcaster his team would win by a score of 2–1 or 3–1. Four days later, he withstood a frenzied Russian attack and his team, a collection of players from two Montreal Canadiens farm clubs, won the game 2–1. When the final siren sounded, a deafening roar filled the Forum. Fans gave him a standing ovation while his teammates carried him on their shoulders.

In 1967, the NHL doubled from 6 to 12 teams, creating more jobs in professional hockey. Plante's former teammate Olmstead became coach of the Oakland Seals. He asked Plante to be the team's goalie consultant. Plante, who had been working as a hockey analyst and as a sales supervisor at Molson Brewery, readily accepted.

He took to the ice during the team's training camp and then, on September 21, he suited up for an exhibition game against the Los Angeles Kings. (Sawchuk was in net for the Kings, starting his only season with the team.) Afterwards, Plante said he had felt great on the ice. There was speculation he would return, but he left the team the next day. The Rangers still owned his playing rights.

1968-69

In the June 1968 intra-league draft, the St. Louis Blues acquired Plante's rights from the Rangers. In the previous season, the Blues had finished third in the West Division, which consisted entirely of expansion teams—and had faced the Canadiens in the Cup final. Although they had lost four straight games, the Blues had acquitted themselves well; each game had been decided by just one goal. The team included established stars such as Hall and Moore. Coach Scotty Bowman felt Plante could make a contribution. Evidently, Plante agreed.

The 39-year-old signed with the Blues. "Life begins at 40 and I feel like a rookie," he told reporters. He added that neither he nor Hall, 36, had anything to prove and would work together for the better of the team. "Nobody wants to take the other's job away," he said.[19]

The goalies proved to be a dynamic duo in the 1968–69 season. Hall finished with a 2.17 goals-against average and a league-leading eight shutouts. Plante posted a 1.96 goals-against average, the best in the NHL. The Blues allowed fewer goals (157) than any other team, so their middle-aged goalies shared the Vezina Trophy—the seventh for Plante and the third for Hall.

PLANTE ALSO made an impression off the ice in St. Louis. Gary Edwards, a Blues backup goalie for two seasons, spent some time living with Plante, whose family was still in Montreal. "He had this one-bedroom apartment with two beds in it. I slept in one of them," Edwards recalls. "I remember Jacques keeping a book filled with notes about every game. He kept track of how many shots had been taken on him, how many goals had been scored against him and who had scored them. He also kept track of his goals-against average. I also remember a bit about his diet. On game days, most of the guys would eat steak, but Jacques always had ground beef. I think it was easier on his stomach. Every morning, he would have a couple pieces of toast with pickled onions on top. I don't know what the appeal was."

> "He was a quiet guy who went his own way, not one of the boys, but that was all right."[27]
>
> *Former Montreal Canadiens teammate* **DOUG HARVEY**, *in 1986*

Edwards recalls teammate Bob Plager once sharing a story about Plante. The defenseman told Edwards some of the players had gathered at a local watering hole after a practice and taken turns buying rounds of drinks. Just before it was Plante's turn, he had left the bar, claiming he had to meet with Bowman. "The next time they went out for drinks, Bobby sat down beside Plante," Edwards says. "When the waitress came by, Bobby said to her, 'Doubles for everybody and this guy sitting next to me is buying the next round!'"

THE BLUES finished first in their division and fourth overall with 88 points. They swept aside the Philadelphia Flyers (61 points) and Los Angeles Kings (58 points) in the first two rounds of the playoffs without losing a game, and then took on Montreal in the final. The Canadiens had finished at the top of the standings (103 points), and they proved too much for St. Louis to handle. The Blues suffered the same fate as their opponents had in the first two rounds and lost the deciding game in their own building.

1969-70

Plante played nearly twice as much as Hall the following season. The Blues finished first in their division and sixth overall with 86 points. They defeated the Minnesota North Stars (60 points) and the Pittsburgh Penguins (64 points) and then met the

Bruins (99 points) in the final. Bobby Orr and Phil Esposito, who had finished first and second respectively in league scoring, led the Bruins to four straight victories—and the team's first Stanley Cup since 1941.

A deflected puck hit Plante in the forehead in Game 1. It shattered his mask and knocked him out cold. He lay on the ice for five minutes before being helped off. He was heard mumbling: "If it wasn't for the mask, I'd be dead." Plante was taken to the Jewish Hospital of St. Louis, where tests revealed he had suffered a serious concussion.[20]

(Plante's teammate Barclay Plager also ended up in the hospital that day. He was rushed there after passing out on the St. Louis bench. X-rays showed a rib separation. "The doctor didn't exactly call it a fracture. He seems to think it was a separation," Plager said. "He said he hadn't seen anything like it before and he's going to write a paper on it.")[21]

That game proved to be Plante's last for the Blues. Unable to protect three goaltenders in the upcoming expansion draft—Vancouver and Buffalo joined the league in 1970—St. Louis traded Plante to Toronto for future considerations. "Age was definitely a factor," said Sidney Salomon III, the Blues vice president. "Plante has been great for St. Louis and great for hockey, but we have to move ahead. I'm sure we'll be criticized for trading such a great player, but we were left with no choice."[22]

1970-73

Toronto had been a mediocre team since winning the Cup in 1967 and continued to be after Plante's arrival. The Leafs bowed out in the quarter-final in each of Plante's first two seasons there, but their aged goalie was top-notch. He played 40 games in the 1970–71 season, posting the best goals-against average (1.88) among NHL starters. (Montreal rookie Ken Dryden recorded a 1.65 goals-against average, but he played in just six regular season games.) Plante was still an elite goalie—and still a loner. "Nobody knew him in Toronto. We never saw him, except at the games and practices," Leafs defenseman Jim McKenney later recalled.[23]

In Toronto, Plante shared the workload with a 25-year-old goaltender who had once idolized him. Bernie Parent had been in the league for five seasons, with Boston and Philadelphia, establishing himself as a good goaltender with great potential. Breaking with tradition, Plante developed a warm relationship with his teammate. He acted as a mentor to Parent, teaching him the finer points of the game. Parent went on to become one of the best goalies in history. "What I got from him was an understanding of the game," Parent says today. "I learned how my defensemen would react to a right-handed shot coming at me. How they would react to a left-handed shot," he says, citing one example. "Of course, my career would have been different if I hadn't worked with Jacques Plante."

PARENT WASN'T the only goalie Plante helped. Before one of the games of the historic Summit Series in 1972, Plante visited Soviet goalie Vladislav Tretiak in the hotel where he and his teammates were staying. Drawing diagrams on a blackboard, Plante showed Tretiak how to face Esposito, Yvan Cournoyer and Paul Henderson. The two goalies needed a translator to communicate, but the message was clear: Plante was showing Tretiak how to shut down Team Canada's offense. As it turned out, the young goalie gave Canadian players fits in the series and emerged as an international star.

TORONTO TRADED Plante to Boston in March 1973. The reigning Stanley Cup champions had lost Gerry Cheevers to the newly formed World Hockey Association (WHA) and were in need of an elite goalie. They put Plante between the pipes in eight regular-season games. He won seven of them and even posted two shutouts. But the Bruins were eliminated by the Rangers (4–1) in the quarter-final. Plante later admitted to losing his nerves in the series. He retired—again.

1973-74

Plante took a job as coach and general manager of the WHA's Quebec Nordiques for the following season. The experiment failed. "I couldn't reach [the players]," he said. "And as manager as well as coach, I was going all the time. I didn't have time to talk to the players enough before games, and when I did talk they didn't listen. Every time I answered the phone there was another problem, another complaint."[24]

In January 1974, the Edmonton Oilers approached Plante, asking if he would trade one of his goalies to them. He suggested he play for them himself.

1974-75

He suited up for the WHA team the following season. But at last, age caught up with him. The 46-year-old goalie suffered a series of injuries, including one to his ear drum that affected his balance. He played in 31 games for the Oilers as they finished ninth in the 14-team league.

In the fall of 1975, Plante's youngest son, Richard, committed suicide. Plante headed home to be with his family but returned to the Oilers training camp a week later. By then, his standing with the Oilers management had deteriorated, along with his health. Before the start of the 1975–76 season, they told him there wasn't space for him on the roster. A week later, the team released a statement saying he had retired.

RETIREMENT

Even after his playing career ended, Plante maintained his ties to the NHL. When Parent fell into a slump after several spectacular seasons with the Philadelphia Flyers—he had rejoined the team in the 1973–74 season—the Flyers recruited Plante to help. Sure enough, Parent returned to form. Plante stayed with the team as its goaltending coach for five seasons.

In September 1978, Plante was inducted into the Hockey Hall of Fame along with five other men, including two former players:

Marcel Pronovost, whom Plante had known since his childhood, and Andy Bathgate, whose shot at Plante's head had changed the face of hockey. At the awards ceremony at the Royal York Hotel—yes, that hotel—Plante posed for a picture with his fellow inductees, all of whom were wearing suits with expansive lapels. There didn't appear to be hard feelings between Plante and Bathgate, but it was hard to tell; Pronovost was standing between them.

Soon after that, Plante moved to Switzerland to work with young players there. He relocated with his second wife, Raymonde Udrisard, who had been his companion since his time with the Nordiques. (Plante and his first wife had divorced in 1972.)

"Sometimes we were on the train all day. Most of the players would play cards, but Jacques wasn't a card player, and neither was I. We would spend some time talking to each other. We would talk about sports and whatever was happening in the news. We both liked to read, too. I remember Jacques reading biographies." —*Former Montreal Canadiens teammate* **JEAN BELIVEAU**

One of his former teams came calling in 1983. Two decades after the Canadiens had traded him away, Plante became the team's goalie coach—and he was delighted to be back. He enjoyed great success there, grooming Steve Penney. The young goaltender became the toast of Montreal in 1984 by winning nine playoff games and notching three shutouts.

In January 1986, Plante became a consultant for the Blues to help the organization develop its young goalies. Plante looked unwell during one trip to St. Louis and was examined by a team doctor. Tests revealed he had advanced stomach cancer. He died in a Geneva hospital a month later.

Family members and friends, including Beliveau, attended his funeral. When Plante's casket was carried from the church, it passed under an arch of hockey sticks held aloft by a team of young hockey players from Quebec who were in Switzerland for a tournament.

Tributes poured in from all corners. "The hockey world has lost one of its greatest stars, a true innovator whose influence helped shape the modern art of goaltending," said NHL president John Ziegler. "Jacques' love of the game, along with his many talents, accomplishments and durability over 17 National Hockey League seasons will always be remembered."[25]

PLANTE · ALL-TIME RANKING*

REGULAR SEASON			PLAYOFFS		
GAMES	WINS	SO	GAMES	WINS	SO
837 [11th]	437 [6th]	82 [5th]	112 [13th]	71 [9th]	14 [5th]

* statistics as of July 2, 2013.

> NHL ALL-STAR TEAM **(1ST)**: 1955–56, 1958–59, 1961–62

> NHL ALL-STAR TEAM **(2ND)**: 1956–57, 1957–58, 1959–60, 1970–71

4

||||||||||||||||||||||||||||||||||||||||||||

THE
JOKER
GUMP WORSLEY

||||||||||||||||||||||||||||||||||||||||||||

"[Gump] had a world-class sense of humour
and love of life that kept his teammates loose
and himself just north of the sanity border."[1]

Columnist **DAVE STUBBS**, in 2007

LUMBERING THROUGH the Montreal Canadiens dressing
room early one season, Gump Worsley paused to greet newcomers. The veteran goalie took stock of their athletic builds, looked
down at his own protruding gut and said dryly, "I've been in the
league a lot of years with this belly. I hope you guys can do as
well as I did." Gilles Tremblay was in the dressing room that day,
and still savors the memory. "Gump always made us laugh," he
says of his former teammate.[2]

Worsley was as fierce a competitor, with as hard an edge, as
any goalie of his era. Yet he stood out. Short and pudgy with a
fleshy face and a brush cut, he looked more like a cartoon character than an elite athlete. Worsley was never at a loss for words.
His wry observations and wisecracks were a source of endless
amusement for players, fans and reporters.

LORNE "GUMP" Worsley was born in Montreal in May 1929, five months before the stock market crashed, flattening world economies and forcing millions to depend on government relief, charity and food handouts. The youngest of three children, he grew up in the working-class neighborhood of Point St. Charles, where life was difficult—and that was on good days. He was three years old when his father, William, lost his job. Lorne later recalled that the family subsisted on a diet of "potatoes and potatoes" until his father found a job five years later.

Lorne dropped out of school at the age of 14 and took a job at Northern Electric (later Nortel Networks), where his father worked. As a messenger boy, he earned a grand total of $9 a week. It wasn't much, but it was enough to buy the two packs of cigarettes he smoked every day. When he wasn't working, he was hanging out with his friends. One of them noted that Worsley wore his hair the same way as one of the characters in the popular comic strip *The Gumps*—sticking straight up—and started calling him "Gump." The nickname stuck.

Worsley was passionate about hockey and enjoyed rough-housing with his friends on the ice. He played in an organized league and was a forward until his teens. He was barely five feet tall when his coach eyeballed him and, displaying keen powers of observation, informed the young athlete he was short. Worsley was advised to switch to goaltending. Hesitant—it was difficult to stay warm in the biting cold while standing in front of the net—but aware that he was more likely to scale Mount Everest than reach six feet, he agreed to become "Gump the Goalie." Worsley became a classic stand-up goalie, but he was so short that he often had to lunge from one side of the net to the other to get even a part of his body in front of the puck. His performance wasn't pretty, but it was effective.

The New York Rangers farm team, the Verdun Cyclones of the Quebec Junior Hockey League, didn't invite Worsley to attend their tryout in the fall of 1946. But he went anyway and, like any good party crasher, he blended in. Playing in a pair of goalie pads he had borrowed from the Montreal Boys' Association, he won a spot on the roster for the 1946–47 season. The team was based in a Francophone area, so Worsley wasn't surprised to discover he was the only Anglophone on the team. But he worked as hard learning French as he did honing his craft and became a top-notch goalie who could swear at referees in la langue de l'amour. After one game, he gave his autograph to a girl named Doreen. The two soon started dating. As fetching as she was, she didn't take his mind off his game. He continued to improve as a stand-up goalie and began to attract attention beyond Verdun.

In the 1948–49 season, Worsley played for Montreal St. Francis Xavier in the MMJHL. He also played two games with the New York Rovers of the Quebec Senior Hockey League. A few months after the season, the Rangers invited him to attend their training camp in upstate New York. He couldn't get time off from his job as an apprentice upholsterer at Canadian National Railway, so he quit and headed to Lake Placid with one pair of slacks and a sport coat crammed into a suitcase his father had loaned him.

Rangers goalie Chuck Rayner, then in the prime of his Hall of Fame career, gave Worsley a warm welcome. But the young goalie wasn't good enough to unseat the veteran, and he was assigned to the Rovers, who had returned to the Eastern Amateur Hockey League. He played very well in the 1949–50 season and helped lead the team to a first-place finish. But that year was memorable for another reason too. After a game in Milwaukee in November, the team boarded a small plane for the trip back to New York. In the middle of the flight, one of Worsley's teammates spotted smoke coming out of the engine. The pilot sprang into action and put out the fire. He made an emergency landing, and the players emerged from the plane shaken but not stirred—all the players, that is, except the goalie. Worsley developed a pathological fear of flying that would later play a role in the course of his career.

► PITCH PERFECT ◄

HOCKEY WAS Worsley's greatest passion but not the only one. He often took to the soccer pitch in the summer, where he proved to be an outstanding forward. He was so good, he was once a member of a Montreal youth all-star team. In September 1948, the Montreal *Gazette* mentioned him in a story about the team. They described the 19-year-old as a "versatile athlete" who has "starred in every sport he has taken up. It's rumoured that he's on the [New York] Rangers reserve list as a hockey goalkeeper."

Later, Worsley played for the Saskatoon Legion of the amateur Saskatoon Senior Soccer League. In the summer of 1952, he played for a Saskatchewan all-star team that squared off in a friendly game against Tottenham Hotspur, a top-tier British team. The game was so lopsided the teams switched goalkeepers at half-time to keep fans interested. In the end, Tottenham annihilated the Canadian squad 18–1. Worsley scored his team's only goal. The Hotspur handbook for that season says "the game was played at the Griffiths Stadium, a useful pitch in very nice surroundings, before a large crowd for the town of some 5,000 spectators, and many thousand more mosquitos."

The following summer, Worsley played for the Montreal Hakoah, a semi-professional team in the Quebec Major League. The Hakoah advanced to the final of the Challenge Trophy, a competition for the winners of a qualifying competition in each province. Worsley, who played center half, was the team captain.

For the following season, Worsley joined the St. Paul Saints, a Rangers affiliate in the United States Hockey League (USHL). He was a standout and was named the league's top rookie as well as its top goaltender. Soon after the season ended, he married Doreen. The young couple spent their honeymoon in New York. On Independence Day, they went to Ebbets Field to see a game between the New York Giants and the Brooklyn Dodgers. Worsley later said it was the highlight of his trip. Whether Doreen was offended, we'll never know.

Worsley's star was on the rise, but he still couldn't outshine Rayner, so the Rangers sent him to the Saskatoon Quakers of the Pacific Coast Hockey League, which was a notch above the USHL. He was stellar again in the 1951–52 season.

NHL

1952-53

Worsley was gearing up for another season in Saskatoon when he got the call he had been waiting for. Rayner had pulled a leg muscle in a pre-season game, and the Rangers wanted Worsley to replace him. After strutting his stuff in several leagues, Worsley finally had the chance to prove himself in the one that mattered most. He joined the Rangers in Detroit on October 9, 1952. Not long after he skated onto the ice at the Olympia, he was fighting the urge to skate back off. From the moment the puck dropped, the Red Wings launched a furious assault on the Rangers net. New York's defense was porous and their goalie had no chance. Detroit jumped to a 3–0 lead in the first period on goals by Ted Lindsay, Alex Delvecchio and Gordie Howe. They went on to win the game 5–3.

The Red Wings finished at the top of the standings that season, whereas the Rangers finished dead last. Still, Worsley played well enough to replace Rayner, who was nine years his senior, as the team's starting goalie. With help from the veteran, who gave him tips on cutting down angles and positioning himself on breakaways, Worsley impressed just about everyone in the hockey world. "I can remember the first time I saw him playing for the New York Rangers, he looked like a kid who had just sneaked over the fence and got into the game," recalled columnist Jim Coleman. "He had closely cropped hair, the Ranger uniform flopped all over him, and he flopped all over the ice. He was just incredible in what he was doing, but he still gave you the impression that he shouldn't be there and had just sneaked in."[3]

Worsley had the fewest wins (13) and the worst goals-against average among starting goalies (3.06), but he won the Calder Memorial Trophy as the NHL's best rookie. Feeling he had earned a raise, Worsley asked the Rangers to add another $500 to his $6,500 salary. In response, they sent him to the Vancouver Canucks of the Western Hockey League.

1953-54

Worsley was defiant. While Johnny Bower tended net in New York, Worsley led the Canucks to a first-place finish. He was named the league's most valuable player, and he won the Outstanding Goalkeeper Award, which was given to the goalie on the team allowing the fewest number of goals in the regular season.

Worsley was none too pleased when Frank Boucher, the Rangers general manager, showed up in Vancouver to present him with the Calder Trophy he had won the previous season. "That burned me up too. I figured if I wasn't good enough to play in New York, I wasn't good enough to accept [the award]," Worsley later said. "Boucher showed up a little drunk at the presentation ceremony and was holding the [trophy] and blabbering away. I thought he would never let go of it. Finally, I got tired of all his mouthings and just grabbed it out of his hand."[4]

Worsley suffered his first of many serious injuries that season when one of his defensemen accidentally rammed him in the back with a stick or knee during a playoff game. The collision affected some nerves and left him unable to move his legs for a few days. His doctor told him he would never play again, but Worsley returned to action and wore a back brace for two years.

1954-63

In the 1954–55 season, Worsley returned to the Rangers and reclaimed his status as the starting goalie. (Bower was assigned to Vancouver but ultimately recovered from the setback; he went on to win four Stanley Cups in Toronto.) Worsley spent the next nine seasons in New York—and they weren't pretty. The Rangers were mediocre at best. They advanced to the play-offs in just four seasons and were eliminated in the first round each time.

New York's defense was so weak, Worsley sometimes faced 50 shots in a game. In one outing, the team was as vigorous as a small dead animal. Squeamish spectators looked away. Afterwards, a reporter asked their shell-shocked goalie which NHL team gave him the most trouble. Without missing a beat he replied: "The New York Rangers."

Worsley was always good for a quote. After a game in which Rangers defenseman Lou Fontinato decked Montreal Canadiens star Maurice "Rocket" Richard, reporters crammed into the tiny Rangers dressing room. They crowded around Fontinato and, undistracted by the players' street clothes hanging from pipes overhead, peppered him with questions. From the other side of the room, an exasperated Worsley exclaimed, "Hey, watch it you guys! The room is starting to tilt."[5]

When Rangers coach Phil Watson publicly complained about the goalie's lack of conditioning and said he had a "beer belly," Worsley had a quick retort. "Beer is the poor man's champagne," he said. "I'm strictly a [rye] man."[6]

But the relationship between coach and goalie was no laughing matter. In fact, it was toxic. "It's not true that Watson and I disliked each other," Worsley later said. "Hate would be a better word."[7] Watson chastised Worsley for his lackadaisical approach to practice, but the defiant goalie said he got more than enough practice in games and saw no need to waste his energy. Journalist Stan Fischler said the interaction between the two men "was almost like a comedy team except that Gump didn't think it was funny, and Watson didn't think it was funny."[8]

> "I always thought that he was ten pounds overweight. I didn't know how he could be so agile by being that much overweight, but that was the Gumper."
>
> *Former New York Rangers teammate*
> **ANDY BATHGATE**

Worsley also continued to contend with an occupational hazard for goalies of the era—injuries. In March 1956, he hurt his knee in the first game of the semifinal against the Montreal Canadiens and missed two of the six games in the series—which the Rangers lost. He underwent surgery on his knee in late May. His luck went from bad to worse in the 1957–58 season. In October, he was sidelined again with a pulled thigh muscle. Marcel Paille was called up from the Providence Reds of the American Hockey League to fill in. He played so well that when Worsley was game-ready a few weeks later, he was sent to Providence to take Paille's place.

Gump was back with the "Broadway Blues" by January, but it wasn't smooth sailing from there. During a game at Madison Square Garden in February 1960, he squared off against the Chicago Blackhawks' Bobby Hull, whose booming slap shot was feared and revered as a weapon of mass destruction. When the Golden Jet cut toward the net, Worsley dove at him. The winger's skate blade sliced through the goalie's catching glove, severing two tendons in his baby finger. The next day, newspapers ran a photo of the doleful netminder looking down at his hand, jowls tumbling over his collar, while team trainer Frank Paice applied bandages.

A year later, Worsley was knocked out cold when the Boston Bruins' Andre Pronovost fired a shot that struck him in the face, above his left eye. The game was delayed as the goalie was carried off the ice. He regained consciousness while being stitched up in the dressing room and, a few minutes later, returned to the ice with two sutures above his eye. The *New York Times* reported that "Gump Worsley of the Rangers had courage enough for two men" in the 5-2 Rangers victory.[9]

In a game just weeks later, Worsley stretched to reach another one of Hull's projectiles and tore a hamstring in his left leg. Once again, he was taken off the ice on a stretcher.

His many injuries, his toxic relationship with his coach and, most of all, the Rangers' poor performance weighed heavily on Worsley. He suffered from insomnia and spent countless nights smoking cigarettes while pacing the floor. In the few hours he did sleep, he dreamt about pucks sailing past him or ripping into his face.

He started to drink heavily. "We ran from bar to bar in those days and you know how many bars there are in New York. About 10,000," Worsley later said. "After most games we'd go out drinking and stay out until the joints closed at four in the morning. We were always there for the last call."[10]

1963-64

Worsley found reason to raise a glass in celebration in June 1963, when the Rangers and the Canadiens completed a multi-player trade that saw Worsley swap places with Jacques Plante. Worsley said he "felt like a man who had just been let out of prison." Although he had grown up in Montreal, he had never dreamt of playing for "Les Habitants." His parents were Scottish immigrants who had cheered on the Montreal Maroons—an early NHL team that drew its support from the city's Anglophone community. Still, he couldn't have been happier to join the Canadiens. The team had won five Stanley Cups in the previous

10 seasons and, with stars such as Jean Beliveau, Bernie "Boom Boom" Geoffrion and the young Yvan Cournoyer, it was poised to win more.

Worsley's first campaign with the Habs wasn't one for the ages. He pulled a hamstring early on. Charlie Hodge took his place and, just as Paille had done six years earlier, played so well he bumped Gump out of a job. Hodge won the Vezina Trophy—then awarded to the starting goalie on the team allowing the fewest goals—while Worsley languished in the American Hockey League. He spent the next year and a half with the Quebec Aces, playing cards with his teammates as they rode the bus from one city to another.

1964-65

Worsley returned to the Canadiens midway through the 1964–65 season, and he put on a stellar performance for the remainder of the campaign. The Canadiens finished the regular season in second place with 83 points.

Worsley's frenetic style and intense desire to win made him a crowd favorite at the Forum. His colorful quips and pudgy appearance only enhanced his appeal. But Canadiens coach Toe Blake had no interest in pinching the goalie's chubby little cheeks. He viewed Worsley's weight as a problem and ordered him to trim down. The goalie went on a diet, laid off the booze and shed 11 pounds. He wasn't quite a string bean by the end of the regular season, but—looking a little like a sweet potato—he weighed a respectable 177 pounds.

The Canadiens beat the Toronto Maple Leafs (74 points) in the semifinal, in six games, and then squared off against the Blackhawks (76 points) in the final. Worsley helped lead the Canadiens to victory in the first two games of that series, but the third one didn't go according to plan. Although the Blackhawks won 3–1, the score was only part of the story. With less than a minute remaining in the game, a brawl broke out. The fans in Chicago Stadium rose to their feet and cheered on their

➤ DOMESTIC DIVA ◄

WORSLEY OFTEN headed to the kitchen in his downtime—but not to eat. He loved to bake and spent hours preparing pastries. When family and friends raved about his pineapple squares, a beaming Worsley christened them "Gumpies." The North Stars once gave him an apron as a Christmas gift.

||||||||||||||||||||||||||||||||||||||||||||||||||||||||||||||

hometown heroes. The decibel level rose with each jab and haymaker. A few minutes in, their attention turned to the Canadiens goalie. Infuriated by their taunts, Worsley charged toward the spectators, but like an enraged walrus in an aquarium, he was foiled by a glass partition. After the game, he claimed he had been hit by empty beverage cups, coins and a slat from a stadium chair. "That's when I blew," Worsley explained. The goalie, a whiskey connoisseur, said "the sale of alcoholic beverages in the rink often incites normally well-behaved hockey addicts to acts of violence."[11]

At some point in the game, Worsley tore a muscle in his right thigh. Hodge took over for the next three games, two of which Chicago won, while Worsley was treated for his injury. He took injections to help ease the pain and was pleased with the results—even though the drug made his breath smell "like the stockyards in summer."[12]

Blake started the veteran goalie in Game 7 at the Forum, guessing that he would be better able than Hodge to handle the pressure of a deciding game. He was right. Beliveau scored on his first shift to get the party started, and Worsley stopped all 20 shots he faced in that game. He made five great saves in the first period alone, stopping two shots fired by the Golden Jet. The Canadiens beat the Blackhawks 4–0 to win their first Stanley Cup in five seasons. The stands erupted when the final siren sounded, and Worsley and defenseman J.C. Tremblay jumped into each other's arms. Worsley later said the five minutes leading up to that moment felt like years. "Nothing has matched that thrill," he later said. "The first Cup victory is always the biggest moment in a hockey player's life."[13]

1965-66

The 1965–66 season was even better for the Habs. They finished at the top of the standings with 90 points. Montreal, like other NHL teams, had adopted a two-goalie system by this point and, in accordance with a new league rule, ensured that a backup goalie was dressed and ready to spring into action for every playoff game.

Worsley and Hodge split goaltending duties. Gump played in 51 games and posted a 2.36 goals-against average. Hodge played in 26 games, recording a 2.58 goals-against average. The pair won the Vezina Trophy.

The Canadiens swept the Leafs (79 points) in the semifinal and then defeated the Red Wings (74 points) to win the Cup for the second straight year. Henri Richard clinched it in sudden death overtime of Game 6 with a goal that was less than illustrious. The Pocket Rocket somehow wound up in the Detroit net along with the puck. The referee ruled that the puck had bounced in off Richard's knee, but Red Wings goalie Roger Crozier insisted Richard had guided the puck into the net with his hand.

Jim Coleman agreed. "There's little Henri sliding along the ice on his knees, in the manner of a child sliding down a snow-clad hill on his toboggan—and, little Henri and the puck and Roger Crozier and the broken hearts of 18 Detroit players all ended up in the Red Wings net. And, Crozier—until he is an old man with a grey beard hanging down to his navel—will now vow that little Henri coyly reached out one little hand and popped the little puck into the pen," he wrote in the *Calgary Herald*. "Certainly, I'm a sorehead."[14]

Detroit's Bill Gadsby said Worsley had not been put to the test in the game. "His underwear can't even be wet," the defense-man griped. Worsley's response was swift—and predictable: "What most people don't know is that my underwear is wet even before the game begins."[15]

1966-67

Midway through the following season, Worsley underwent surgery to remove cartilage from his right knee. He was sidelined for a month, leaving outstanding rookie Rogie Vachon to take his place. No sooner had he returned to the ice than he collided with the Bruins' Johnny Bucyk and sprained his knee. He missed another month.

Worsley suffered a mild concussion in one of the few games he played in the 1966–67 season. But the mishap didn't involve another player, the puck or even the galvanized steel posts that framed his net. At one point in a game at Madison Square Garden, an overzealous fan hurled an egg at the ice. It hit Worsley in the head with such velocity, it scrambled his brain and forced him to leave the game. Police marched the malefactor into the Canadiens' dressing room after the game, presented him to Worsley and asked the goalie if he wanted to press charges. Like a Roman emperor deciding the fate of a stricken gladiator, Worsley paused to consider his options. He sized up the fan, a high school student who looked like he was about to faint, and

➤ PROTECTING THE "MELON" ◄

LEGENDARY GOALIE Jacques Plante first donned a mask in 1959, and most of his contemporaries soon followed suit. But Worsley resisted, saying that wearing one made him feel uncomfortably hot and prevented him from seeing the puck when it was at his feet. Still, his reluctance puzzled the many fans who had heard *Hockey Night in Canada* broadcaster Danny Gallivan say, "It looks like the Gumper has taken one on the melon!"

"Somebody once said to him, 'You've never worn a face mask?'" Minnesota North Stars teammate Lou Nanne later recalled. "Gump [who had about 200 stitches in his face] replied, 'You think I'd look like this if I did?'"[24]

Finally, at the urging of Cesare Maniago, his goaltending partner in Minnesota, Worsley relented. He played the last six games of his 931-game NHL career wearing a mask. He was the second-to-last big-league goalie to wear one. Only Andy Brown, who played five seasons in the NHL and three in the World Hockey Association in the 1970s, held out longer.

||||||||||||||||||||||||||||||||||||||||||||||||||||||||||||||||||

turned his thumb up. The kid was released, proving that Worsley was nothing if not merciful.

That egg wasn't the only object hurled at the goalie during his NHL career. Montreal fans would often litter the ice with rubber galoshes—no doubt representing a boon for shoe repairmen from Beaconsfield to Verdun—whereas spectators in Chicago and New York would leave the ice strewn with ball bearings. In one incident at Madison Square Garden, a fan tossed a paper bag onto the ice. It landed in front of Worsley, who peeked inside and spotted a ham and cheese sandwich.

The Canadiens finished second that season with 77 points. They swept the Rangers (72 points) in the semifinal but didn't repeat as champions. The grizzled Leafs (75 points), whose average age was a geriatric 31, rose from their walkers for one last hurrah, beating the Canadiens in six games to win Toronto's 13th, and last, Stanley Cup.

1967-68

The Canadiens and their star goalie were back to their winning ways in the 1967–68 season. The Habs notched 94 points to finish first in the league, which had doubled in size from 6 to 12 teams. Worsley played in 40 of 74 regular-season games, posting a 1.98 goals-against average. It was the best average, by far, of all the starting goalies. He and Vachon, who posted a 2.48 goals-against average, won the Vezina Trophy.

The Canadiens swept the Bruins (84 points) in the quarterfinal and then beat Chicago (80 points) in a five-game semifinal. In the fourth tilt against the Blackhawks, Worsley collided with his old nemesis, the Golden Jet. The netminder whacked his own neck on the goal post and was carried off the ice on a stretcher. He was diagnosed with a sprained neck and was fitted with a protective neck collar. He sat out the fifth and deciding game of the series. But he was back in net for the final against the St. Louis Blues (70 points). Montreal swept the series, leading the *New York Times* to rave about the "controlled madness" of the Canadiens offense. The paper reported that in the final game, the Habs "unleashed a final-period drive that enabled them to catch, and defeat, the St. Louis Blues, 3–2."[16]

Worsley was sensational. He started in 11 of his team's 13 post-season games and won all of them. He allowed just 21 goals in total. But he fell short of winning the coveted Conn Smythe

Award for the league's top playoff performer. It went to Blues goalie Glenn Hall. Although he had lost 10 of the 18 post-season games in which he had started, voters felt Hall had carried the Blues to the final and kept the scores respectable.

> "Gump didn't like it when I shot the puck high on him during practices. He once said, 'Damn you! You don't have to do that in practice!' I said, 'Gump, I have to have confidence in my shot. So when I shoot on you in practice, I have to do what I do in games. Where else am I going to work on my shot?'"
>
> **ANDY BATHGATE**

Worsley soared to new heights that season, but his trip was not without turbulence. In the expanded league, teams had to travel from one side of the continent to the other. That meant more plane flights for all the players, including the notorious white-knuckle flyer. On one Canadiens flight, the plane hit an air pocket as a flight attendant was serving coffee. She lost her footing and spilled coffee over Beliveau. When the team arrived at their destination, an airline agent offered to buy the hockey star a new suit. "Forget about Beliveau," an ashen-faced Worsley piped in. "How about my jockey shorts? They got soiled too."[17]

1968-69

A year later, in November 1968, Worsley was playing well, but he was emotionally drained by rocky relations with the Canadiens' new head coach, Claude Ruel, and by the unrelenting pressure of playing in hockey-mad Montreal. His nerves were already frayed when the Canadiens boarded a flight to Chicago. The plane hit turbulence and dropped 10,000 feet before the pilot righted the craft. As soon as the plane landed, Worsley announced he was retiring and waved goodbye to his teammates. Hours later, they were flying to Los Angeles for a game against the Kings while he was headed to Montreal—on a train. A few days later, Canadiens general manager Sam Pollock convinced the goalie to see a psychiatrist. Worsley visited the therapist every day for about a month. He returned to the Canadiens lineup in January and was "thrown in the barrel" for a game against the Blackhawks. Life returned to normal—or at least to the way it had always been.

He and Vachon, whose star was on the rise, helped lead the Canadiens to the top of the regular-season standings again. The Habs finished with 103 points, 3 more than the second-place Bruins. The Canadiens swept aside the Rangers (91 points) in four games in the quarter-final, beat the Bruins in a six-game semifinal and then won their second straight Cup by battering the Blues (88 points) in a four-game sweep.

Worsley suffered a dislocated finger in Game 4 against Boston when he put his glove in front of his face to prevent a shot from shattering his schnoz. Vachon replaced him for the rest of the playoffs and played so well he was considered a favorite for the Conn Smythe Trophy. (Instead, it went to the Canadiens' promising young defenseman, Serge Savard.)

Worsley watched the second game of the final with his friend Yogi Berra. After the game, Worsley invited Berra, then coach of the New York Mets, into the Montreal dressing room. No sooner had Berra walked through the door than he was approached by Canadiens trainer Larry Aubut, who ordered him to put out his cigarette. The baseball legend gave the trainer a long, hard look—then did as he was told.

1969-74

Worsley returned to the Canadiens for the start of the 1969–70 season but didn't stay long. Ruel continued to chastise Worsley for his slack approach to practices. He also favored Vachon, giving the young goalie much more playing time than the veteran. A month into the season, Ruel and Worsley weren't even on speaking terms.

Pollock assigned Worsley to the Montreal Voyageurs of the American Hockey League, but the goalie wouldn't go. When he was suspended for not reporting to the farm team, Worsley announced his retirement. He headed back home to Beloeil, situated about 20 miles east of Montreal, where he got reacquainted with his family—which then included Doreen and four children, Lorne Jr., Dean, Drew and Lianne—and promoted a brand of hockey sticks.

He was easing into civilian life when he got a phone call from the general manager of the expansion Minnesota North Stars. Wren Blair wanted Worsley on his roster. Blair made a good offer, but it wasn't enough to persuade Worsley to come out of retirement. The deal was sealed, however, when Wren pointed out that, because Minnesota was in the central part of North America, the North Stars traveled less than other NHL teams. "That's how we got him," Lou Nanne, who played for the North Stars, said years later. He added that Worsley never overcame his fear of flying. "I used to sit behind him on our charter flights...we'd take off, and I'd reach up and shake his chair, and he'd about have a heart attack."[18]

WORSLEY JOINED the North Stars in February 1970 and shared goaltending duties with Cesare Maniago. Although the men were polar opposites in appearance—Maniago was seven inches taller than the vertically challenged Worsley—they became fast friends.

Worsley made an impression on his teammates. "We had a training camp in Winnipeg, and we started dry-land training," former teammate Tom Reid recalled in 2007. "We'd run up and down hills, run around the track, do firemen's carries. We were all told to bring running shoes and shorts. One day we're running on the track and I look over and there's Gump. He's got on black wingtip brogues, with knee-high black socks and a pair of shorts, smoking a cigarette, and walking. Gump was always one of the centers of attention, because he was so comical."[19]

➤ PAYING TRIBUTE TO "GUMPER" ◄

THE GUMPER'S appeal has transcended hockey to such an extent he's been immortalized in songs by two Canadian indie rock bands.

The Weakerthans put out a song called "Elegy for Gump Worsley" in 2007, a few months after the goalie died. It commended him for inspiring "a nation of pudgy boys." In 1995, Huevos Rancheros recorded an instrumental song called "Gump Worsley's Lament" for the compilation album *Johnny Hanson Presents: Puck Rock.* "I grew up playing street hockey," says Calgary-based guitarist Brent J. Cooper, when asked about the genesis of his band's song. "I was a goalie, so the names of famous NHL goalies were always floating around in my head. I like the name 'Gump Worsley.' It has a nice ring to it. 'Ken Dryden's Lament' wouldn't work as well as a song title."

But what did Worsley have to lament? "Well, a few things, I guess," Cooper continues. "For starters, he once suffered a concussion when he was hit by hard-boiled egg." The musician gives Worsley credit for being "a real character. Does he have a stamp yet? There really should be a Gump Worsley stamp."

Worsley spent most of his time in Minnesota as a backup goalie, but—with three individual NHL trophies on his mantel and four Stanley Cup rings in his jewelry box—he had nothing left to prove. He enjoyed playing in Minnesota and it showed. His enthusiasm helped lift the team into the playoffs for four straight seasons. But the "Gumper," as he was affectionately known by adoring Minnesota fans, was getting long in the tooth—and that showed too.

> "I met Gump in the coffee shop at MLG before one big game. I asked him, 'Gump, do you get really nervous before a game like this?' He raised his coffee cup and I saw that his hand was shaking. He said, 'Did you ever see whitecaps on a cup of coffee?'"
>
> *Sports broadcaster and author*
> **BRIAN MCFARLANE**

He was more injury-prone than ever. Six weeks into the 1970–71 season, when he was 41 years old, he collided with a teammate in a pre-game skate and tore a muscle in his right shoulder. He sat out for a couple of weeks. The following season, trainers had to use oxygen to revive him after a collision sent him headfirst into the crossbar in the opening round of the play-offs. A hamstring injury sidelined him for five weeks in the 1972–73 season, and he appeared in just 12 games. Beat and beaten up, Worsley decided to retire. But the North Stars were loath to see the goalie go, so they made him an offer that would see him stay with the club for five more seasons, the first as a player and the next four as a scout. He accepted.

In the third period of his final NHL game, in April 1974, Worsley gave up three goals in less than five minutes. The last of those was scored by Dave Schultz, who was born in 1949, the year Worsley started his professional career. Worsley unfastened his goalie pads for the last time and became a North Stars scout.

RETIREMENT

During his 14 years as a scout, Worsley looked at a lot of NHL prospects, including goalies. "For me, only one thing [matters]," he explained. "Does he keep the flippin' puck out of the flippin' net? If he can do that consistently and in tough situations, I don't give a hoot about style or technique."[20]

Worsley was thrilled when he was inducted into the Hockey Hall of Fame in 1980. "You always hope that one day you'll make it…and this is it," he said when he got the news. "It's just great."[21]

At the ceremony, he faced a barrage of reporters' questions for the first time since his playing days. They asked him what he did when he wasn't scouting. "Just like a schoolteacher in the summer—nothing." And what about flying? "I fly now that I'm scouting for Minnesota, but I don't like it any more than I did then. I went to see a shrink about it and he didn't help me any."[22]

His wit never dulled, but his health declined in his golden years. He had a heart attack in January 2007 and, five days later, died at his home in Beloeil. He was 77. Tributes arrived from around the hockey world in the following days, but none were more fitting than the one from the man who had sat behind Worsley on dozens of flights in and out of Minnesota. "Worsley was one of the first real characters in the NHL," Nanne said. "He had a lot of personality and really showed the human side of the game. He didn't look like an athlete, and he smoked like a chimney between periods, but he was terrific when he put the pads on."[23]

WORSLEY · ALL-TIME RANKING*

REGULAR SEASON			PLAYOFFS		
GAMES	WINS	SO	GAMES	WINS	SO
861 [10th]	335 [18th]	43 [31st]	70 [32nd]	40 [23rd]	5 [36th]

* statistics as of July 2, 2013.

> NHL ALL-STAR TEAM **(1ST)**: 1967–68

> NHL ALL-STAR TEAM **(2ND)**: 1965–66

5

|||||||||||||||||||||||||||||||||||||||||||||

THE
GENTLEMAN
JOHNNY BOWER

|||||||||||||||||||||||||||||||||||||||||||||

"If you don't like Johnny Bower,
there's not much hope for you."[1]

St. Louis Blues coach
LYNN PATRICK, in 1976

JOHNNY BOWER sat down in the Toronto Maple Leafs
dressing room after a practice in 1968 and unlaced his goalie
pads. Soon afterwards, they disappeared. More than four
decades later, a fan named Roger Spivey presented the pads to
the Leafs legend and explained that Bower's teammate, the late
Tim Horton, had given them to Spivey's mother years before.
Spivey had worn them as a teenager. The gesture moved Bower
to tears.

Days later, Bower showed a writer the old leather-covered
pads in the garage of his suburban Toronto home. He beamed as
he propped them against his calves. "Look there," he said, pointing at initials etched on the sides of the pads. "J.B. They're mine,
all right!"

Reclining in a chair in his living room, Bower spent the next
hour gamely answering questions he had been asked countless

times over the years. He talked about the four Stanley Cup victories, his individual awards and his former teammates. "Geez," he said, clasping together hands as big as pizza trays, "What a great bunch of guys!"

When the interview ended, the writer headed to the door. Bower called her into the dining room. He signed a puck and several copies of a photo showing him in his prime—wearing his Leafs jersey with his arms wrapped around the Cup. She thanked him and left. She took a few steps down the driveway and then stopped and turned. Bower was calling to her. "Thanks for dropping by!" he said, waving. "Merry Christmas!"

He was one of the nicest people she had ever met—and she wasn't the first person to feel that way. During his illustrious NHL career, Bower earned a reputation for being not just a gifted athlete and a dogged competitor but also a gentleman. He remains so to this day.

BORN JOHN KISZKAN in November 1924, he grew up in Prince Albert, Saskatchewan, a small community on the banks of the North Saskatchewan River. There were few jobs during the Depression. Most families struggled to make ends meet, and the Kiszkan family was no exception. John, one of only two sons among nine children, earned money delivering the local newspaper, but it was not enough to buy him hockey equipment.

Nonetheless, on winter mornings, he bundled up and walked to an outdoor rink, where he and his friends played shinny for hours at a time. His skates, which an older player had given to him, were much too big, so he often played without them—an inconvenience that prompted him to become a goalie.

He stood like a sentry at his post in front of a makeshift net, even when the plummeting temperature robbed him of feeling in his fingers and toes. He wore pads fashioned from a discarded mattress and used a stick that his father, John Sr., had carved from a tree branch. It was too heavy for the young goalie to lift, so he stood in net with his stick resting on the ice like a cinder block.

➤ SEARED BY A BRANDING IRON ◄

LIKE MOST goalies of his generation, Bower didn't wear a mask until the twilight of his career. In his prime, he stared down opposition forwards barefaced. Top shooters such as Jean Beliveau and Bernie "Boom Boom" Geoffrion gave him pause, but he didn't lose sleep over anyone—except Bobby Hull. The Ontario farm boy, whose arms were as big as the columns of a Roman amphitheater, was famous for his booming slap shot, clocked at 120 miles per hour.

In one game against the Chicago Blackhawks, Bower managed to get his left leg in front of a Hull drive. Despite his protective padding, the goalie limped off the ice at the end of the game with a badly bruised knee.

Once, when Hull scored on a shot from 60 feet out, Bower was as dumbstruck as the spectators. He described the shot as "a black blur. It was heading right for my right ear," the goalie said. "I straightened up and tried to take it on my chest but it was too fast and crashed in off my forearm. It felt like I had been seared by a branding iron. Beliveau fires most of his shots low, just off the ice. Hull throws a high, hard one. It's a rising shot and heavy as a lead weight. When you catch one, it just about tears your hand loose from the wrist."[35]

Years later, during a shooting drill before a game at Maple Leaf Gardens, Hull unleashed a shot that shattered Harold Ballard's nose in four places. The puck hit the Leafs owner while he was sitting in an executive suite reading a program.

Bower still shudders when he remembers the Golden Jet's booming shot. "I just stood there and did this," he says, moving his right hand across his chest in the sign of the cross.

HE STARTED playing organized hockey, hoping to follow in the footsteps of celebrated Boston Bruins goalie Frank Brimsek, but he put his career on hold when war broke out on foreign shores in 1939. Kiszkan managed to join the army, though he was only 15, three years younger than the minimum age required for enlistment, and was sent to Vernon, B.C., for training.

Officials there soon found out Kiszkan was underage, so he was forced to cool his heels in B.C. for two years. When he was finally sent to England, he trained as a gunner in the Queen's Own Cameron Highlanders of Canada. He was supposed to take part in the Battle of Dieppe—a 1942 Allied attack on a German-occupied port in France—but instead ended up convalescing in a British hospital with a respiratory infection. He was also diagnosed with rheumatoid arthritis, which was most acute in his hands, and was eventually sent home.

> "If you play your heart out, the Toronto fans will give you a lot of credit, even if you don't play well every night. They love their hockey and, of course, they want the Stanley Cup really badly."
>
> **JOHNNY BOWER**

His health improved, but the pain in his hands never went away. "Eventually, when I got older, especially once I started playing goal for a living, I got used to the pain," he says. "It's like nothing. You know it's there. It's just throbbing, throbbing, throbbing."[2]

KISZKAN RETURNED to the ice for part of the 1944–45 season and played for the Prince Albert Black Hawks of the Saskatchewan Junior Hockey League. He led the league with a 2.57 goals-against average and attracted the attention of scouts from the American Hockey League (AHL).

He turned professional the following season, playing for the Cleveland Barons. Now known as Johnny Bower—he had legally changed his name in response to a split in his family—he established himself as one of the league's best goalies. For his first four years in Cleveland, he shared goaltending duties with Roger Bessette. In the 1947–48 season, the pair posted a 27-game unbeaten streak and lifted the Barons to the league title.

NHL

1953-54

Bower's success drew the attention of the New York Rangers, who recruited him to play during the 1953–54 season. He was almost 30 years old when he made his NHL debut. Under the tutelage of coach Frank Boucher, Bower played 70 games for the NHL club and notched a solid 2.60 goals-against average.

Five decades later, he still flinches when he recalls playing at Madison Square Garden. When New York fans were frustrated with their middling team, they hurled chairs and other objects at Bower. A spectator once threw a dead fish at him, but the goalie refused to pick it up, worried that it might be a bomb.

Convinced that Bower gave up too many rebounds, the Rangers sent him packing at the end of the season and tapped veteran Gump Worsley to be their starter. Bower was disappointed. "I thought I was as good as Worsley, but they kept Gump and I was sent down to the minors," he said five years later, adding that the Rangers never gave him "a real chance to remain in the National Hockey League."[3]

1954-57

Bower spent the next three seasons bouncing around between teams. He played seven games for the Rangers and suited up for the Vancouver Canucks of the Western Hockey League as well as his former team, the Providence Reds. But he was undaunted. "I lost a lot of confidence through that experience, but I didn't give in. I knew NHL scouts would be watching me. I kept saying to myself, 'John, you have to think positively.' I couldn't go to sleep every night worrying about every move I made on the ice."

Looking back, Bower attributes much of his perseverance to the support of his wife, Nancy, whom he had married in 1948. "In many games, I played poorly and let in some bad goals. But I never considered giving up," he says. "My wife pushed me pretty good. She was a big factor."

1957-58

Bower landed back in Cleveland in the 1957–58 season and thrived there. Late in the season, he headed into a game against Providence, hoping to post a league-record-breaking ninth shutout. He was just minutes away from doing that when an opponent's foot found Bower's midsection and the goalie fell to the ice clutching his ribs. He was carried off on a stretcher and remained sidelined for three weeks.

But he returned to the game in time for the playoffs and turned in a stellar performance against the Springfield Indians, the Boston Bruins farm team. The Indians general manager, Punch Imlach, was impressed.

THE LEAFS had finished dead last in the 1957–58 season. Stafford Smythe, head of the committee that ran Toronto's hockey operations, hoped a new goalie would improve the team's fortunes. The Leafs claimed Bower in the inter-league draft in June 1958.

Bower was reluctant to join the club at first. He, Nancy and their two children, John Jr. and Cindy (Barbara would arrive two years later) were comfortable in Cleveland. Besides, he was a star in the AHL, having played on four championship teams and been named the league's best player three times. He was already 33 years old, and he doubted the Leafs were serious about making him their starting goalie.

He considered hanging up his skates and returning to Prince Albert to tend to his hamburger joint, an establishment columnist Milt Dunnell generously described as a "Saskatchewan culinary and culture center."[4] But with encouragement from Barons general manager Jim Hendy, who stood to receive some financial compensation for his goalie, Bower took a second crack at the NHL. He signed a two-year contract with the Leafs. It stipulated that he could return to Cleveland if he didn't make the Leafs roster.

Three decades after taking his first tentative steps on an outdoor rink in central Saskatchewan, Bower arrived in Toronto amid the clatter of streetcars, the shouts of newsboys and the distant hum of traffic on a newly built expressway. About eight goalies took to the ice during training camp, but Bower, who was much more experienced, stood out from the rest. He didn't wear a mask, but he was ferocious in protecting his net. At a time when goalies were expected to stand as erect as the Queen's Guard, Bower routinely dove headfirst at shooters, extending his stick to knock the puck loose. Impressed with his poke check and his expertise at cutting down angles, the Leafs added him to the roster.

1958-60

He shared the workload with Ed Chadwick, who had been the Leafs starter the previous two seasons. The men became fast friends, even though they were competing for the top job. On one occasion, when Bower's equipment failed to arrive in time for a practice, Chadwick lent him his own.

With Imlach now at the helm as general manager and coach, the Leafs began their slow march up the standings. Thanks to a late surge in the 1958–59 season, they won the fourth and final playoff berth. Bower was tapped to start in the post-season.

The Leafs, who had finished with 65 points, scored a surprising upset in the first round, beating the favored Boston Bruins (73 points) four games to three. In the final game, the puck

➤ "HONKY THE ◄ CHRISTMAS GOOSE"

I N NOVEMBER 1965 a CBC radio employee named Chip Young wrote the lyrics for a Christmas song called "Honky the Christmas Goose." He recruited Bower, whom he described as "the friendliest man in Canada," to record the song. After drinking tea with honey for a week, Bower headed into the studio with his son, John Jr., and a group of neighborhood kids who had agreed to be the backup singers. Johnny Bower with "Little John and the Rinky Dinks" recorded the song and another called "Banjo Mule."

"The night we recorded the songs the lights went out and I nearly died," Bower said later that month. "I'm no Sinatra but I didn't think my voice would wreck the hydro. I was glad to learn that I hadn't blown all the fuses... I was a soprano back home before my voice changed. Now I guess I'm a cracked bass."[36]

"Musically, that was really a tough year for me," Bower said decades later. "We were bucking the Beatles at the time."[37]

The record was released in time for Christmas and became a big hit. It sold more than 40,000 copies, making it the best-selling Canadian record ever made to that point.

Almost 30 years later, when Bower confessed to a reporter that he didn't own a copy of the record, fan Don Fountain gave his copy to the legendary goalie. "All those stories about Johnny being such a kind man are true," Fountain said. "We visited with him for about an hour and he treated us like family."[38]

smashed into the face of Boston goalie Harry Lumley, splitting his upper lip, breaking a real tooth in half and knocking out a false one. He skated off the ice spitting blood and received dental care. When he returned to his net 30 minutes later, he made sensational saves on three Toronto players. But he couldn't stop Gerry Ehman, who scored with less than three minutes remaining in the third period to give the Leafs a 3–2 victory. "The mouth hurts quite a bit," a dejected Lumley said afterwards in the Bruins dressing room. "But I don't know which hurts most— the mouth or the losing." Imlach was giddy. "We're going to take the whole thing," he said, looking ahead to the final. "I have no doubt about it."[5]

Toronto met the powerful Montreal Canadiens (91 points) in the final. The Leafs put up a good fight, but the Habs, who had just eliminated the Chicago Blackhawks (69 points), beat the Leafs four games to one to win their fourth straight Cup. Imlach had to eat his words, but Smythe was unbowed. "The Canadiens had better take a good look at the Stanley Cup because it's the last time they're going to see it for a long time," Smythe said. "This club is on its way."[6]

THE LEAFS continued to improve the following season. Forwards Bob Pulford and George Armstrong emerged as two of the league's top scorers and, with help from rugged defenseman Horton, formed a potent offense. Bower was solid in net.

The Leafs finished second overall, with 79 points, and faced the Detroit Red Wings (67 points) in the semifinal. Bower didn't blink in his showdown with superstar Gordie Howe. Time and again, the goalie shut down the forward, who had won the NHL scoring title five times and had been named the league's most valuable player four times. But there were no hard feelings between the rivals. They were good friends who had spent many summer days together, fishing in their native Saskatchewan. After Bower turned aside one of his shots, Howe skated past the goalie and leaned in to him. "When we get out in the boat next summer," he said with a sly smile, "you're going into the lake." The Leafs clipped the Red Wings in a six-game series.[7]

The Leafs met the powerful Montreal Canadiens (92 points) in the final for the second straight year. It was a David-and-Goliath showdown that didn't unfold according to the script. In this version, the giant picked up the future king and crushed him between his thumb and index finger. The Leafs fell in four straight games and were out-scored 15-5.

1960-61

The Leafs continued to improve in the 1960-61 season, thanks to the contribution of certain top players. After three full seasons in the NHL, a strapping young forward emerged as an offensive threat. Frank Mahovlich led the Leafs in scoring that season and finished third in the league. Teammate Red Kelly was one step behind, finishing sixth overall—not bad for a player who had been a defenseman until the previous season. Rookie Dave Keon, a great skater, made an immediate impact at both ends of the ice.

The Leafs were first in the standings when they rolled into Detroit for a game in February. In the third period, Detroit's Howie Young collided with Bower when the goaltender came out of his net to clear a puck. Bower headed to the dressing room for treatment. He later returned to the ice, but his left leg folded as he tried to make a routine save. "He looked like a wounded duck trying to get off the water as he staggered to his feet," according to one report. Ignoring Imlach's entreaties to head to the bench, Bower made an acrobatic dive to stop Alex Delvecchio on a late breakaway. Imlach later described Bower, who had suffered a pulled hamstring, as the gutsiest goaltender in hockey.[8]

Bower sat out 12 games that season, but he still managed to win more games (33) than any other goalie, and he had the best goals-against average (2.50) among all starters, except for the Canadiens' Charlie Hodge, who had played 28 fewer games.

With Bower in net and steadfast defensemen such as Horton, Bob Baun, Carl Brewer and Allan Stanley on the blue line, the Leafs allowed the fewest goals in the NHL. Bower won the Vezina Trophy, which was then given annually to the goalie(s) on the team allowing the fewest goals.

The Leafs and Canadiens waged a pitched battle for first place in the regular season. Montreal came out on top with 92 points, and the Leafs finished just 2 points behind, in second place. Toronto met Detroit in the semifinal again, but the outcome was different this time. The Red Wings (66 points) flew past the Leafs, who were hampered by injuries, and won the series four games to one. (Detroit squared off against Chicago in the final and lost four games to two.)

1961-62

Bower suffered a bruised ankle early in the 1961–62 season but returned to the ice and finished the season with more wins (31) than any other goalie except Montreal's Jacques Plante (42).

Once again, the Canadiens (98 points) finished first in the standings, with the Leafs (85 points) one spot behind. Toronto was considered a strong contender heading into the playoffs, and many fans expected the Leafs to make quick work of the lowly Rangers (64 points). But the Rangers fought hard, coming back from a two-game deficit to win the third and fourth games.

Game 5 was a fierce contest. It ended when Kelly scored four minutes into the second overtime period to give the Leafs a 3–2 win. He became an instant hero in Maple Leaf Gardens, but it was the veteran Rangers goalie who received the lion's share of the praise. "This writer never has seen better playoff goalkeeping than [Gump] Worsley threw at the Leafs, but it was not enough to turn the tide in New York's favor," wrote columnist Red Burnett. "In all, Gump kicked out 56 shots, of which about 20 appeared labelled. When you can't win with goalkeeping like that you don't have much hope."[9]

Before celebrating with his teammates, Bower skated across the ice toward the man who had taken his job eight years before. He shook Worsley's hand. "I told him he was great," Bower said. "He grabbed my hand, looked at that wildly cheering crowd and said, 'John, you were just as good or we would have won. We sure as h— gave them their money's worth.'"[10]

The Leafs clinched that series two nights later by trouncing the Rangers 7-1 and then squared off against the Chicago Blackhawks (75 points) in the final. Momentum swung back and forth in that series until Game 5, when the Leafs thumped the Blackhawks 8-4 to take the series lead. Bower sat out that game with a pulled groin. He spent the rest of the series on the sidelines, and backup Don Simmons took his place in net.

In Chicago two nights later, Blackhawks goalie Glenn Hall made 27 saves in the first two periods—including 6 in which he stopped Toronto snipers at close range—and another 8 in the third frame. Early in the third period, teammate Bobby Hull opened the scoring when he intercepted a Leafs clearing pass and blasted in a shot from 20 feet out. Jubilant fans threw hats, beer cans, toilet paper, colored ink, a water bomb and eggs onto the ice. But the celebrations didn't last long. With Keon, Pulford and Kelly firing on all cylinders, the Leafs scored two unanswered goals to win the game—and their first Cup in 11 years. In the dressing room afterwards, an exuberant Mahovlich picked up the 35-pound trophy and held it high above his head. "We've got it fellows," he yelled. "Just take a look at it!"[11]

Six weeks later, a helicopter pilot found the remains of Bill Barilko, a defenseman who had scored the winning goal in the Leafs' previous Cup victory, in 1951, and then had disappeared on a fishing trip.

1962-63

In the 1962–63 season, the Leafs finished first overall with 82 points, 1 more than the second-place Blackhawks.

Toronto stormed past Montreal (79 points) in the semifinal. The Leafs clinched the series in Game 5, thanks mostly to Keon, who notched two goals and an assist, and Bower, who posted his second shutout of the series. When the game ended in a 5–0 Toronto victory, 14,000 fans at the Gardens rose to give the goalie a standing ovation as his teammates showed their love by giving him a "mauling," according to Burnett. "John, gifted with the knowledge and wisdom of at least 39 years and the rubber legs and reflexes of a teenager, was tremendous through this Stanley Cup semi final," the columnist wrote.[12]

Someone snapped a picture of Bower and his son after the game, and the photo ran in a Toronto newspaper the next day. Sporting a crew cut, the boy is seen smiling ear to ear while clasping his father's arm in the Leafs dressing room. "Johnny Bower, 9, is proudest and happiest lad in town as he poses with pop after the game," the caption read.[13]

Less than a week later, Bower was in the dressing room to suit up for the first game of the final against Detroit. The Red Wings (77 points) had the league's top scorer in Howe and one of the best goalies in Terry Sawchuk, but they couldn't manhandle the Leafs. The Leafs held the Red Wings to just 10 goals in five games. Keon scored two shorthanded goals in Game 5 to give the Leafs a 3–1 win—and their second straight Cup.

The next day, the players were driven through Toronto's financial district for a ticker tape parade. For the second year in a row, tens of thousands of fans lined the streets to show their love. Six hundred policemen lined the route.

1963-64

Those celebrations seemed like a distant memory just a month into the 1963–64 season. Toronto was treading water in the middle of the standings and threatening to sink to the bottom. The players' spirits were low, and Imlach was irate. He barked at players in the dressing room and openly criticized those he felt were playing poorly. Bower was the target of at least one outburst.

But even in trying times, the goalie remained a gentleman. During a game against Montreal in January, Canadiens enforcer John Ferguson crashed into the boards behind the Leafs net and collapsed on the ice. Bower skated to his side to ensure he was okay. Imlach was enraged. "I don't know what Bower said to him, but I don't like it. We're here for one thing only—to win. We're not running a kindergarten." Bower helped the Leafs notch a 6–1 victory, but that did little to placate Imlach.[14]

He announced that Bower was sitting out for a week because he had a sore hand. Skeptical reporters were banned from the Leafs dressing room. "According to an official announcement from the Leafs, Bower will be resting a bruised hand. But it's no secret to those who watched Thursday's practice session that the ancient netminder stomped off in a huff after being rebuked by manager-coach Punch Imlach," wrote one reporter. "Imlach told Bower his job was strictly stopping shots, not worrying about the condition of opposing National Hockey League forwards who happened to crash into the boards near Bower's cage... Imlach's attitude is: let them fall where they will. Bower disagreed. Bower is benched."[15]

Bower was riding the pine a week later, when his team's predicament worsened. The Leafs suffered a humiliating 11–0 loss at Maple Leaf Gardens to the lowly Boston Bruins.

IN DESPERATION, Imlach orchestrated a blockbuster trade that saw Andy Bathgate, the NHL's leading scorer (along with Hull) in the 1961–62 season, join the Leafs. He arrived in Toronto with fellow forward Don McKenney.

Right after the trade, the Leafs took on the Rangers in back-to-back games. Toronto won the first matchup 5–2 and the second one 4–3. McKenney notched a goal and an assist on Saturday and added a goal on Sunday.

THE KING OF
PRINCE ALBERT

IN 2009, Bower returned to his hometown, Prince Albert, for the dedication of the Johnny Bower Lobby in a local arena. He had a tight schedule, but at the request of mayor Jim Scarrow, he took the time to visit an ailing First Nations man in the hospital. "Long John had his chest pressed up against the X-ray machine when we walked in," Scarrow recalls. "But as soon as he saw Johnny, his face just lit up. Bower was beaming too."

Scarrow had met Bower decades earlier. "He was a household name back then. He had a wonderful sense of humour and an incredible smile. People remember him as a kind person, one who would give you the shirt off his back."

The Leafs lost only 4 of the 15 games remaining in the regular season after the trade, and Bathgate collected 18 points. Toronto finished third in the standings, with 78 points, and faced the first-place Canadiens (85 points) in the semifinal. The teams battled hard, pushing the series to seven games. In the last tilt, Bower stopped 38 shots to help the Leafs clinch a 3–1 victory. "We were two goals down, came back and were stopped by Bower," Montreal general manager Frank Selke said about the goalie, who was named the first star of the game. "He's a great goal-tender. It eases the pain if you lose to a nice guy like Bower."[16]

The Leafs took on the Red Wings (71 points) in the final. Detroit had staged an upset in the semifinal by beating the Blackhawks (84 points) in seven games—and they proved hard to handle. In fact, the Leafs were trailing three games to two when the teams met for Game 6 at Olympia Stadium in Detroit. In the third period, Howe blasted a shot that hit Baun in the ankle. The defenseman suffered a hairline fracture and was carried off the ice on a stretcher. After a doctor froze the ankle, Baun slid his skate back on and hobbled to the bench. The teams continued to duke it out, and regulation time ended in a 3–3 tie. In overtime, Baun took a pass from Pulford and put a shot over Sawchuk's shoulder. The spectators sat in stunned silence.

Bower deserved much of the credit for the win—at least according to Keon. "Before we came back and Bobby scored that goal, we had been losing by one in the third period. [Detroit forwards] Norm Ullman and Larry Jeffrey got in all alone on Johnny," Keon said 45 years later. "Norm passed and Larry shot and, somehow, Johnny reached back and made the save. Right then I knew we had won the Stanley Cup. We were kind of dead on the bench, everybody tired, but when John made that save, we knew we would come back."[17]

Two days later, the puck dropped in the Gardens for the deciding game. The Leafs won 4–0 to clinch their third straight Cup. When the final buzzer sounded, their elated goalie threw his stick in the air. The piece of wood returned with a vengeance, smacking him on the nose and slicing a cut that needed seven stitches. "I didn't even feel it, I was so excited. I kept holding my hand to my self-inflicted wound, pinching it, to squeeze it together and stop the bleeding. I was happy," Bower said.[18]

Two months later, Detroit left Sawchuk unprotected in the intra-league draft, either because they were confident in the abilities of upstart Roger Crozier, who would be named the NHL's best rookie in the 1964–65 season, or as Howe suggested, because they figured no one would take a chance on the

34-year-old Sawchuk. The Leafs jumped at the chance to add him to their roster. If Bower was worried about his job, he didn't show it. He applauded the trade and said he was convinced the Leafs would win another Cup because Sawchuk was "the best goaltender there is in the league."[19]

1964-66

The Leafs didn't come close to laying their hands on Lord Stanley's Cup the following two seasons. The Canadiens eliminated them in the semifinal both years. But Toronto's middle-aged goalies acquitted themselves well, sharing the Vezina Trophy in the first of those seasons.

1966-67

The first part of the 1966–67 season played out like the opening bars of a dirge. The Leafs lost 10 games in a row in late January and early February, sending Imlach to the hospital with exhaustion. The team regained some equilibrium in his absence and mounted a 10-game winning streak. They ended the season in third place overall, with 75 points. That won them a spot in the playoffs—and a date with the mighty Blackhawks.

The Hawks had shot to the top of the standings that season, finishing with 94 points. Armed with a powerful slap shot, Hull had scored more goals than any other NHL player that season. He had help from Stan Mikita, who had won the league's scoring title, and Kenny Wharram, who had tied Howe for fourth overall in scoring. Hall, an established star, shared the net with Denis DeJordy. Together they had won the Vezina Trophy that season.

Toronto was a squad of grizzled veterans, with eight players over the age of 35. Bower, 42, and Sawchuk, 37, were two of the three oldest goalies in the NHL. No one gave them a chance against Chicago.

Bower injured his thumb before the playoffs, ensuring that his partner would start in the opening round. Sawchuk

➤ AGELESS WONDER ◄

THROUGHOUT MOST of his career, Bower kept his teammates, the media and the fans in the dark about his true age. His coach, Punch Imlach, once said Bower had lied about his age so often the goalie himself wasn't sure of it. Bower became eligible for his NHL pension when he turned 45 in November 1969. He informed Clarence Campbell, but the league president wouldn't take his word for it. He ordered Bower to produce a birth certificate—which the goalie did in short order. The enduring mystery about Bower's true age was finally solved in the last of his 15 NHL seasons.

||||||||||||||||||||||||||||||||||||||||||||||||||||||||||||||||||||||||

floundered in the first game, prompting fans in Chicago Stadium to sing "Goodnight, Terry" during a 5–2 Leafs loss. But the Leafs bounced back to win four of the next five games, and much of the credit went to Sawchuk, who allowed just six goals in that span. He shut down Hull in the last two games.

Rookie Brian Conacher was also celebrated for his contribution. He scored two goals in his team's 3–1 victory in Game 6. "The puck went by [Glenn] Hall's left side and Conacher jumped in the air with joy when it hit the net," a reporter wrote about Conacher's unassisted second goal. "But he missed his landing and slid face-first into the Chicago goal. As he picked himself up, the crowd gave him a thunderous ovation."[20]

AFTER ELIMINATING the NHL's top team, the Leafs headed into the final against a Canadiens squad (77 points) that was brimming with confidence after sweeping aside the Rangers (72 points) in the semifinal. When the puck dropped in Montreal on April 20, 1967, Sawchuk was between the pipes. He allowed five goals and was pulled just five minutes into the third period. Bower allowed just one goal, but the speedy Habs won 6–2. Henri "Pocket Rocket" Richard notched a hat trick.

Bower shut down the Habs in the next game as the Leafs won 3–0. The goalie "threw a zero at the Habs here Saturday afternoon and changed the whole outlook of the Stanley Cup carnival," wrote Dunnell. "Instead of wondering mildly whether Leafs would manage to win a game (they succumbed in four last year) Montreal partisans stumbled out of the Forum mumbling that Punch Imlach must be equipping his goalies with monkey glands."[21]

Bower was also a standout in Game 3, which lasted almost 90 minutes. He made 60 saves, and the Leafs won 3–2 in the second overtime period. Bower robbed a handful of Montreal attackers, including Yvan Cournoyer, who had three great scoring chances. After the game, the veteran goalie quickly changed into his street clothes and rushed home to get some much-needed sleep. He left his coach behind to sing his praises. "Bower is the oldest guy, playing the toughest position of all in the fastest game there is," Imlach said. "Sure, he's amazing. Name me somebody in any sport who compares with him."[22]

Bower was supposed to start in Game 4, but during a pre-game warm-up, he stretched to stop a drive by teammate Larry Hillman and pulled a hamstring. He skated off the ice and didn't return. In the dressing room, Montreal players breathed a collective sigh of relief. "Bower had been murder to us in the [previous] two games," Habs coach Toe Blake explained later. Sawchuk started in goal. For the second time in the series, he floundered in net, and Montreal posted a 6–2 win.[23]

With Bower barely able to walk, Imlach had no choice but to start Sawchuk in the next game. He stood his ground this time, helping the Leafs post a 4-1 victory and pull ahead in the series, three games to two.

The Leafs flew home and had a brisk skate at the Gardens. While his teammates were on the ice, Bower was in the whirlpool. He took a steam bath afterwards to soothe his injured thigh—but it didn't do much good.

The next day, the Leafs gathered in the dressing room for Game 6. The players, many of whom had been teammates for years, knew the roster would be dismantled at the end of the season. Many of the veterans, their joints aching from countless body blows delivered and received, would retire. Others would be plucked from the roster by one of the six new teams joining the league the following season. It was the end of an era.

Breaking with character, Imlach showed a sentimental side. "It's been said that I stuck with the old men so long we couldn't possibly win the Stanley Cup," he told his players. "For some of you, it's a farewell." He paused then continued, returning to form. "Now, go out there and put that puck down their throats!" Imlach told Bower to dress for the game, only so that the goalie could be on the bench with his teammates. Bower did as he was told, Dunnell reported, adding that the goalie "would have squatted on the time clock in a bikini if Imlach had asked."[24]

With Bower on the sidelines, the team looked to Sawchuk to hold the fort—and he didn't disappoint. The crowd roared with approval as he kicked aside one Montreal shot after another. He frustrated a raft of Montreal shooters through 60 minutes, even robbing star Jean Beliveau twice on close-in chances. He made 40 saves overall as the Leafs won 3-1, and Armstrong, the captain, hoisted the Stanley Cup for the fourth time in six seasons.

Doused in champagne after the game, the players tossed Imlach and his assistant, King Clancy, into the shower fully clothed. Imlach emerged sopping wet to tell reporters that this Cup victory was the sweetest of all four. "We sure as hell ruined the Canadiens' plans to display the Cup at Expo 67," he said, "and [we] completed a centennial project on our own hook."[25]

Three days later, the 48th Highlanders band led the players in a cavalcade through the streets of downtown Toronto. They were showered with ticker tape and confetti. Some 25,000 fans greeted their heroes when they arrived at Nathan Phillips Square. Mayor William Dennison introduced each player to the cheering crowd, and Armstrong accepted a gold watch on behalf of the club. Later, the players gathered at the Gardens for a staff celebration—except Baun, who had missed the day's festivities to go fishing with his sons.

1967-70

After eight seasons as a mainstay of the Leafs lineup, Kelly retired and took a job as coach of the new Los Angeles Kings. He acquired Sawchuk when the Leafs left the goalie unprotected in the June expansion draft.

Back in Toronto, many of the Leafs' top scorers were in the lineup for the start of the 1967–68 season, but not all of them were happy. Some chafed at Imlach's hard-nosed leadership style.

Mahovlich was miserable. A few weeks into the season, the 29-year-old star fell ill on a train before it left for Detroit, where the Leafs were scheduled to take on the Red Wings. He was admitted to hospital suffering from acute depression and tension. Mahovlich took to the ice at a figure skating club as a form of therapy, and four weeks later, he returned to the Leafs lineup. But Imlach was fed up with his temperamental star and sent him to Detroit as part of a blockbuster seven-player trade that brought Paul Henderson and Norm Ullman to Toronto. Imlach hoped the change would breathe new life into his team, but it didn't. The defending Stanley Cup champions failed to make the playoffs.

IN THE 1968–69 season, the Leafs (85 points) finished fourth in the East Division and fifth overall. Having squeaked into the playoffs, they squared off against the Bruins (100 points) in the opening round.

Midway through the first game, Toronto defenseman Pat Quinn laid his elbow or shoulder (depending whom you ask) into Bobby Orr's head and knocked the superstar unconscious. The fans in Boston Garden were enraged, and with Orr en route to the hospital, they tried to attack Quinn in the penalty box. Leafs players rushed to his defense, swinging their sticks in the air to keep the fans at bay. A Lucite panel behind the penalty box was shattered, and police moved in to escort Quinn to the dressing room. A dustup between opposing players also caused delays, but the contest did eventually end. With Phil Esposito leading the charge, the Bruins clobbered the Leafs 10–0.

The carnage continued the next night, when the Bruins mowed down the Leafs 7–0. Three days later, Boston completed a four-game sweep of Toronto. Just minutes later, the Leafs president fired Imlach. "That's it, the end of the road; the end of the Imlach era," Smythe said. When media suggested that Imlach might stay on as general manager, Smythe's response was unequivocal. "No, he's fired. I am buying up the last year of his contract and we parted friends." The story ran with a photo showing Imlach slumped in a chair holding his hand up to his face, looking as though he wanted to disappear under his fedora.[26]

Toronto players heard the news while unlacing their skates in the dressing room. "That's it for me," the ever-loyal Bower said. "I'm leaving with him. He was the reason I stayed around. I thought I could help him in this rebuilding season. Personally, I thought he did a great job with the green defensemen. We might have gone further if a few guys had shown a little more desire."[27]

ARMSTRONG LATER convinced Bower to stick around for the 1969–70 season. The goalie turned 45 in November, becoming the first NHL player to become eligible for a pension while still active. "It's the desire that you have, that you want to win," he says today, explaining why he played as long as he did. "You play from your heart, mostly. Also, it was a livelihood for me. You have to work for something, and we were working for the fans. You have to give something back to them."

That season, the Leafs went with three goalies—Bower, Bruce Gamble and Marvin Edwards—leaving Bower with limited ice time. He didn't start in a game until December, when he played against the Canadiens. The Leafs were leading 3–2 at the end of the second period, but the Habs stormed back and scored four goals in the last frame. Montreal won 6–3. Media attributed the loss to defensive lapses, particularly by Horton. But Bower leapt to his teammate's defense and blamed himself. "If I hadn't dropped too soon, I would have had [Jacques] Lemaire's shot," he said. "If I stay up, he doesn't beat me."[28]

Bower was sidelined with a knee injury a few weeks later and found it challenging to return to game shape. That frustration, combined with his failing vision—he was having a hard time handling long shots due to shortsightedness—persuaded him to call it quits. In March, he hung up his skates to become a scout and goalie coach for the Leafs. "I don't feel too bad about bowing out of active playing," Bower said. "I thought it would be worse than it is. I felt better when [Leafs general manager Jim] Gregory offered me a job with the organization because I'm still going to be with the players. I'm going to enjoy it real well."[29]

When Bower was elected to the Hockey Hall of Fame six years later, columnist Jim Proudfoot sang his praises. "Four Stanley Cups, two Vezinas, one all-star nomination. All accomplished after joining the Leafs at 34, presumably well past his prime," he wrote. "What none of this conveys is the warmth and decency of Johnny Bower as a person."[30]

RETIREMENT

Bower never played another minute in the NHL, but he came close. At one point in the 1979–80 season, the Leafs suffered so many injuries an elephant could have thundered through the dressing room without brushing up against a healthy player. Bower, who laced up for the occasional practice at the time, volunteered to return to duty in the Leafs net. Jaws dropped. "Someone once suggested Johnny Bower was so good he could probably stop pucks while sitting in a rocking chair," one reporter wrote, "and we might finally see if that's true."[31]

When reporters reminded Bower he was nearing 60, he was coy. "Well, I don't know how old I am," he replied with a mischievous smile. "I volunteered for this job and I just hope and pray I'm not needed."

"I don't know whether Johnny can see that well," confessed Imlach, who had returned as Leafs coach that season. "But I used to say that when I coached him he never let us down … He has to be the greatest competitor I have ever seen."[32]

Bower didn't lace up that night—flu-stricken Paul Harrison managed to take to the ice—and the Leafs lost to Montreal, leaving some fans to wonder how the team would have fared with the "geriatric goalie" in net.

ON A LATER scouting trip in Providence, Rhode Island, Bower ran into Tom Army, who had been a color commentator on radio broadcasts of Reds games when Bower played for the team. "I saw John in the hall and decided to approach him. I started to introduce myself, and before I could finish he said, 'For Christ's sake, Tom, I know who you are!' I couldn't believe he remembered me. I offered to send him some old photos of the Reds championship team I had found in my cellar. He thanked me for offering, and was very gracious, but he told me to keep it. He said the Rhode Island Reds Heritage Society should have it. What a humble guy. You would never know he's a star. He's just a great guy."

In the 1980s, Bower took part in some charity golf tournaments. Decades between the pipes had left so much scar tissue in his hands that he couldn't rotate them enough to master his swing. But that didn't deter him. "If he hit a bad shot he would get really angry at me," Bathgate says about his longtime friend and golfing buddy. "But then he started going to the driving range to practice and he started to improve. He got better. After a while he could play a reasonable game."

Since leaving the Leafs organization in 1990, Bower has endorsed newly built homes, street hockey nets and a myriad of other products. In 2011, he released his own line of wine: Johnny Bower Merlot, produced by a winery in Beamsville, Ontario. A winery spokeswoman said the wine had been designed to match the former goalie's status as a "vintage hockey player."[33]

He has also continued to appear at countless events, for both commercial and charitable causes. At one event, the 86-year-old sat a table for 90 minutes, signing autographs, posing for photos and chatting with his fans. "I find it very flattering that they know me no matter where I go [in Toronto]...I guess the worry is when they don't ask to talk to you," he told one reporter. "These folks paid my salary at one time. Maybe they didn't, but their parents and grandparents did. It costs you nothing to stop and smile and say: 'Nice to meet you.'"[34]

BOWER · ALL-TIME RANKING*

REGULAR SEASON			PLAYOFFS		
GAMES	**WINS**	**SO**	**GAMES**	**WINS**	**SO**
552 [51st]	250 [46th]	37 [39th]	74 [25th]	35 [27th]	5 [36th]

* statistics as of July 2, 2013.

> NHL ALL-STAR TEAM **(1ST)**: 1960–61

6

||||||||||||||||||||||||||||||||||||||||||

THE BON
VIVANT
BERNIE PARENT

||||||||||||||||||||||||||||||||||||||||||

"He is a free-spirited guy.
He is a fun person, and he is happy."

Parent's business manager
DEAN SMITH

RELAXING IN A hotel restaurant with a writer, Bernie Parent shares his outlook on life. "There are two ways you can live. Either you're miserable or you're happy. It's simple," he says. "You choose." With neatly combed silver hair and a matching goatee, he could be a retired therapist. But then a boy wearing a Philadelphia Flyers jersey approaches the table to ask for an autograph, and it's clear that this man didn't spend his career counseling people with acute stress or helping couples overcome marital problems.

The conversation turns to hockey, and he's asked to confirm a rumor: Is it true he used to smell his teammates' shoes? His smile broadens. "Yes, that was me. I would smell their shoes— but only before they wore them," he confesses. "You know, there is a beauty to the smell of new leather, perfume or the scent you pick up when you walk through a field," he continues without a wink, a smile or any other indication he might be kidding around. "For me, this is another way to enjoy the magic of life."

Parent had an illustrious NHL career, and he embraced every magical part of it—from his Stanley Cup victories to his individual awards and, yes, even his teammates' footwear.

BERNIE PARENT was born in April 1945, the youngest of seven children. The family home was not far from the Montreal Forum, home of Les Habitants. Like kids across Quebec, Parent followed the Montreal Canadiens with religious fervor. He idolized Habs goalie Jacques Plante and spent hours camped outside the home of Plante's sister, who lived nearby, waiting to catch a glimpse of his hero. Too intimidated to approach the NHL star, Parent hid in the bushes and stared in amazement as Plante strode across the lawn.

Parent's parents, Claude and Emilie, emphasized the importance of education, but he wasn't an enthusiastic student. He and his friends spent entire afternoons chasing a tennis ball through the slush-filled streets of east Montreal. He couldn't gain much traction wearing oversized galoshes, but that didn't dampen his enthusiasm for these impromptu games.

When he found a pair of skates under the Christmas tree, Parent turned his attention to the ice, and a star was born—at least in the mind of the pudgy seven-year-old Habs fan. He wasn't a fast skater, so he backed into the goal crease and stayed there. It wasn't love at first blocked shot. Little Bernie hated wearing the bulky equipment, which took up as much space as he did and was difficult to move in—but he persevered.

After he allowed 20 goals in one organized game, the 11-year-old spent a month practicing his craft. He returned to the ice with a swagger rarely seen in a goalie barely tall enough to touch the crossbar. He played well in his next outing, helping his team record a 5–3 victory. Parent continued to hone his skills, playing on outdoor rinks in sub-zero temperatures.

Like most of his peers, he became a classic stand-up goaltender—and he didn't have much choice, as he saw it. The cold stiffened his limbs to such an extent that he sometimes dropped to the ice like a popsicle tumbling from a freezer door.

Parent hit his stride playing for a local Junior B team. "Backed by the goaltending magic of Bernie Parent, Rosemount Bombers kept their slim Metropolitan Junior Hockey League playoff chances alive by blanking Verdun Maple Leafs 3–0 before 4,491 boisterous fans at the Verdun Auditorium yesterday," the Montreal *Gazette* reported in March 1963. The article applauded the 17-year-old goalie for being "particularly larcenous" on a winger named Bob Berry, foiling him on "two close-in power play thrusts."[1]

Parent was so consistently "larcenous" he drew the attention of the Niagara Falls Flyers, an Ontario Hockey Association (OHA) team sponsored by the Boston Bruins. The Flyers recruited him for the 1963–64 season, and he ventured into the wilds of English Canada for the first time. "I went to Niagara Falls. If I had played it safe and stayed at home, I would have missed out on the whole journey that got me to where I am now," Parent says. "One decision can change your whole life."

Parent distinguished himself playing in an arena just a few blocks from the wax museums and neon lights of the main strip. The OHA named him the league's top goalie at the end of his rookie season. In his second season, he helped the team clinch the Memorial Cup, the top prize in Canadian junior hockey. He allowed just 19 goals in 13 games, recording a 1.63 goals-against average. A reporter sang the goalie's praises after the Flyers trounced the Edmonton Oil Kings 8–1 in the final game. "Parent is a big stand-up goalie," he wrote in the *Edmonton Journal*. "He's one of the best juniors I have ever seen."[2]

Parent's language skills didn't develop as readily as his game in those years, but that didn't prevent him from making friends. In fact, it helped. His teammates respected his determination to speak English and delighted in his good-natured response to ribbing about his poor grammar or pronunciation. They were sorry to see him go when, in the summer of 1965, the Bruins signed him and sent him to the Great Plains to lace up for the Oklahoma City Blazers of the Central Professional Hockey League.

NHL

1965-67

A month into the 1965–66 season, the Bruins were languishing at the bottom of the NHL standings and both their goalies, Ed Johnston and Gerry Cheevers, were sidelined with injuries. Parent headed to Chicago and laced up for a game against the league-leading Blackhawks. In his NHL debut, he turned aside 40 shots in a 2–2 draw.

Parent was in the Bruins net again for their next game against the Blackhawks. In that contest, hockey's most feared sniper, Bobby Hull, unleashed a slap shot that ripped through the air and smashed into Parent's hand, sending a torrent of pain up his arm. "The Golden Jet blazed one shot at Boston's rookie goalie, Bernie Parent, that nearly tore the youngster's hand off," a wire service reported after the Blackhawks victory "Parent, who again stood out in the Bruins nets, suffered an injured finger on the play and had to leave the game late in the third period when the finger began to bother him."[3] The rookie's initiation was complete.

Parent played in 39 NHL games that season, 6 more than Johnston and 32 more than Cheevers, performing admirably for the mediocre Bruins, who missed the playoffs that year and the next. (Before Bobby Orr and Phil Esposito lifted Boston to the top of the standings in the early 1970s, the team was the runt of the NHL litter.)

Parent showed a lot of promise, but that didn't endear him to hard-nosed Harry Sinden, who took over as Bruins coach in May 1966. He shook his head in disgust as Parent ate, drank and made merry with the conviction of a rock star backstage. Sinden questioned the work ethic of the young goalie, who had also developed a taste for cigars. The coach put him on the bench and left him there for most of the 1966–67 season. Parent looked on as Johnston and Cheevers split goaltending duties. He played in just 18 games that season, winning just four of them. More than once, a chorus of boos echoed through Boston Garden after he had given up a soft goal.

The Bruins left him unprotected in the expansion draft, when the NHL expanded from six to 12 teams. The Philadelphia Flyers picked him up along with fellow goalie Doug Favell.

1967-70

The new team finished first in the West Division, which consisted entirely of expansion teams, and sixth overall. The Flyers put up a good fight against the St. Louis Blues in the first round of the playoffs, pushing the quarter-final series to seven games before being eliminated. Parent and Favell were a big factor in the team's success.

But the Flyers began to flounder. The Blues swept them aside in the first round of the 1969 playoffs, and Philadelphia missed the playoffs altogether the following season.

Injuries and inconsistent play pushed Favell to the sidelines, and Parent emerged as the starting goalie. Before long, the French-Canadian kid became a fan favorite in Philly. He was also popular among his teammates, who appreciated his ability to give or take a joke with aplomb. They howled with laughter in the dressing room and on the team bus when Parent shared stories; his words burst from his mouth in a rapid-fire jumble, and his stories often collapsed in a heap of broken syntax.

Team executives liked Parent too, but that didn't prevent them from dangling him as trade bait in an attempt to add some firepower to the roster. Four months into the 1970–71 season, the Flyers gave up Parent in a complicated three-way trade. Parent was devastated. He held back tears as he packed up his car and headed north with his wife, Carol, their two young sons, Bernie Jr. and Chuck, the family dog and two gerbils.

1970-72

"My career wasn't going well when I landed in Toronto," Parent says now, looking back. "I had talent but I was lost, going in circles... it was like I was crawling through the swamp. Little did I know that when you hit bottom, sometimes it's good because it drives you in a different direction."

His tears dried up when he realized who he would be joining in Toronto—the man he used to study while hiding in the bushes of a neighbor's lawn. Plante, then in the twilight of his legendary career, was the Leafs starter that season. He was in his forties but was still in a class of his own, midway through a season in which he would notch an incredible 1.88 goals-against average—better than that of every NHL goalie except the Canadiens' Ken Dryden, who played in just six games.

The two new teammates were polar opposites in terms of temperament. Plante was as sullen as Parent was chipper. While Parent bonded with his teammates, Plante kept his distance. Yet the veteran warmed to the upstart and took him under his wing. Plante taught Parent to cut down angles, reducing the amount of net space open to shooters, and to steer shots toward the corner boards to avoid giving up rebounds. Following his mentor's advice, Parent made subtle adjustments to his game. He started placing his weight on his right leg (his stick side) rather than his left, to improve his balance. He also worked on his mental game and spent hours visualizing himself making saves in every situation. "I would sit there on the bench and watch Plante play," says Parent. "I thought, 'Wow.' He was very creative. He was the one who introduced the mask. He was the one who went behind the net to play the puck. I said to myself, 'That is what I want to do.' I asked him to teach me and he said, 'Sure.'"

Plante's influence was considerable. The similarities between the two goalies—on the ice, at least—were striking. Minnesota

North Stars goalie Gump Worsley, then near the end of his storied career, described Parent as "a carbon copy" of Plante. Parent's play improved dramatically. "He had quick hands and he
played angles well," said Johnny Bower, who had ended an illustrious playing career with the Leafs just before Parent arrived.
"He wouldn't race out to the shooter. He would edge out to cut
down the angle. Before the shooter knew it, he would run out
of real estate. By the time the shooter was ready to let the shot
go, there wasn't much of the net exposed. [Parent] basically
said to the shooter, 'Go ahead, try to beat me. You're not going
to score.'"

Parent's teammates warmed to him in Toronto too. Bower
described him as a "team joker" who would "keep the guys loose
and alive in the dressing room by cracking jokes and pulling
pranks."[4]

The Leafs were a middling team during Parent's time there.
In both seasons, they were eliminated in the first round of the
playoffs. No one attributed the team's lack of success to their
goaltenders. In fact, Parent was a man in demand. The Miami
Screaming Eagles, a franchise with the new World Hockey Association (WHA), offered the 27-year-old goalie a five-year contract
worth $750,000. Bombastic Leafs owner Harold Ballard—whose
penny-pinching and bad management ultimately made him
public enemy number one in Toronto—refused to match that
offer. Parent packed his bags, and Plante looked on with pride as
his hatchling left the nest.

1972-73

No sooner had the ink dried on Parent's contract than the
Screaming Eagles moved from Miami to Philadelphia and
became the Blazers. (Team ownership was not happy with the
arena in Miami; it had no air conditioning and an open roof.)

Parent started off on the wrong foot in the WHA. In fact,
he broke it while making a routine save just weeks into the
season and sat out for a month. When he returned, Parent

➤ PLAY IT AGAIN, KATE ◄

THREE DECADES after Kate Smith sang a stirring rendition of "God Bless America" on her radio show, the Broad Street Bullies made it their unofficial anthem. They played a recording of the song before a home game against the Toronto Maple Leafs in December 1969. Philadelphia won the game—and a superstition was born. The Flyers began to see the song as a good luck charm.

When Smith showed up at the Spectrum for the opening game of the 1973–74 season, the crowd went wild. She belted out the song and—wouldn't you know it—the Flyers won again. Soon, Smith was striking more terror in the hearts of visiting players than Dave "the Hammer" Schultz. Before the sixth game of the 1974 Stanley Cup final, Boston Bruins star Phil Esposito presented Smith with a bouquet of flowers, hoping to reverse the hex. It was no use. The Flyers won the game—and the Cup.

The opening strains of the song tied opponents' stomachs in knots, but by the second verse, even they had succumbed to its charms. Former Montreal Canadiens goalie Ken Dryden remembers vividly the start of the third game of the 1976 Cup final. "Finally, blackened ice surface, the gate opens up, red carpet, spotlight, Kate Smith," Dryden recalled years later. "I was standing beside Jimmy Roberts on the blue line and here's Jimmy, who by this time is about 35 years old and he's seen it all and done it all, and we're standing there belting out, 'God Bless America.' I mean from the bottom of our lungs we're really belting it out."[17]

Smith died in June 1986. A year later, the Flyers announced plans for a memorial—an eight-foot statue to be displayed outside the Spectrum. "Kate Smith was a great, great lady," said

Flyers president Jay Snider. "She was an inspiration not only to the Flyers, but to our entire country."[18]

To this day, the Flyers show a video of her singing "God Bless America" before important games.

||||||||||||||||||||||||||||||||||||||||||||||||||||||||||||||||||||||||||

continued to face a barrage of shots in every game. His valiant efforts to keep the scores respectable went unnoticed by most sports fans because they didn't go to the games—the Philadelphia Blazers played before mostly empty houses. Teammate Derek Sanderson recalled one grim outing—an exhibition game in Sherbrooke, Quebec. "Parent stood there during the national anthem and counted the people. He could count the crowd," Sanderson told author and sports broadcaster Evan Weiner. "There were 62 people. He said 'Derek, I am not playing before this sparse crowd. I am not going to injure myself with nobody watching.' And he left." Sanderson headed to the dressing room, hoping to convince Parent to return. He still remembers the conversation. "Bernie said, 'Derek, listen, you can get hurt every time you lace them up. I'm not playing in front of 62 people.' I said, 'Bernie, you're right,' and I took my skates off too."[5]

With the team's financial troubles growing, the checks stopped coming. Parent was not amused. He left the Blazers after the first game of the playoffs over a contract dispute. Coach John McKenzie called him a "selfish baby,"[6] and after the Cleveland Crusaders swept the Blazers aside in four games in their series, Philadelphia president Dick Olson vowed that Parent would never again wear the Blazers jersey, whose garish orange and yellow hues represented nothing less than an affront to human decency. That was just fine with Parent.

He wanted to return to the NHL but not to play in Toronto. He asked Ballard to trade his rights back to the Flyers, and the Leafs owner agreed. In May 1973, Parent switched places with his former goaltending partner Doug Favell. Favell went to Toronto, where he spent three disappointing seasons, and Parent headed to Philadelphia—where he played two of the best seasons ever recorded by a goalie.

1973-74

Parent headed back to Broad Street, but like the university grad who returns to his parents' home to find his bedroom has been turned into a storage area, the goalie discovered the landscape had changed in his absence. Favell, an acrobatic netminder with a flair for the dramatic, had become a fan favorite and his departure had upset many of the faithful. Fans grew crankier during Parent's first game back, an exhibition game against the New York Rangers. New York scored seven goals in short order, and Flyers coach Fred Shero pulled Parent as an act of mercy. But the rocky start soon became a distant memory.

The Flyers had a solid nucleus of young players, including talented forwards such as Bobby Clarke, Bill Barber and Rick MacLeish, as well as some good role players. Most of them were hard as nails—none more so than the "Hammer." Dave Schultz was an enforcer par excellence. The tall, mustachioed forward intimidated opponents and routinely pummeled them into submission. He recorded 472 minutes in penalties in the 1974–75 season, a record that still stands. In Philadelphia, he was embraced as a working class hero; elsewhere, he was accused of assault—not just on the ice but on the senses. He warbled his way through a song called "The Penalty Box," which opened with a jaunty piano riff—think of mood music in a saloon—and Schultz singing the line, "Baby, how long will ya keep me in the penalty box?" "What did I think? As a singer, Schultz was a great fighter," Parent later said.[7]

PARENT WON the hearts and minds of just about everyone— and not just because of his success on the ice. Fans found his animated and sometimes unintelligible speech endearing. Teammates laughed sharing stories about his unusual game-day rituals—he would eat a 16-ounce steak with exactly 10 mushrooms, take a nap with his dog Tinker Bell and then wake up to watch the Three Stooges—and his appreciation for what he considered the finer things in life, including the smell of shoe leather.

They also appreciated his ability to lighten the mood during tense moments. More than once, Parent called over a teammate at a critical moment in a game to engage in idle banter. "In the middle of the heat of battle he would do this," recalled teammate Bill Clement. "That's a great memory."[8] "Bernie was always full of life and energy," remembers Bob "Mad Dog" Kelly. "He would play pranks on his teammates and tell jokes. Bernie knew how to lighten the mood. And he kept on getting better. Not just his play but everything about him."

Reporters who crowded into the Flyers dressing room after games often received a warm welcome from Parent. He would stop what he was doing, smile widely and say, "Some fun, eh?"

THE NEWLY minted "Broad Street Bullies" ended the 1973–74 season with an incredible 112 points, good enough to place first in their division and second overall. Bobby Orr and the Big, Bad Bruins finished just one point ahead.

Parent was given much of the credit. He led the league in wins (47), shutouts (12) and goals-against average (1.89). He also saw more action than any other goalie. He played in 73 games that season, 3 more than second-place finisher Tony Esposito of the Chicago Blackhawks. Parent and Esposito were co-winners of the Vezina Trophy, which was then given to the goalie(s) on the team allowing the fewest goals. (Both Philadelphia and Chicago allowed 164 goals that season.)

The Flyers swept aside the Atlanta Flames (74 points) in four games in the quarter-final and then confronted the Rangers (94 points) in a dramatic semifinal. Philadelphia went on the attack right away. In Game 1, Flyers attackers racked up four goals at one end of the ice, while their goalie held the line at the other end. Parent stonewalled the Rangers offense, and the Flyers recorded a 4-0 win.

> "It's 60 minutes of hell. It must be like jumping out of an airplane. Before you do it, you want to think about anything else but what you're going to do."[20]
>
> **BERNIE PARENT**

The series was a fierce battle that went the distance—in one sordid incident, Schultz grabbed Rangers defenseman Dale Rolfe and beat him senseless. The Flyers won the seventh game 4-3, thanks to a stellar performance by Parent and teammate Gary Dornhoefer, who scored two key goals.

The Flyers then headed to Boston to take on the formidable Bruins in the final. Twelve days later, the series culminated with a dramatic Flyers win in Game 6 at the Spectrum. The Flyers scored a goal in the first period and didn't need any more than that. Parent didn't allow a single goal. No one blinked when he was awarded the Conn Smythe Trophy as the most valuable player in the playoffs. Late in that game, Parent called over teammate Simon Nolet. "From the bench I see Simon give him an annoyed wave and skate away," Clarke recalled years later. "I asked him 'What did that crazy bleeper say?' and Simon told me he was bragging about his new golf clubs."[9] A few minutes later, the Flyers had become the first expansion team to win the Stanley Cup.

"When time ran out, the Spectrum just exploded with noise," Parent later recalled, adding that so many people rushed onto the ice he could barely move. He and Clarke were forced to abandon plans to hoist the Cup on a celebratory lap around the ice. "The dressing room was a madhouse with people and cameras. Players were hugging and slapping each other on the back. When I had the chance, I moved into the medical room," Parent remembered. "Clarkie, Ross Lonsberry and a couple other players were there too. We just had to get away from the people and microphones and be by ourselves." Reporters found him there, lying on the trainer's table, drinking beer.[10]

More than 2 million people packed the streets of Philadelphia for the team's victory parade. Wild-eyed fans mobbed Parent and his teammates, leading police to fear for the athletes' safety. Kelly has vivid memories of the day. "When you're stuck in a parade, and you've had a few beers, you need to go to the bathroom. So at one point…" He starts to laugh. "At one point, Bernie got out of the car and walked up to a house on Broad Street. The people let him in to use the bathroom. When he was done, they removed the toilet seat. He signed it for them and they framed it."

1974-75

A few months later, the Flyers picked up where they had left off. They were a tour de force in the 1974–75 season, winning more regular-season games (51) than any other team. They tied the Buffalo Sabres and the Montreal Canadiens for most points (113) in the league.

Parent was dominant. For the second straight season, he led the league in wins (44), shutouts (12) and goals-against average (2.03). He won the Vezina Trophy again. This time, he didn't have to share it. Cars drove through the streets of Philadelphia with bumper stickers that read, "Only the Lord saves more than Bernie Parent." Fans hung banners with the same message on the walls of the Spectrum, where they chanted, "Bern-ie, Bern-ie," even before Parent stepped on the ice in his distinctive white fiberglass mask.

The Flyers beat the Leafs (78 points) in the quarter-final, winning the series in four games, and then met the New York Islanders (88 points) in the semifinal. That series didn't start well for Philadelphia's favorite son. During the Game 1 warm-up, Parent moved to block a shot by Dornhoefer. The goalie's stick got caught in his pads, leaving some of his leg exposed. The puck hit him square on the knee, sending him off the ice and onto a pair of crutches.

The Flyers won that game and the next with Wayne Stephenson in net. Parent ditched his crutches and took to the ice for Game 3 on Long Island. He posted a shutout as the Flyers won 1–0. The Islanders stormed back to win the next three games, sending the series to Philadelphia for a seventh and deciding game. Singer Kate Smith made an appearance, firing up the crowd with her popular rendition of "God Bless America." The Flyers were fired up too. They beat the Islanders 4–1.

The Sabres arrived two days later to start the Stanley Cup final. Led by the "French Connection," a line consisting of three skillful French Canadians (Gilbert Perreault, Rick Martin and Rene Robert), the Sabres were a serious threat.

The series started as a straightforward affair. With Clarke buzzing all over the ice, the Flyers jumped to a two-game lead. But the third game, in Buffalo, assumed the dimensions of a Monty Python movie. At one point, a bat flew across the ice. Parent raised his stick and took a swing at it but missed. The Sabres' Jim Lorentz had better luck. He made contact with the rodent, and it fell to the ice in a lifeless heap. MacLeish retrieved the corpse and, with a funeral march playing ever so faintly in his head, dumped it in the penalty box. Some fans were amused, but others were concerned the Flyers sniper would contract rabies.

And that was just the beginning.

➤ THE CURIOUS CASE ◄ OF THE MISSING MASK

ONE OF the most bizarre incidents in Parent's career started when he was playing for the Toronto Maple Leafs and ended more than 40 years later.

When a bench-clearing brawl erupted during a playoff game in New York in 1971, New York Rangers captain Vic Hadfield ripped off Parent's mask and threw it into the frenzied crowd at Madison Square Garden. Parent pleaded for its return and police scoured the stands—but to no avail.

Since he had no backup mask, Parent had to choose between playing without face protection and not playing at all. He chose the latter. Maple Leafs coach John McLellan begged him to change his mind, but Parent was adamant. "I said, 'What are you, crazy?'" Parent recalled years later. "'I'm not going back in there without my mask!'" Jacques Plante, famous for being the first NHL goalie to wear a mask, took Parent's place.

In June 2012, a sports memorabilia collector shipped the mask to Parent, asking him to authenticate it. Goalie and mask were reunited for a few days—and it felt so good. The collector said he would donate the mask to the Hockey Hall of Fame after his death.[19]

The game soon heated up. Literally. It was hot and humid outside, and because the Buffalo Auditorium didn't have air conditioning, the arena soon felt like a sauna. With the temperature soaring to 90 degrees Fahrenheit, a fog descended on the ice. Referees stopped play and arena workers ran onto the ice waving white bedsheets in an attempt to clear things up. They weren't entirely successful, but the game continued anyway. Spectators, already feeling faint, had to strain to see the ice. Players could only see each other from the waist up. The Sabres won the game 5–4 in overtime—and the fortunate few fans who could see the ice were delighted.

The teams split the next two games and then met at the Aud for Game 6. Parent shut out the Sabres as the Flyers posted a 2–0 victory to clinch the Cup. Once again, Parent was awarded the Conn Smythe Trophy. Days later, more than 2 million people jammed the streets of Philadelphia for the victory parade.

Parent was in great spirits as he prepared to relax on his boat and do some deep sea fishing. His mood improved during the summer, when the Flyers offered him a lifetime contract.

1975-76

Every great story has a third act, and Parent's saga was no exception. Before the 1975–76 season started, he had back surgery to repair a disk that was putting pressure on a nerve. He was forced to look on as Stephenson took his place between the pipes. Parent returned to action late in the season and played in just 11 games. He was no longer dominant, but he was good enough to help the Flyers, who had finished first in the new Patrick Division and second overall with 118 points, beat the Leafs (83 points) in a seven-game quarter-final and the Bruins (113 points) in a five-game semifinal.

The Flyers were matched up against the Canadiens (127 points) in the final. Parent and his teammates arrived in Montreal determined to defend their title, but the Habs proved too hot to handle. With finesse players such as Guy Lafleur and

Steve Shutt in fine form and workhorses such as Bob Gainey and Doug Risebrough chipping in, Montreal won the series in four games straight.

"Montreal Canadiens' Stanley Cup victory at the expense of Philadelphia's Broad Street Bullies is being characterized as a triumph of brains over brawn, class over vulgarity, artistry over labor, finesse over crudeness," observed columnist Jim Proudfoot. He added that by beating the Flyers, "Canadiens demonstrated that might isn't necessarily right."[11]

1976-79

In the next three seasons, the Flyers bowed out of the playoffs twice in the semifinal and once in the quarter-final. Those were challenging times for Parent. He was excellent on occasion—he led the league in shutouts (7) in the 1977–78 season—but not on a consistent basis. He was delighted when his former mentor, Plante, became the Flyers goalie coach. The Zen master watched his pupil in action and noticed that the goalie was sitting back on his heels and backing into the crease. Plante instructed Parent to snap out of it—and he did. His performance improved, and his career seemed to be back on track.

But his comeback ended on a cold afternoon in February 1979. During a tussle in front of the net during a game against the Rangers, Flyers defensemen Jimmy Watson accidentally poked his stick blade through the right eyehole of Parent's mask. The goalie pushed his mask off his face and made a beeline for the bench. He was escorted to the dressing room and rushed to hospital. The lens of the eye had been destroyed, and tendons on either side of it had been torn. Parent couldn't see out of his injured eye or out of the other one; the shock had rendered it useless. He was blind for two weeks. Parent regained his vision, but his depth perception was compromised. His career was over.

He stepped before the microphones on May 31, 1979. Sporting a full beard and wearing dark glasses, he announced his retirement. "I'm only 34, and I wanted to play at least five more

➤ "CHEESY" KEEPS ◄
'EM IN STITCHES

GERRY CHEEVERS and Parent joined the Boston Bruins at the same time, in 1965. But when Parent headed to Philadelphia two years later, Cheevers stayed and became an integral part of the Big Bad Bruins, who won two championships in three seasons. He earned a reputation for being aggressive and for roaming out of his net. But he's best remembered for his iconic mask—a plain white shield with black stitches painted on it.

"In one practice a puck jumped and hit my mask," Cheevers says. "It hit me so lightly, it wouldn't have knocked me over even if I had been playing without a mask. But I pretended to faint and allowed them to wheel me into the dressing room. Five minutes later, [Coach] Harry Sinden walked in and said, 'You're not injured. Get your ass out there.' Our trainer, John Forestall, said, 'Wait a minute.' He came over with a Sharpie and drew a 12-stitch cut above my right eye. He told Sinden I was indeed cut. We all had a chuckle over that."

From then on, the goalie painted a stitch on his mask every time he took a puck or a stick to the face.

"Cheesy" retired after the 1979–80 season, hanging up his skates—and his mask—almost two decades after suiting up for his first NHL game. The mask, one of the most celebrated in hockey history, now hangs on the wall of his grandson's bedroom.

years. But they tell me I can't," he said in a low, halting voice. "Hockey has been good to me. Philadelphia fans great, and management super."[12] Parent had little more to say.

"He gave us some of the greatest goaltending ever seen anywhere," mournful Flyers general manager Keith Allen told reporters. "We'd have never won the two Stanley Cups without him."[13]

RETIREMENT

The Flyers made Parent a goaltending coach a few months later, giving him the opportunity to work beside Plante. "It's nice to get involved in a game that I've played for 25 years," Parent said. "It will make my retirement much easier."[14]

The Flyers retired Parent's jersey in a ceremony before the opening game of the 1979–80 season. When plans were announced, the retired goalie told reporters he feared the experience would be like attending his own funeral. But during the event itself he was beaming, more animated than your average corpse. Wearing a white Flyers sweater over his suit, Parent stood at center ice beneath a scoreboard flashing the word "Bernie" and waved to fans who cheered as a banner was raised to the rafters.

Despite his new status as an éminence grise in the sports world, Parent had trouble adapting to retirement. His spirits flagged, and he lapsed into a deep depression. He started using alcohol as a crutch, turning from a social drinker into an alcoholic. His relationships grew strained.

"There is a built-in discipline to playing any sport, a structure that keeps you within certain bounds," he says today. "I played hockey for 25 years. All of a sudden, I couldn't play anymore. The discipline was gone, and it was easy to drift away. When I played, from the time I was 12 years old, I would look at myself in the mirror it was always the hockey player I was looking at," he explains. "Then when my career was over. One day I looked at myself in the mirror and asked, 'Who are you?' Tough question, eh? I had no clue who I was as an individual."

One day he walked out of the family home and didn't come back for three days. When he returned in a cab—he couldn't find his car—he went upstairs to his bedroom and fell asleep. He had reached a breaking point. Desperate for help, he joined Alcoholics Anonymous and started to rebuild his life. By the summer of 1980, he had found new purpose. He dedicated himself to a career in public relations. "I'm happy with Bernie Parent, the human being," he said in a candid moment. "I don't need the stuff anymore."[15]

> "Knowing that Bernie was back there made us cockier and allowed us to play loose. We were a young group just needing to add a couple more pieces to the puzzle, and Bernie gave us that confidence."
>
> *Former Philadelphia Flyers teammate*
> **BOB "MAD DOG" KELLY**

IN 1981, Parent became a mentor to a young goalie who had idolized him. With his guidance, Sweden's Pelle Lindbergh turned from a talented but erratic young goalie into one of the best in the NHL. When Lindbergh won the Vezina Trophy in 1985, he dedicated it to Parent. (Since 1981, the award has been awarded based on merit alone.)

Five months later, an intoxicated Lindbergh drove his Porsche into a New Jersey schoolhouse. His death sent shockwaves through the sports world. Shaken, Parent flew to Sweden for the funeral and attended a memorial service at the Spectrum, telling the crowd he felt like he had lost a son.

IN 1984, Parent was inducted into the Hockey Hall of Fame with two other retired stars, Phil Esposito and Jacques Lemaire. Bernie, Carol and their three children, Bernie Jr., Chuck and Kim, were on hand to celebrate. "It's so very difficult to explain how fantastic I feel," Parent said when he found out he would be the first Flyer to be inducted. "The feeling I have now is like 10 years ago, when we won the Stanley Cup."[16]

Nine years later, Parent endured upheaval again. He stepped down as Philadelphia's goalie coach, and his marriage ended soon after. He faced an uncertain future, but Parent, the eternal optimist, soon found a new niche for himself doing public appearances and pursuing other business ventures. In 2011, he published a self-help book called *Journey through Risk and Fear*.

In December 2011, Parent announced that he would participate in an alumni game before the upcoming NHL Winter Classic, an annual event in which a regular season NHL game is played outdoors. Excitement built in the following weeks and reached a crescendo on the day of the game, December 31.

When Parent appeared in his Flyers uniform with a broad smile and his signature white mask tipped back on his head, the 45,000 fans at Citizen Bank Park gave him a rapturous welcome.

In his old post between the pipes, he stopped all five shots he faced as the crowd chanted "Bern-ie, Bern-ie!" He skated off the ice after five minutes and was later named the game's first star.

Brian Propp, an all-star with the Flyers in the 1980s, also played in the game. He was as happy to see Bernie as the fans. "When he played, he was one of the best goaltenders in the world," Propp says about Parent. "He's such a great person, to everybody. He makes everybody smile and really gives of himself. He's really a pleasure to be around."

PARENT · ALL-TIME RANKING*

REGULAR SEASON			PLAYOFFS		
GAMES	WINS	SO	GAMES	WINS	SO
608 [39th]	271 [37th]	54 [20th]	71 [29th]	38 [25th]	6 [23rd]

* statistics as of July 2, 2013.

> NHL ALL-STAR TEAM **(1ST)**: 1973–74, 1974–75

7

THE
SCHOLAR
KEN DRYDEN

"Reporters know he is polite, bright and intelligent.
They do not get 'deathless' quotes from him."[1]
Columnist **JIM MCKAY**, in 1976

FIVE MONTHS AFTER Montreal Canadiens goalie Ken
Dryden was named the most valuable player of the 1971 playoffs,
he answered a reporter's questions about facing Bobby Orr and
the Big, Bad Bruins. Then the conversation took a turn. When
asked what he had done following his team's Stanley Cup victory, he revealed that he had gone to Washington, D.C., to work
with consumer advocate Ralph Nader. "I worked on a program
to organize sport and commercial fishermen into a national arm
to combat water pollution," explained the young man, sporting
horn-rimmed glasses and pork chop sideburns. "What I learned
was that there is a tremendous inertia in the people, and there
are many serious problems involving government and bureau-
cracy. I'm writing an article on the subject right now." "Yes,"
came the reporter's response, "I suppose that your writing keeps
you from being bored when you're not studying law or playing
hockey. A fellow has to fill in his free time."[2]

From the beginning to the end of his storied NHL career, Dryden's interests extended far beyond hockey—an inclination that made him a goalie as unique as he was accomplished.

KEN DRYDEN was born in Hamilton, Ontario, in August 1947 and grew up in suburban Toronto. When he wasn't at school, he spent hours shooting tennis balls at the garage door of the family home he shared with his parents, Murray and Margaret, and his siblings, Dave and Judy. Murray, who sold bricks and building materials, paved the backyard with asphalt when Dryden was six years old, turning it into a year-round hockey rink. The Dryden brothers and their friends spent hours there, chasing tennis balls from end to end.

Scrambling across the asphalt in rubber boots, Dryden imagined he was Gordie Howe, speeding up the ice at Maple Leaf Gardens, spurred on by the deafening roar of the crowd. At other times, he guarded his net and, as Johnny Bower or Terry Sawchuk, dazzled spectators with acrobatic saves. "Sports were part of growing up—and anything you did, you did seriously and with ambition to become very good at it. But we never saw ourselves playing in the NHL," Dryden says today. "That was on television."

When he started playing organized hockey, he became a goalie, just as his older brother had done years before. He played for Humber Valley in the Metro Toronto Hockey League. A natural athlete and big for his age, Dryden competed with kids who were two years older than him. He joined the Etobicoke Indians, a Junior B team in the Ontario Hockey Association (OHA), for the 1964–65 season. Dryden played all his minor hockey in the Toronto area, but the Leafs didn't notice him. The Boston Bruins were more on the ball—but not much. They selected him in the NHL draft of unsigned amateurs in June 1964 and then traded his rights to Montreal.

Like other budding hockey stars, Dryden spent hours on the ice, honing his skills. But unlike the others, Dryden was just as dedicated to his studies and was determined to get a good education. "Our parents, like most parents at the time, hadn't gone to university, but they had been able to create this amazing world," explains Dryden. "Canada was booming. They thought, 'If we can create this kind of world without a university education, imagine what [our] university-educated children could do,' It was just part of the air that we breathed at the time—that going to university is what we were going to be doing."

When he graduated from high school, the Canadiens encouraged the teenager to head 62 miles east to play for the Peterborough Petes, a Junior A team in the OHA, and attend Trent University. But Dryden had his sights set on an Ivy League school. He accepted a scholarship at Cornell University, in Ithaca, New York. At the time, it was almost unheard of for a promising young player to choose collegiate over junior hockey. A handful of NHL players earned university degrees, but they pursued their studies in the off-season.

In Ithaca, Dryden studied history and suited up for Cornell's Big Red, which competed in the highest division of the NCAA hockey program. He attracted attention the moment he stepped onto the ice. He was six-foot-four and weighed more than 200 pounds. Not only did he tower over other goalies—often the smallest players on the ice—but also over all the other players. Craning their necks to size him up, his teammates feared he would be too big and slow to be a top-notch goalie. Their concerns were unfounded. Dryden took up so much space, shooters had to strain their eyes to find open space in the net. But he had those areas covered too. He was quick and routinely grabbed pucks heading to the top left corner, his glove hand flashing across the net like a bolt of lightning.

During his three seasons with the Big Red, the team won the Division I title one year (1966–67) and finished second in another (1968–69). Dryden was the backbone of the team. He won 76 games, lost four and tied one, posting an incredible 1.65 goals-against average. He was an all-American in each of those seasons and was named the league's best player in the 1968–69 season.

"Ken was very obviously an academic and a serious thinker," recalls Cornell teammate Bob Kinasewich. "He was not a drinker. He was not a carouser. But when we had team get-togethers, Ken would be there—and you knew he was there as part of the team."

Another teammate, Murray Deathe, has similar recollections of the goalie. "Ken didn't drink... if he did go out to a bar, and there were five people there, everybody bought a round, until it came to Ken's turn, and he left. I don't want to say that he was... he wasn't cheap, but he certainly did spend his money wisely. Also, he would have conversations with anybody about anything, and he always wanted to learn. He's a very curious individual."

Dryden's on-ice exploits impressed officials at Hockey Canada, which had just been established. At their request, he flew to Sweden to join the Canadian national team after it had suffered a 7–1 loss to the Soviet Union. With Dryden in net, the Canadians shut down the Americans 1–0.

A few months later, Dryden graduated with a history degree, determined to pursue a career in law.

THE CANADIENS wanted him to play with the Montreal Voyageurs, their American Hockey League affiliate, and were willing to let him attend law school at the same time. But Dryden doubted that would be possible; the demands of professional hockey were too great. Once again, he followed his own path. Aware that the International Ice Hockey Federation (IIHF) had granted Hockey Canada permission to offer some players professional contracts, Dryden signed a three-year deal with the national team. It was based in Winnipeg, which was also home to the University of Manitoba. "The Canadiens thought I would go to McGill law school while playing pro in Montreal. At first I was interested, but when I realized I couldn't combine the two, I decided against it," he explained. "This way, I'll be able to go to law school and also play hockey. International hockey is exciting—and then there's the extra kick of travelling to Europe for games."[3]

Newspapers ran a photo of Dryden—long hair tucked behind his ears and a moustache spreading the length of his upper lip—standing beside a national team official, who looked like one of Snow White's dwarfs next to the hulking athlete. "He is a tall, husky young man and he is probably the biggest goalkeeper in the business," one reporter wrote about Dryden. "But for all his bulk, he moves quickly and has a good pair of hands."[4]

Dryden, whose salary covered little more than his living and education expenses, enrolled at the University of Manitoba in the fall of 1969. He and his teammates flew to the Soviet Union for a series of games against Soviet and Finnish teams. They won four games and lost one, to the "Wings of the Soviets." The Canadians also played games elsewhere in the region. The road trip had some memorable moments both on and off the ice.

In Moscow, coaches couldn't leave their hotel because the streets were cordoned off for the state funeral of a Soviet military officer and politician. They had to cool their heels in the lobby while, according to reports, the players "practiced gaily without supervision" at Lenin Stadium. In another incident, Hockey Canada executive A.J. "Buck" Houle kept the entire team sitting in the lobby of a Bratislava hotel one night to protest accommodations; six players had been assigned to rooms that didn't have baths or showers. The sit-in lasted for three hours before hotel management agreed to change the Canadians' rooms.[5]

The Canadians were back home a few weeks later to play the Soviets in eight games across the country. Dryden, who split goaltending duties with Wayne Stephenson, played a game in Vancouver five days before Christmas. The Soviets buzzed around the Canadian net like angry hornets. Dryden allowed nine goals on 44 shots.

BIG BROTHER IS WATCHING

Ken Dryden was still in diapers when his brother Dave, six years older, started playing street hockey near the family home in Toronto. When a local team requested Dave's services, he turned his attention to organized hockey.

In his third season of Junior A, the 20-year-old goalie played one game for the New York Rangers, and figured that would be the beginning and end of his NHL career. But four years later, in the 1965-66 season, he was on the Chicago Blackhawks roster as a backup to Glenn Hall. After three seasons with the club, he joined the Buffalo Sabres. He played against his brother in a game in March 1971, and the two shook hands at center ice after the Habs' 5–2 win. In 1974, he jumped to the World Hockey Association, where he played one season with the Chicago Cougars and then headed to Edmonton.

In net for the Oilers, he became one of the league's best goalies. In the 1978–79 season, he played in 63 games, recording the best goals-against average (2.86) and finishing in a four-way tie for most shutouts (three). He was named the league's best goalie and its most valuable player.

"Sure, I wanted to win Stanley Cups," Dave Dryden says today, comparing his career to that of his famous kid brother. "But looking back at some of the games I played in, I can say I was the best goaltender in the world that night. I can say, nobody could have played better than I did that night."

During his career, he tinkered endlessly with his equipment (and later spent some time as an equipment consultant for the NHL)—and legions of goalies are indebted to him for that. He developed the fiberglass-and-cage mask that is now de rigueur in the NHL, and he introduced upper-body armor, which combines comprehensive shoulder and chest protection. In no small way, this piece of equipment has contributed to the soaring popularity of the butterfly technique—goalies are more inclined to drop to their knees when they know they will be able to stand up with their parts intact.

"I had so many things happen in my career," says Dryden. "How lucky am I that it turned out that way?"

||||||||||||||||||||||||||||||||||||||||||||||||||||||||||||||||||

The IIHF soon changed its mind about allowing the Canadians to include professionals on their national team. In response, Canada withdrew its offer to host the 1970 worlds. The national program began to flounder. Dryden left the team. A few months later, he and his wife, Lynda, headed to Europe for a camping tour.

NHL

1970-71

Once again, the Canadiens urged Dryden to turn professional. This time he agreed. He signed with the Voyageurs ahead of the 1970–71 season. The terms of the contract allowed him to pursue his studies at McGill University. He attended just one practice a week and played in just five games before Christmas. Dryden believes he was fortunate that the Canadiens were willing to accommodate him. "Other NHL teams would have said, 'No, you can't be both a professional hockey player and a student. You have to make your choice,'" he says. "If I had been faced with that choice, I would have chosen to stop playing hockey, and I would have continued going to law school."

Dryden often rushed from class to practice. While his teammates flipped through the pages of sports magazines on road trips to Rhode Island or Massachusetts, their goalie had his nose in his textbooks. His academic pursuits didn't put him at odds with his teammates. "Goalies are understood to be different. Forwards like to think of goalies as different. Defensemen like to think of goalies as different. They're almost unsettled if a goalie doesn't seem different to them," he explains. "In some way, [pursuing a law degree] was my eccentricity. As Jacques Plante's eccentricity may have been knitting and somebody else's was whatever, this was mine. And my teammates would say, 'Well, what do you expect? He's a goalie.'"

One day, Voyageurs coach Floyd Curry approached Dryden in the dressing room. He handed the young goalie a plane ticket and told him he was going to join the Habs. Dryden pulled the hallowed *bleu, blanc* and *rouge* jersey over his head one night in October and skated onto the ice at Boston Garden for his first NHL game. More than 14,000 Bruins fans watched him lead the Habs to a 5–4 victory over the defending Stanley Cup champions. Dryden made 42 saves in the exhibition game, many of them spectacular. He won praise from all quarters and might have stayed with the Canadiens if he wasn't intent on finishing law school.

Dryden played in 33 games for the Voyageurs that season, recording 16 wins, 7 losses and 8 ties. He posted three shutouts and finished with a 2.65 goals-against average.

THE HABS were deep in talent at the time. The team had won two Stanley Cups in the previous three seasons under the leadership of captain Jean Beliveau. He was nearing the end of his storied career but was still one of the strongest skaters in the league and a big scoring threat. Yvan Cournoyer, known as the

"Roadrunner" because of his blazing speed, was at the peak of his powers. He finished 13th in league scoring that season. That tied him with Frank Mahovlich, whom the Canadiens had acquired from Detroit in January. Veterans J.C. Tremblay, Terry Harper and Jacques Laperriere formed a steady, physical presence on the blue line. Montreal also had a strong netminder. Rogie Vachon had emerged as a top-notch goalie when he replaced an injured Gump Worsley in the 1966–67 post-season, and he had played a pivotal role in the Habs' recent Stanley Cup victories. The Canadiens ended the 1970–71 season with 97 points, good enough for third in the East Division and fourth overall.

The Habs called up Dryden late in the regular season to give him some more big-league experience. It was customary for the Habs' top prospects to serve a lengthy apprenticeship before being added to the roster. After watching one game from the press box, Dryden suited up for a road game against the Pittsburgh Penguins. He allowed just one goal as the Canadiens beat the Penguins 5-1. He started in 5 of the next 10 regular-season games and won all of them. He allowed just nine goals in that span, posting a sparkling 1.65 goals-against average.

No one doubted that Dryden had a future in the NHL. But no one expected him to be the Canadiens starter in the post-season. He was a rookie, after all. But Montreal coach Al Mac-Neil surprised everyone by putting Dryden in net for the start of the playoffs, a quarter-final matchup against the Bruins. Boston fans squealed in delight, sure the young goalie couldn't handle the Bruins. Boston had just posted a regular season to remember. Four of the league's five top scorers played for the Bruins. Phil Esposito led the NHL with 152 points. He was followed by Orr, with 139. The team had scored 399 goals overall—108 more than the Canadiens, who were second in that category. Boston had ended the season with an astounding 121 points, securing its status as the undisputed heavyweight champion of the hockey world. A second straight Stanley Cup victory seemed inevitable.

The Bruins won the first game 3–1 thanks to goalie Gerry Cheevers, who made two spectacular saves on Cournoyer. Orr scored a short-handed goal and notched an assist, but the game wasn't his proudest moment. When referee John Ashley called a holding penalty on him in the third period, Orr protested. In response, the official tacked on a misconduct penalty. After serving his sentence, Orr charged out of the penalty box, pushed a linesman aside and, with steam coming out of his ears, made a beeline for Ashley. His teammates intervened—as much to save the referee's life as to keep their star player from being tossed out of the series. The Bruins realized their work was cut out for them. Dryden rose to the challenge, stopping 39 shots in front of 15,000 Boston fans.

The goalie's performance drew rave reviews. "Their rookie Ken Dryden, earned his master's degree in goaltending," a Boston reporter said. He added that Dryden would be a great lawyer one day if he could defend clients as well as he defended his goal crease.[6]

Dryden's response? Meh. After the game he admitted he had been nervous—but only in the first few minutes.[7]

The Bruins burst out of the gate in the next game and delighted the hometown crowd by jumping to a 5–1 lead. But then the tide turned. With veteran Beliveau leading the charge and rookie Dryden holding the fort, the Habs took control of the game and notched a 7–5 victory. The Boston players skated off the ice feeling like they'd been whacked over the head with a cast-iron skillet.

The series turned into a dog fight. The teams split the next four games. Momentum shifted many times, but one thing remained consistent—the brilliant goaltending of the Canadiens' new netminder. Dryden stopped the NHL's top scorers time and again, leaving Esposito and Orr smashing their sticks on the ice in frustration. "Throughout the four games of the series, the dominant Montreal figure has been Dryden," columnist Jim Coleman wrote before Game 5. "Never has a rookie survived unflinchingly such a baptism of fire. Dryden has held Phil Esposito to one goal; he has blanked Johnny Bucyk and Ken Hodge. That trio scored 170 goals for Boston during the regular season."[8]

The teams headed to Boston for Game 7, with the Bruins hoping their boisterous fans would give them the boost they needed. But as it turned out, the crowd's support wasn't enough. Dryden was spectacular. He made one acrobatic save after another, including dramatic glove saves on Orr and Esposito. Against all odds, the Habs beat the Bruins 4–2 and advanced to the semifinal. "It was such an overwhelming experience. When you're thrown into deep water and you don't know whether you can swim, you don't notice how fancy your strokes are," Dryden said later. "You're just trying to keep your head above water. So I think it was maybe when the whole playoffs were over that first year that I stepped back and said Geez, I made it. I'm here. I'm okay."[9]

"Throughout his pro career Dryden has been something of a different creature than your average hockey player. Where most of his peers on the ice dropped out of high school to devote themselves to hockey, Dryden not only graduated from an institution of higher learning, but completed a law degree while performing in the big league."[31]

Reporter **HUBERT BAUCH**, *in* 1979

The Canadiens defeated the Minnesota North Stars (72 points) in six games and then took on the Chicago Blackhawks (107 points) in the final. In that series, Dryden came face to face with Bobby Hull, who had finished fifth in scoring that season behind four Bruins. His ferocious slap shot had led many goalies to wave the white flag of surrender, but Dryden was unfazed. He stopped the Golden Jet and his teammates time and again.

Montreal beat Chicago 3–2 in Game 7, winning the series and the Stanley Cup.

Dryden—who had headed into the post-season with just six regular-season NHL games under his belt—had played in all 20 playoff games and had posted a 3.00 goals-against average. His heroics earned him the Conn Smythe Trophy as the most valuable player in the playoffs. The next day, Dryden and his teammates rode through the streets of Montreal in a victory parade. Undeterred by the heat, crowds lined St. Catherine Street to see the players, perched on convertibles, pass by on their way to city hall. The center of attention was a tall young man wearing glasses, a pink shirt and a loud tie—Dryden, celebrating his first of many Stanley Cup victories.

1971-72

While Montreal players unwound on the links that summer, Dryden worked on the water pollution project with Ralph Nader; in the fall, he returned to Canada to pursue legal studies part-time and, of course, to play hockey. He reported to the Canadiens training camp in the fall of 1971, concerned that his success the previous spring had been a fluke. "I was wondering if, in the cold light of day of the following season, it was going to revert back to me being a Humber Valley goalie," he said. "I was wondering if it was going to fall apart."[10]

His fears were unfounded. He was anointed the Habs starter, leading Vachon to request a trade. Dryden played in 64 of the 78 regular season games—and would have played more if not for a mid-season back injury—notching more wins (39) than any other goalie in the league. He also recorded eight shutouts, just one less than league leader Tony Esposito.

But there was no miracle on ice for the Habs this year. They were eliminated by the Rangers in the first round of the playoffs. Although his team lost the sixth and deciding game 3–2, Dryden was named one of the game's three stars, along with the Rangers' Walt Tkaczuk and Bill Fairbairn. Waiting for the announcement, the goalie stood near the boards with his chin resting on his stick and his eyes downcast. One observer reported seeing Dryden "reaching up with his arm every once in a while to brush away a tear."[11]

The following month, Dryden was awarded the Calder Memorial Trophy as the league's best rookie, narrowly beating sniper Rick Martin of the Buffalo Sabres. (Dryden hadn't been eligible the previous season, because he hadn't played enough regular season games.)

IN AUGUST, Dryden and more than 30 of his peers gathered in Toronto to prepare for an eight-game series pitting the NHL's best Canadian players against the top players from the Soviet Union. When training camp opened, coach Harry Sinden confessed he didn't know what to expect from the Soviets—he couldn't watch footage of their last five world championship finals because the video player at Maple Leaf Gardens was on the fritz—but the Canadians weren't too concerned. Word on the street was that the Soviets passed too much and their snipers couldn't hit the broad side of a barn in southern Siberia. Sure, they had won nine world and three Olympic titles in the past decade. But they had never faced the best Canadian players—professionals were barred from international competition at the time. A team of NHL stars would declaw the Russian bear without a problem. Dryden wasn't so sure. "Just because a North American says the Russians pass too much, that doesn't necessarily mean it is so. It may be true in our judgment, but the Russians still could be right," he told reporters three days before the start of the series. He recalled playing against the Soviets in international competition. "I'd get set for a shot. They wouldn't shoot. They'd pass instead," he said. "Against our national team, they looked devastating by passing right into the net."[12]

On September 2, thousands of Canadians settled into their seats at the Montreal Forum, and millions more gathered around their television sets, prepared to watch their heroes go to town on the Soviets. Early on, the game unfolded according to the script, with the Canadians scoring two quick goals in the first period. But then, as Gerald Eskenazi of the *New York Times* reported, "strange things happened." The Soviets stormed back. Valeri Kharlamov, Alexander Yakushev and their teammates bore down on the Canadian net using feints, change of pace and intricate passing to set the Canadians back on their heels. The Soviets netted seven goals, whereas the Canadians managed just one more. Spectators sat in stunned silence.

It was a crushing defeat. "In a shock to Canada's nervous system, the remarkably controlled Soviet Union national team tonight trounced the National Hockey League's finest players, 7–3, in the first meeting between the world's top professional and amateur hockey teams," Eskenazi recounted. He chided the Canadians for being condescending toward the Soviets before the game—the NHLers had ridiculed their opponents' $20 skates and outmoded helmets. The Soviets "left bottles of Italian mineral water outside their hotel rooms, along with empties of tonic water and Coke. In short, they were different," Eskenazi wrote. "And tonight they were better."

He said Dryden "discovered what happens when the Soviet passing is uninterrupted," noting that the goalie was "helpless" on the first Soviet goal.[13] "They got to almost every loose puck before we did. We didn't play our game at all," Dryden said. "After they tied it up, we started playing a panic type of game. Sometimes there were five men all going for the puck at once."[14]

The Canadians managed to regroup. Sinden made some changes for the second game. He put Tony Esposito in net, and the goalie played an instrumental role in the Canadians' 4–1 victory in Toronto. He also played a pivotal role in the third game, a 4–4 tie in Winnipeg. Many observers thought the score would have been much higher if not for the heroics of Esposito and his Soviet counterpart, Vladislav Tretiak.

Dryden was back between the pipes for the fourth game, in Vancouver. He didn't look any better than he had in Montreal, and neither did his teammates. The Canadians lost 5–3 in a game described as "a dreadful spectacle."[15] Fans at the Pacific Coliseum roared their disapproval, and the Canadian players were subjected to a chorus of boos as they skated off the ice at the end of the game.

In a post-game television interview, Phil Esposito was defiant. "For the people across Canada, we tried. We gave it our best. For the people that booed us … all of us guys are really disheartened, and we're disillusioned and we're disappointed in some of the people," he said, sweat dripping from his face onto his red-and-white jersey. "Even though we play in the United States, and earn money in the United States, Canada is still our home and that's the only reason we come, and I don't think it's fair that we should be booed."

"What happened was this," Dryden told columnist Frank Orr. "We were going to have a big party and the Russians spoiled it." Orr tipped his hat to the "erudite goalie" for his thoughtful analysis of fan reaction, saying he summed it up "perhaps the best."[16]

The Soviets had Team Canada on the ropes when the series moved to Moscow. Soviet coach Vsevelod Bobrov told reporters he expected the Canadians to improve—in part because they had learned a thing or two from the Soviets—but he didn't seem alarmed. He noted that the Canadians were slow to recover in their own end and mount a counter-attack. Furthermore, he added, Dryden tended to get confused when the puck was close to the net.[17]

On September 22, more than 14,000 fans crowded Luzhniki Ice Palace for the fifth game of the series. Esposito was between the pipes. Team Canada dominated the first two periods and was up 3–0 heading into the second intermission. But the Soviets bounced back, scoring five goals in the third period and allowing just one. It was a 5–4 Soviet victory.

The Canadians eked out a 3–2 victory in the sixth game. Dryden played well, but the game is best remembered for one of the most infamous episodes in hockey history. In the heat

➤ STRIKE A POSE ◀

WHEN HOCKEY fans tuned in to *Hockey Night in Canada* to watch the Montreal Canadiens play the Boston Bruins in the 1971 playoffs, they heard the voice of Danny Gallivan. "Into Bucyk and... blocked by the long arm of Ken Dryden!" he announced excitedly in one game. "I don't know if the Bruins are firing right into him, but the pads, the arms, the glove always seem to be there!"

Then the whistle blew and, as Gallivan continued to sing Dryden's praises, the goalie stood up with his stick extending the full length of his body. He put his hands on top of his stick and rested his chin on top of his hands. He stayed like that for a minute or two, waiting for play to resume. The odd stance sparked a conversation among fans that continues to this day. What, they wonder, was that about?

Some people think that when Dryden assumed that stance, which he did throughout his career, he was deep in thought. "Now, we all know that lawyers like to think about what they're going to say before they say it," said Hall of Fame goalie Johnny Bower, "and when Ken would lean on his stick, I always had the feeling that he was thinking about the players that were on the ice against the Canadiens."[30]

But that's not the case. "It was just a resting position," Dryden explains. "The traditional resting position for a goalie used to be just bending over and leaning on top of his pads. Well, I was taller, so [standing] was easier for me ... It's kind of weird that it has become an iconic image. Usually the enduring image of a player is one of action. But mine is of inaction. I'm not doing the splits; I'm not catching a puck. I'm just standing there."

of battle, Canadian forward Bobby Clarke pulled his stick back with both hands and, with one fell swoop, smashed Kharlamov's ankle. The Soviets' best player limped off the ice. He was forced to sit out the seventh game and was hobbled for the eighth. To this day, many fans view the incident as the turning point of the series.

Esposito started in the seventh game and played well throughout, especially in the second period, when he made some spectacular saves. Late in the third period, Paul Henderson, who had started the series as a bit player, scored his second game-winning goal of the series. The Canadians won 4–3.

Sinden decided to start Dryden in the final game. By that point, the tension was almost unbearable. To win the series, the Canadians had to win the game; if the contest ended in a tie, the Soviets would win the series on goal differential.

The Canadians felt it was their patriotic duty to win—the series had come to represent a battle between opposing political systems—and they skated onto the ice like soldiers marching into battle. The millions of Canadians who gathered around television sets in homes, offices and schools held their collective breath as Phil Esposito and Vladimir Shadrin crouched low over the ice, sticks drawn back, waiting for the puck to drop. The tension escalated from the moment the game began. Tempers flared on the ice when an official made some questionable calls, and off the ice—Canadian players reached over the boards with their sticks to threaten Soviet military officers trying to apprehend Alan Eagleson, a player agent who had helped organize the tournament.

Dryden shut down the Soviets in the third period as the Canadians rallied from a 5–3 deficit to win the game 6–5. When they clinched it with just seconds remaining—and broadcaster Foster Hewitt exclaimed, "Henderson has scored for Canada!"—the Canadian players leapt in the air in jubilation. As their fans in Moscow and across Canada sprang out of their seats, pumping their fists, Dryden and his teammates wrapped each other in bear hugs. Soon afterwards, the team received a telegram from Canadian prime minister Pierre Trudeau, who was preparing for the upcoming federal election. "The election campaign and virtually every other activity in Canada came to a standstill this afternoon while Canadians watched game number eight in the great hockey series," he said. "The country is now in a state of enthusiastic revelry following your tremendous victory. From start to finish, these games have been exciting and filled with tension, but only one word describes today's result: Wow."[18]

It was a memorable moment in the history of Canada—and in the life of one of the country's most celebrated athletes. "It was the absolute worst of moments and the absolute best of moments," Dryden said years later. "It was tied together. When you have the two of those things tied together, it's the most special of times."[19]

1972-73

The NHL season started a week later. The Habs bounced back from their disappointment in the previous season and, over the next five months, marched to the top of the league. They finished first in the regular season, with 120 points.

Dryden played a pivotal role in the team's success. Although he missed a few weeks with a strained back in the middle of the season, he ended up with the most wins (33) and the best goals-against average (2.26) among starters. He and Roy Edwards of the Detroit Red Wings tied for the most shutouts (6). Dryden was awarded the Vezina Trophy, which at the time was given to the goalie(s) on the team allowing the fewest goals.

In the playoffs, the Habs eliminated the Sabres (88 points) in six games, dispatched the Philadelphia Flyers (85 points) in five and then won the Cup by defeating the Blackhawks (93 points) in six games. "Their objective achieved, the Montreal Canadiens took turns sipping champagne from the coveted Stanley Cup, which they earned Thursday night with a hard-fought 6–4 victory over the Chicago Black Hawks," a wire service reported. "Aside from a shout here and there, there was no whooping it up, no hollering and no spraying of champagne. They were tired, weary warriors. They had done their job. The Stanley Cup now goes back to Montreal, where they feel it belongs."[20]

1973-74

Having been crowned ruler of the goaltending universe, Dryden was poised to continue his reign. But it was not to be. Although he was widely regarded as the best goalie in hockey, a handful of other netminders were earning more money than him. He asked for a raise and, when the Canadiens balked, he quit. Dryden, who had completed his law degree, announced his plans to intern at a Toronto firm. "It's a matter of pride," he said at a press conference. "You see someone else and where they are with their team. I could name six goalies at the start of last year that were higher paid than I was. That bothers me."[21]

Dryden's departure sent the Canadiens into a tailspin. While he earned $134 a week as an articling student, three goalies took turns in the Canadiens net, none of whom could fill Dryden's sizeable shoes. The Canadiens finished fourth in the league in scoring and allowed 56 more goals than they had the previous season. The Rangers eliminated the Habs in the first round of the playoffs. The disappointment made the Canadiens more amenable to contract negotiations with Dryden. In May 1974, the two sides reached a deal that would pay Dryden $200,000 per season, more than double what he had been earning a year earlier. After months of wearing a suit and tie, Dryden showed up for work in the fall of 1974 wearing a Canadiens jersey.

1974-1975

The Canadiens tied with the Sabres and the Flyers for most points (113) in the 1974–75 season, but Dryden was not spectacular. He played in just 56 of the team's 80 games and didn't finish among the top three goaltenders in wins, shutouts or goals-against average. He ended up with a 2.69 goals-against average, the worst of his NHL career.

The Canadiens bowed out in the semifinal, losing to the Sabres in six games. In the final tilt, a 4–3 Sabres win, Dryden made two costly errors. "Never since he came up to the Canadiens with one of the most memorable goaltending performances in hockey history—miracle playoffs of 1971—has Ken Dryden been plunged into such an abysmal gloom as he was last night," wrote one reporter.[22]

1975-76

The Habs returned to form the following season. By the end of December, they were leading the NHL with 58 points. Montreal snipers Guy Lafleur and Pete Mahovlich were first and fifth respectively in league scoring. It was the perfect time for a showdown with another powerhouse. Excitement reached a fever pitch in Montreal when members of the Red Army marched into the Forum on New Year's Eve for a game against the Canadiens as part of a tournament pitting teams from the Soviet Championship League against top NHL clubs. The Red Army team included Kharlamov, Tretiak and other players who had become household names in Canada during the Summit Series. Fans on both sides of the Atlantic Ocean were anxious to see how the Soviets would fare against the NHL's top team.

From start to finish, the Montreal squad was firing on all pistons. Lafleur, who would win the NHL scoring title that season, Mahovlich and their teammates skated circles around their opponents and, with tenacious forechecking, forced them into making bad passes. The Habs fired 38 shots on net, 25 more than the Soviets. They dominated the game—yet it ended in a 3–3 tie. "The obvious question then is, if the Canadiens were so good, why didn't they win? There were two reasons," reported Al Strachan of the Montreal *Gazette*. "One was Vladislav Tretiak.

The other was Ken Dryden. Tretiak was extremely sharp as he repeatedly robbed the Canadiens on scoring chances," Strachan continued. "Dryden, on the other hand, did not come up with the big game that would have made the score reflect the play."[23]

Dryden admitted he could have played better. "I had an awful lot of shots at my glove tonight and they were just dropping out of it," he said, looking down at the floor. "It's very upsetting to me. Here we played as well as we could and we came out with only a tie."[24]

THAT GAME was soon a distant memory. The Canadiens were so dominant that season they finished first in the standings with 127 points, 9 more than the second-place Flyers. Dryden finished first among goalies in wins (42), shutouts (8) and goals against average (2.03). He won his second Vezina Trophy.

The Habs dispatched the Blackhawks (82 points) and the New York Islanders (101 points) without much problem and then squared off against the Flyers in the final. It was a clash of polar opposites. The Flyers were as brutish as the Canadiens were skillful. The "Broad Street Bullies" had won two consecutive Stanley Cups in part by beating their opponents into submission and were loathed around the league.

Hockey purists were hoping for a resounding Montreal victory, and they weren't disappointed. The Habs swept the Flyers

"I'd always thought of myself dipping and darting across the goal mouth with all the grace of a wood nymph, while violins played in the background and everybody in the stands went 'ooh' and 'ahh' at my performance. I thought of myself as Nureyev on ice. But on TV I realized that I was a dump truck. I was an elephant on wheels."[32]

KEN DRYDEN, *after seeing televised images of himself in the 1971 playoffs*

aside in four games, sending the bullies down Broad Street with bruised egos. Dryden deserved much of the credit. He allowed just 25 goals in 13 playoff games to finish with a 1.92 goals-against average. "The Canadians are famous for their speed and their offense, and they still skate and shoot with dizzying skill," one reporter observed, "but this year they have become a defensive power as well."[25]

1976-79

Like Trajan ruling over a vast Roman Empire, the Habs imposed their will on opponents in every corner of the league for the next three seasons. They lost just 35 of 240 regular-season games during that span and twice finished at the top of the standings. They also won the Cup in each of those seasons, defeating the Bruins in two finals (1977 and 1978) and the Rangers in one (1979).

Lafleur led the charge. He won the scoring title twice and was twice named the league's most valuable player. He was once named the most valuable player in the post-season. Larry Robinson was just as integral to the Habs' success. The star of an elite defense corps that also included Serge Savard and Guy Lapointe, the towering defenseman made headlines around the league with his body checks. He was named the NHL's top defenseman once in that three-year span and, like Lafleur, was once named the most valuable player in the playoffs.

Dryden was all but unbeatable in net. The "Octopus" recorded the most wins among goalies in one of those seasons and, in the other two, posted the second-most wins. He also twice led the league in shutouts and once finished second in that category. In each of those three seasons, he posted the best goals-against average among starters and shared the Vezina Trophy with his backup, Michel "Bunny" Larocque.

Some of his critics dismissed Dryden's success, insisting that any goalie could have done just as well playing on that team.

The Habs were so good, they reasoned, Dryden faced far fewer shots than his peers around the league. But his supporters leapt to his defense, insisting that spending long stretches of time in complete solitude makes a goalie's job more, not less, challenging. "Critics say he only had 18 or 20 or 25 shots a game. Well, I think that's a credit to Kenny in that he kept his concentration," Robinson said years later. "You talk to any goaltender and [they will tell you] the hardest thing is when you're only getting a few shots here and there."[26]

"When he let in a couple of bad goals, he was unhappy—and you could see it in his face," says Rejean Houle, a Habs forward for most of the 1970s. "But he would never blame his defenseman or other players around him... He would accept the blame without any problem. But I don't remember seeing him have two bad games in a row," adds Houle. "He was always ready for the game, a true professional who really cared. Without him, we would never have won the Cups that we won."

Two months after he lifted the Cup for the sixth time, Dryden announced he was retiring. He said he had accomplished all he could in hockey and it was time to move on. At a press conference, he told reporters there were some things he hoped he would "have the ability to do."[27] As it turned out, he had the ability to do a lot of things. In the next three decades, he forged careers in writing, politics and business.

RETIREMENT

Soon after he retired, Dryden and his family—his wife, Lynda, and their children, Sarah and Michael—moved to England. The family stayed there for three years, during which time he wrote *The Game*. The book chronicled his last season in Montreal and took a broader look at the game and its place in Canadian culture. To this day, *The Game* is often described as the best hockey book ever written and one of the best sports books of all time. Since its release in 1983, Dryden has written four other books, covering topics as diverse as hockey, education and Canada's place in the world.

Dryden returned to hockey in 1997 as president of the Toronto Maple Leafs. He stayed in that role until 2003, when the position was eliminated. Although Dryden received mixed reviews for his performance, the Leafs' record improved during his tenure. In the 1998–99 season, they made the playoffs for the first time in three years and then made the playoffs in each of the following five seasons, twice advancing to the Eastern Conference final.

Dryden had always been interested in politics. His work with Ralph Nader took place near the beginning of his playing career; near the end, he became a member of Ontario premier William Davis's advisory committee on confederation. In January 1979, he attended a conference with some of the heaviest hitters in Canadian politics, including Davis and governor general Roland Michener. "If Dryden does want to get deeper into politics he can well afford to wait until his playing career is over," the Montreal *Gazette* reported. "At that time he can be judged on what he says without his goals against average forcing itself into consideration."[28]

Five years later, Dryden became Ontario's first youth commissioner. Then, in 2004, he jumped deeper into the political fray. He ran for the House of Commons as a Liberal candidate in Toronto. He was successful in that federal election and in the two that followed, managing to keep his seat even after the Conservatives assumed power. In 2008, he made a failed bid for the Liberal party leadership. Three years later, he was voted out of office.

Dryden has made contributions in many areas of Canadian life, but across the country, he's known first and foremost as one of hockey's greatest goaltenders. Habs fans applauded when he was inducted into the Hockey Hall of Fame in 1983 and when the Canadiens retired his jersey in 2007. Two years later, they gathered at the Bell Centre—the Canadiens' home since 1996—to join Dryden and other "oldtimers" to celebrate the Canadiens' 100th anniversary. The ceremony included a short skate-around. To prepare for it, Dryden had shown up at the arena earlier in the day and strapped on a pair of goalie pads. He spoke about how odd it felt to do that for the first time since 1979. "Typically, Dryden went on to discuss his concern about 'balance points in contemporary equipment,'" one reporter said. "It's a phrase not often heard in today's dressing rooms."[29]

DRYDEN · ALL-TIME RANKING*

REGULAR SEASON			PLAYOFFS		
GAMES	WINS	SO	GAMES	WINS	SO
397 [93rd]	258 [43rd]	46 [27th]	112 [13th]	80 [6th]	10 [10th]

* statistics as of July 2, 2013.

> NHL ALL-STAR TEAM **(1ST)**: 1972–73, 1975–76, 1976–77, 1977–78, 1978–79

> NHL ALL-STAR TEAM **(2ND)**: 1971–72

8

||||||||||||||||||||||||||||||||||||||||||

THE
WARRIOR
RON HEXTALL

||||||||||||||||||||||||||||||||||||||||||

"Ronnie has probably gotten himself in trouble on a
couple of occasions that [cemented] his persona or image
as being a villain. But he plays a very aggressive and
intense style of goal and he's revolutionizing the position."[1]
Philadelphia Flyers coach **MIKE KEENAN**, in 1988.

IN THE WEEKS leading up to the 1987 Canada Cup, the top
Canadian players spent hours doing skating, passing and shooting drills. They aimed to thwart the Soviet assault on the summit of world hockey, and no one was more committed than the
Philadelphia Flyers' Ron Hextall, who had just emerged as one
of the NHL's best goaltenders in his rookie season.

In a scrimmage before the start of the tournament, he and
teammate Sylvain Turgeon of the Hartford Whalers battled for
the puck. The tussle ended with Hextall's stick crashing into the
forward's arm and breaking it. Hextall said it was an accident,
but not everyone believed him. "It's obvious that this player is
uncontrollable," Whalers president and general manager Emile
Francis said, "and by a stupid act he has put an outstanding
player out of the Canada Cup."[2]

Hextall was as combative as he was talented. Brandishing his stick like a weapon, he attacked opponents in front of the net and along the boards. He racked up penalty minutes at a torrid pace and was suspended more than once. He was also excellent at handling the puck, completing precision passes to teammates breaking out of the defensive zone and shooting the puck at the opposing team's net. Hextall's ferocity vaulted him to the pinnacle of hockey.

RON HEXTALL was born in May 1964 in Brandon, Manitoba, an agricultural center 124 miles west of Winnipeg. But he didn't grow up playing hockey on a frozen pond in rural Canada, with frost-bitten toes and a toque on his head. He spent much of his childhood in big American cities. His father, Bryan Hextall Jr., was a professional hockey player who skated for three different NHL teams during his eight-season career. When he moved from one team to another, he took his wife and three children, Tracy, Rod and Ron, with him.

It was a mixed blessing for Ron. He faced the awkwardness of being the new kid in class more often than he would have liked, but he had opportunities his classmates didn't. He often went to practices with his father and spent hours with his nose pressed up against the glass, watching NHL players put through their paces. He sometimes skated onto the ice to take pointers from goalies on his father's teams. "Dan Bouchard used to stand behind me and move me across the crease to help me with angles," Hextall recalled years later. "Jimmy Rutherford worked with me, too. He even gave me one of his old masks."[3] In the summer, he trained at hockey camps run by his father.

Ron's uncle and grandfather were also in the business. Dennis Hextall played in the NHL for 12 seasons, starting in 1968. Bryan Hextall Sr. spent 11 seasons with the New York Rangers, starting in 1937. He led the NHL in goals twice (1939–40 and 1940–41) and won the overall scoring title once (1941–42). He also scored the Stanley Cup–winning goal in 1940.

Ron broke with family tradition and decided not to play forward. Instead, he set out to follow in the footsteps of NHL goalies such as Tony Esposito and spent hours sketching pictures of them. His parents were supportive, though his father urged him to try other positions first, to hone his skating skills. Fay Hextall drove her son to games and practices and, as doting mothers have been doing for generations, spent hours at a time standing on the driveway of the family home, firing wrist shots at her youngest child.

Not yet able to grow a playoff beard, little Ron was a far cry from an NHL star. Still, his mother knew he was destined for greatness. "I felt from a young age that he would make it," she said. "He had a love for the game that frankly I didn't see in too many of the players that his father played with."[4]

WHEN RON was 12 years old, his father retired from professional hockey, and the Hextall family moved back to Brandon. Ron had a rude awakening when he played his first organized game there. A handful of seasons in mediocre leagues south of the border had not prepared him for competition in Canada. The game was faster, and the players were more skilled. Ron had some catching up to do but hadn't quite done it by the time he started junior hockey in 1980.

The young goalie had ample opportunity to hone his skills during his first three seasons as a junior. His teams were so weak, he routinely faced more shots than the victims of the Saint Valentine's Day Massacre. In one of his games between the pipes for the Melville Millionaires of the Saskatchewan Junior Hockey League, the puck was fired at him 105 times. The team lost 21–2, but the consensus was that the score would have been even more lopsided if not for Hextall. He was named the first star of the game.

Hextall joined the Brandon Wheat Kings of the Western Hockey League (WHL) in 1981. In his first two seasons there, his team didn't fare much better than the Millionaires. The Wheat

Kings were dethroned in the first round of the 1981–82 playoffs and didn't even advance to the post-season the following year.

But Hextall made an impression. From the moment he charged onto the ice with his head down and his nostrils flared at the start of each game until he removed his mask at the final buzzer, electricity coursed through his veins. He stood impatiently while the national anthem played, shifting his weight from one foot to the other. He slammed his stick against the goal posts while getting set for a face-off in his zone and sometimes went for a short skate after letting in a goal.

Hextall loved to skate with the puck and often carried it up the ice before passing it to a teammate or shooting it toward the other team's net. "I can't say I planned on being a puck-moving goaltender when I was a kid," he says today. "It just sort of evolved over the years. Also, I remember being at my father's practices and seeing Jimmy Rutherford shoot the puck at the boards, lifting it off the ice. I still remember that vision and thinking it was one of the coolest things. For what reason? I have absolutely no idea. But that was one of the things that, as a kid, stuck in my mind." Other players marveled at his offensive skills, but his coaches weren't impressed. They urged him to stop playing like a third defenseman and warned him that he wouldn't make it to the NHL unless he did.

Hextall scared people. He shouted at referees and waged war on opponents. "Let me just tell you that I'm not like that off the ice," he says, laughing. "I'm not really sure where that came from. When I go out to compete I'm an aggressive personality. I can't say I watched somebody growing up and said, 'I'm going to be like him.' I just felt that I was at my best when I competed hard and I was a little bit aggressive."

His ferocity gave Philadelphia Flyers scout Gerry Melnyk a warm, fuzzy feeling; less than a decade earlier, the Flyers had won two straight Stanley Cups primarily by beating the living daylights out of their opponents. Melnyk convinced team executives that Hextall would be a good fit, and they chose him in the sixth round of the 1982 NHL draft. He was 119th overall.

In the 1983–84 season, his third and final one in the WHL, Hextall played in 46 games. He recorded 29 wins, more than the total from his previous two seasons combined. His goals-against average (4.27) dropped below 5.00 for the first time. He also set a single-season league record with 117 penalty minutes.

Hextall arrived at the Flyers training camp in the fall of 1984 expecting to win a spot on the roster. Instead, he was dispatched to the farm system and stayed there for the next two seasons. He made an impression while playing for the Hershey Bears of the American Hockey League (AHL). The team finished first in the 1985–86 regular season, and Hextall won 30 of the 59 games in which he played. He posted a 3.41 goals-against average and was named the league's best rookie. Of course, the season wasn't all sunshine and lollipops. In the conference final against the St. Catharines Saints, which the Bears ultimately won, Hextall reportedly took on three players in a single bench-clearing brawl.

NHL

1986-1987

Hextall headed to the Flyers training camp in September 1986 feeling cocky. As tall as Ken Dryden and as scrappy as Battlin' Billy Smith, who used his stick like a scythe, Hextall turned heads. But the Flyers had a good goaltender in Bob Froese—who had tied for most wins (21) among goalies the previous season—so coach Mike Keenan considered Hextall a long shot to make the roster. He soon changed his mind. The young goalie played so well in four exhibition games, Keenan put him in net for the opening game of the regular season.

In his NHL debut, Hextall faced the powerful Edmonton Oilers and one of the best hockey players in history, Wayne

||||||||||||||||||||||||||||||||||||||||||||||||||||||||||||||||||||

➤ GREAT GRANDPA ◄

HEXTALL'S grandfather, Bryan Hextall, was inducted into the Hockey Hall of Fame in 1969, in recognition of a great career that spanned 11 seasons. When he scored the winning goal for the New York Rangers in the 1940 Stanley Cup final, reporters sang his praises:

"The Leafs opened overtime in command. Bob Heron then Don Metz whaled shots at Kerr. They were hard drives, but high. Kerr loves that kind," Andy Lytle reported in the *Toronto Daily Star*.

"There were line changes. Apps for us, Hextall, that clever little monkey, Watson and Hiller for them. 'Look out!' said a man harshly, 'This spells trouble.'

"He had hardly spoken ere the 'pest' line rushed three abreast… Quick passes… a lusty back-hand heave by Hextall…

"The red beacon shone. Blue-shirted figures danced madly. The glittering lights on our hockey hopes went 'pffhut.' Blackout for at least a year."[24]

||||||||||||||||||||||||||||||||||||||||||||||||||||||||||||||||||||

Gretzky. Hextall allowed a goal on the first shot he faced, but the brash young goalie wasn't rattled. He stopped every shot for the remainder of the game, and the Flyers notched a 2–1 victory. "On a night of surprises in the NHL, the biggest one of all was the goaltender that Philadelphia Flyers coach Mike Keenan named to start against the Edmonton Oilers," a wire service reported. "Hextall was the surprise starter opening night over Froese, who led the NHL in goals-against average last year. Keenan said he decided to give Hextall the start over Froese to show his confidence in the 22-year-old sixth-round draft choice."[5]

The big kid between the pipes helped lead the Flyers to finish first in the Patrick Division and second in the league, with 100 points, in the 1986–87 regular season. (The Oilers finished with 106 points.) Hextall had the most wins (37) and the best save percentage (.902) among starting goalies. His 3.00 goals-against average was second only to Patrick Roy (2.93) of the Montreal Canadiens, who played 20 fewer games than Hextall. At the end of the regular season he was awarded the Vezina Trophy as the NHL's best goalie (Until 1981, the award was given to the goalie, or goalies, on the team allowing the fewest goals during the regular season; since then, it has been awarded based on merit.)

Hextall was as combative in his first NHL season as he had ever been, if not more so. He pushed and shoved unwanted guests on his doorstep and whacked them with his stick for good measure. In late January, he watched from the bench as his team lost 4–3 to the New Jersey Devils. It was too much to take. At the end of the game, Hextall leapt off the bench and lunged at New Jersey goalie Alain Chevrier, who was 7 inches shorter and 12 pounds lighter. "It was the kind of assault that if committed outside a hockey rink would be subject, on conviction, to a prison sentence," the *Washington Post* reported. The paper went on to note that Chevrier emerged from the altercation with scratches on his face. "The guy went for my eyes," the goalie said. "The Flyers' bench had been getting on me all night, calling me names and trying to get me off my game. Hextall had the biggest mouth. But I never expected something like that." But to Hextall, it was just another day at the office. "It's nothing," he said. "We just went at it."[6]

With Hextall at his combative best, the Flyers advanced through the first three rounds of the playoffs, defeating the New York Rangers (76 points), the New York Islanders (82 points) and the Montreal Canadiens (92 points) respectively. "Hextall is a cocky son of a gun," Canadiens coach Jean Perron said before Game 5 of the Prince of Wales Conference final. "He plays music by banging on the posts. He charges over like a bull and challenges our bench in warm-ups. It's part of him getting fired up."[7]

The Flyers took on the Oilers in the final. Edmonton was leading the series two games to one when the teams squared off for Game 4 at the Spectrum in Philadelphia.

Hextall went to battle as soon as he stepped on the ice. In the pre-game warm-up, the Oilers' Kevin Lowe shot the puck too close to Hextall—at least, in the goalie's estimation. Hextall swung his stick at Lowe, prompting players from both teams to crowd around center ice prepared to drop their gloves. Cooler heads prevailed—but not for long. In the third period, Hextall disagreed with a call made by referee Andy Van Hellemond and gave him an earful. The goalie was rewarded for his efforts with a 10-minute misconduct penalty.

Soon afterwards, the Oilers' Glenn Anderson closed in on the Flyers net and fired a shot. Hextall trapped the puck against the goal post, and Anderson swung his stick at it. He made contact with Hextall's pads and darted off before the goalie could react. Hextall was seething. During a play in front of the net a few minutes later, he drew his stick back with both hands and, like a lumberjack bringing down a tree, swung at the back of Kent Nilsson's legs. The Oilers forward fell to the ice and lay facedown for a few minutes before being helped to his feet. Hextall got a five-minute penalty.

Nilsson was furious. "If he's not suspended for that what is a player going to be suspended for in this league? It was obvious he was going to hit the first Oiler coming by," the Swede said later, standing in the dressing room with an ice pack strapped to his leg. "I just happened to walk into the worst two-hander I ever got."[8]

Hextall told reporters his slash was meant to be payback. He thought he was targeting Anderson, not Nilsson. The crime had been a case of mistaken identity. "If somebody slaps you in the face, you're going to slap him back," Hextall said. "It's not like [Anderson] gave me a touch to jar the puck. What's he going to do next, break my arm? I'm sorry it was Nilsson and not Anderson I hit, but I just reacted. At the time, it seemed the right thing to do."[9]

The Oilers went on to win the game 4–1. The Flyers won the next two contests to force a seventh game. Heading into that tilt, Gretzky shared his thoughts about the series and, more specifically, about Philadelphia's goalie. "Hextall is probably the best goaltender I've ever played against in the NHL," he said. "Just when you think you are going to bombard him, he comes up strong. It seems every game we start up 2–0 and 3–0, and he comes up with big saves. That's been the difference."[10]

Edmonton had won back-to-back Cups before the marauding Habs rode in from the east to lay claim to hockey's Holy Grail in the 1985–86 season. A year had passed since then, and Edmonton fans wanted the Cup back where it belonged—in the hands of the "Great One." Hextall did all he could to prevent that from happening. Up on his feet and down on the ice—on his stomach and even his behind—he stopped one shot after another. But in the end, it wasn't enough. The Oilers won the game 3–1, and Gretzky hoisted the Cup in front of a jubilant crowd.

"The guy I'm sad for is Ronnie Hextall," Flyers teammate Rick Tocchet said afterwards. "I mean, that guy, he was unbelievable tonight. I thought fate was going to give it to him tonight. He was just like God out there."[11] Hextall was awarded the Conn Smythe Trophy as the most valuable player in the playoffs, becoming just the fourth player from a losing side to win that honor.

"Ron Hextall played the pipes splendidly. Left, right, left, right, left, right, he clanked the posts with his big stick," the *Pittsburgh Post-Gazette* reported. "After performing the ritual in 92 games, Philadelphia's rookie goalie was revered by opponents, reviled by their fans and respected enough to be voted the Stanley Cup playoffs' Most Valuable Player."

"He was our Gretzky, he was our key," said Chico Resch, the Flyers' veteran goaltender and Hextall's mentor. "I'm keeping tapes of his performance just in case I have to teach young goalies how to play the game. He is today one of the greatest, and he will, in five to 10 years, be the greatest."[12]

1987-92

Seven years before Hextall's rookie season, in a game between the New York Islanders and the Colorado Rockies, another goalie made NHL history. When a delayed penalty was called against an Islander early in the third period, the Rockies pulled their goalie and sent out an extra attacker. A few seconds later, a Colorado player accidentally shot the puck the length of the ice and into his own empty net. The goal was awarded to the last Islander to touch the puck—goalie Billy Smith. He became the first NHL goalie to be credited with a goal.

Hextall intended to go a step farther. Having honed his puck-handling skills for years, he set out to become the first NHL goalie to score a "true" goal by shooting the puck into the net himself. "Hextall has it all planned," *Sports Illustrated* reported two months after the goalie made his NHL debut. "With the opposition's net empty, he will make a save, whistle a wrist shot the length of the ice and watch the puck pucker the back of the net. He can hear it now. 'Goal by number 27, Ron Hextall....'"[13]

Hextall made good on his promise a year later. In the final minutes of a December 1987 game against Boston, the Bruins pulled their goalie in favor of an extra attacker. Hextall grabbed a loose puck and shot it high in the air. It landed near the Boston blue line and skidded into the empty net, putting the Flyers ahead 5–2. Hextall's jubilant teammates leapt over the boards and rushed to congratulate him. Spectators rose to their feet to give him a standing ovation. "I don't mean to sound cocky," the goalie later told reporters, "but I knew I could do it. It was a matter of when."[14]

"I remember how excited my teammates were," Hextall says today. "Their reaction was almost over the top, to be honest. I thought [scoring the goal] was kind of neat, but not to the degree they did … It was like we had won a playoff game. I just said, 'Guys, settle down!' It was the celebration that made the goal special to me."

"In his rookie year, he played as well as any goaltender I have ever seen—and I have seen a lot of them."

Former Philadelphia Flyers teammate **MARK HOWE**

Hextall's goal-scoring streak didn't end there. Late in a game against the Washington Capitals in the division semifinal of the 1988–89 playoffs, Washington pulled its goalie for an extra attacker. Hextall took control of the puck and shot it at the empty net. Mission accomplished. Hextall became the first goalie in NHL history to score a true goal in the post-season.

FOR MOST of the five seasons following their appearance in the 1987 Stanley Cup final, the Flyers struggled—the team missed the playoffs three times in that span—and so did Hextall. Scoring exploits notwithstanding, the goalie failed to match the brilliance of his rookie season. He was hampered by numerous injuries and more angry outbursts. In each of his first two seasons in the NHL, Hextall amassed 104 regular-season penalty minutes. He was the first goalie in NHL history to be penalized more than 100 minutes. In his third season, 1988–89, he collected 113.

That season, Hextall allowed nine goals on 26 shots in the fifth game of the division final. When his frustration reached a critical mass, he argued with officials and got into shoving matches with Pittsburgh Penguins players. He even chased one of them around the ice, drawing a 10-minute misconduct penalty. "I just wanted to fight," Hextall explained. "It was no big deal. I was frustrated to say the least."[15] In the last minute of the game—after Hextall had been given the hook not once, but twice—Penguins fans in Civic Arena rose to their feet chanting, "We want Hextall! We want Hextall!" When his replacement, Ken Wregget, was thrown out following a dustup, Hextall was sent back onto the ice. The Pittsburgh fans, who had been waving "Hex Towels" all night, were elated. They anticipated another Penguins goal. But the last few seconds passed without scoring. The Flyers lost 10–7.

The Flyers bounced back to win the next two games and the series.

Hextall's antics continued in the next playoff round, the conference final. In the second game of the series against Montreal, Canadiens defenseman Chris Chelios used his elbow to smash Brian Propp into the glass. The Flyers sniper wound up in the hospital with a concussion. Chelios was not penalized, so Hextall took matters into his own hands later in the series. In the dying minutes of Game 6, when it was clear Montreal would win the game and the series, Hextall made a beeline for Chelios as the defenseman skated along the boards to the right of the Flyers net. Hextall swung the butt end of his stick at Chelios's head, grazing his helmet. Chelios fell to the ice and Hextall pounced on him, flailing at him with his fists. Hextall lost his jersey in the melee but hung on to his blocker. He lost that a few seconds later when he reached over a linesman and flung it at Chelios, who was being escorted off the ice.

BILLY SMITH:
PUBLIC ENEMY NUMBER ONE

YEARS BEFORE Hextall was first described as an "uncontrollable" NHL goalie, Billy Smith was earning similar reviews for wielding his stick like a machete. During the New York Islanders' heyday, opponents knew better than to skate too close to the team's combative goalie. No one was spared, not even the Great One.

In the second game of the 1983 Stanley Cup finals, "Battlin' Billy" reached behind his net and swung his stick at Wayne Gretzky, hitting him above the knee. The Edmonton Oilers' star fell to the ice. He stood up and confronted Smith. In the end, Gretzky didn't attack the goalie—but media, which had already denounced Smith as "Public Enemy Number One" for his belligerent play, railed against him. It hardly mattered.

The Islanders went on to sweep the Oilers in that series and win their fourth straight Cup. Smith took home the Conn Smythe Trophy. Also that season, he won the William M. Jennings Trophy as the goalie on the team allowing the fewest goals. The year before, he had won the Vezina Trophy and had been named to the first all-star team.

Twenty-four years after he retired, Smith is remembered as a clutch goalie—and as one who set an improbable record. In a game against the Colorado Rockies in November 1979, Rockies defenseman Rob Ramage accidentally put the puck in his own net. Smith had been the last Islander player to touch the puck, and so he became the first NHL goaltender to be credited with a goal. Looking back, Smith is unassuming. "It wasn't as nice as what Hexy did to score his," he says.[26]

"I saw him and I said, 'The hell with that,' and I went after him," Hextall said later. "It wasn't premeditated...but he tried to knock Brian Propp's head off. I think we owed him something."[16] "Just before that happened, our coach called a time-out and gave us a pep talk," remembers teammate Mark Howe. "He said, 'If we're going to go down, let's do it with pride and dignity.' Well, we lost the face-off and Montreal gained possession. Chelios ended up in our end. I was chasing after him, but I was too far behind to catch up. Then I looked up and saw Hexy skating out of his net to confront Chelios. I laughed at the irony. I thought to myself, 'Hexy's the only guy who didn't hear the coach's pep talk!' But that's Hexy, through and through."

Vigilante justice belongs in movies—Charles Bronson, take a bow—but not in hockey. At least, that's what the league decided. It gave Hextall a 12-game suspension, to be served at the start of the 1989–90 season. "Everyone respected Hextall for sticking up for a teammate," Propp says today. "He didn't deserve that suspension. Chelios should have been suspended for twice that number of games. I felt [Hextall's suspension] was a bad call—and it hurt us going into the next season."

That wasn't Hextall's first suspension—he had missed the first eight games of the 1987–88 season as punishment for slashing the Oilers' Nilsson—and it wouldn't be the last.

Hextall returned to the ice in early November after serving his suspension and settling a contract dispute. In his first game back, against the Toronto Maple Leafs, he pulled his groin. He sat out for almost two weeks. His luck then turned from bad to worse. In subsequent months, he suffered more groin problems and pulled a hamstring. He ended up playing just eight games in the 1989–90 season.

"It was an awful feeling for me to sit out," he told hockey broadcaster Dick Irvin Jr. "I remember thinking that there I was, 25 years old and my career might be finished. I'm not a real spiritual guy, but I must admit I said a prayer or two just to play until I was 32. At that point I was scared, very scared, that I was finished."[17]

He suffered injuries the following season too, including a torn ligament in his left knee, and played just 36 games.

But Hextall was unbroken. In an exhibition game before the 1991–92 regular season, he got into a dustup with Detroit Red Wings enforcer Jim Cummins. Officials gave Hextall a major penalty for slashing and Cummins a match penalty for attempt to injure. When the league reviewed the incident a week later, it suspended Hextall for six regular-season games and Cummins for three.

Hextall's life changed in June 1992, when he was sent to the Quebec Nordiques along with Peter Forsberg and four other active players, two first-round draft picks and a large sum of money in exchange for Eric Lindros. The Nordiques had picked the young phenom in the 1991 entry draft, but he had refused to play for the team.

1992-94

The next two seasons were a roller-coaster ride for Hextall, featuring dramatic highs and lows. Despite his initial concerns about moving his family to a French-speaking area, his wife, Diane, settled in quite nicely, as did their kids. Hextall did too. Although he missed 14 games with a thigh injury, he recorded 29 wins in 54 games and helped the Nordiques advance to the post-season for the first time since 1987.

Hextall was outstanding early in the first round of the playoffs, the Adams Division semifinal, and the Nordiques beat the Canadiens in the first two games. But then the wheels fell off. The hated Habs overtook the Nordiques and won the series in six games.

In the final tilt, Hextall was pulled after allowing five goals in a 6–2 loss. "I played poorly in Game 5 and not much better tonight" he said afterwards. "Goaltending proved the biggest

➤ PRACTICE MAKES PERFECT ◄

HEXTALL WAS a warrior in practice as well as games. Mark Howe, his teammate in Philadelphia, has vivid memories of those sessions. "He was just so intense all the time. We used to play with him a bit. When Hexy was on the right side of the net during practice, taking shots from some of the guys, Brian [Propp] would tuck in a puck on the left side. It drove Hexy absolutely crazy." But it delighted Propp. "Sometimes I would just stand at the net and shoot the puck again and again until it went in," he says. "It would just drive him crazy. I liked to see how far I could go before he would flip his lid."

"He was very systematic about the way he did things," recalls Howe. "Perhaps it was superstition. He ended every practice with me taking a shot on him. Someone would stand in the corner and pass the puck to me. I would shoot the puck low to Hexy's glove side. He would stop the puck and then skate off the ice. I remember once, after we had lost four or five games, I broke with the tradition. I refused to shoot the puck at him at the end of practice and he got mad. In the locker room, he gave me a hard time about it. I said, 'Hexy, whatever you're doing ain't working so I'm changing it for you.'"

difference," a wire service reported. "Quebec City native Patrick Roy played his best hockey of the season in the Montreal net, while Ron Hextall's play in the Nordiques net dropped sharply in the last two games after four brilliant outings."[18]

LESS THAN two months later, Hextall was on the move again. The Nordiques sent him to the Islanders.

Hextall was shaky early in the 1993–94 season as the team lost six of its first seven games. In a home game against the New Jersey Devils, he allowed six goals in the first two periods. Fans heckled him and cheered sarcastically every time he touched the puck without letting it in the net. He was pulled after the second period and looked on helplessly as his team fell to the Devils 6–3.

But he soon regained his composure. He went on to post five shutouts that season, the best regular-season total of his career. He also recorded a 3.08 goals-against average, the best since his rookie season. But his performance dipped again in the first round of the post-season. Playing in three games of the eastern conference quarter-final against the New York Rangers, he allowed 16 goals and posted a 6.08 goals-against average—the worst of his career. The Rangers swept aside the Islanders in four games. Many people felt Hextall was washed up, but Flyers general manager Bobby Clarke thought otherwise. A few months later, he acquired Hextall in a trade.

1994-99

Hextall's return to the City of Brotherly Love breathed new life into his game. His next few seasons were some of the best of his career. With "Hexy" back between the pipes in the 1994–95 season, the Flyers made the playoffs for the first time in six years. They won their first two series against the Buffalo Sabres and the New York Rangers and then took on the Devils in the conference final.

Hextall struggled in the first two games, both resounding victories by the Devils, but bounced back with some stellar play. In the end, it wasn't enough. The Devils won the series in six games. (They then swept the Detroit Red Wings to win the Cup.) Hextall took some heat over his inconsistency during the series, but many observers credited him with keeping the Flyers in contention.

Hextall silenced many critics in the 1995–96 season. Along with Detroit's Chris Osgood, he had the best goals-against average (2.17) among NHL goalies who played at least half the games that season. He also posted his best-ever save percentage (.913).

Hextall showed new poise in the first round of the playoffs, the conference quarter-final, against the Tampa Bay Lightning. The fifth game was a rough-and-tumble affair. Players exchanged blows more than once, racking up almost 150 penalty minutes overall. But Hextall wasn't penalized. He kept his temper in check, even after Lightning defenseman David Shaw skated behind the net during a Tampa Bay power play and smashed the goalie into the boards. Hextall reacted instantly, shaking his left hand to release it from his catching glove. But then he stopped. Seeing that the referee was about to call a penalty on Shaw, Hextall chose not to throw any punches. Shaw did a double take. Fans gasped in disbelief. The Earth stood still. "I was tired," Hextall said with a shrug. "We were killing a penalty."

His teammates attributed the 4–1 victory to their goalie. "Hexy's our backbone," said forward Joel Otto. "His whole season has been unbelievable," added defenseman Karl Dykhuis. "I don't see the other goalies that much, but I can't believe they could be any better."[19]

Philadelphia won the series and advanced to the conference semifinal. They were eliminated by the Florida Panthers in six games, but few blamed Hextall for the loss. The veteran played in all 12 playoff games, recording a 2.13 goal-against average and a .915 save percentage.

Led by the "Legion of Doom," a high-scoring forward line consisting of Lindros, John LeClair and Mikael Renberg, the Flyers finished second in the conference and fourth overall with 103 points in the 1996-97 season. They made quick work of three teams in the playoffs—the Pittsburgh Penguins (84 points), the Buffalo Sabres (92 points) and the New York Rangers (86 points). But they collapsed in the Stanley Cup final. Detroit (94 points) won the series in four straight games, forcing the Flyers to end their season standing on the ice at Joe Louis Arena, watching Red Wings captain Steve Yzerman hoist the Stanley Cup.

Hextall had some good moments in the next two seasons—he notched a 2.17 goals against average in the 1997–98 season—but not many. His performance started to lag, and he came under fire for allowing too many soft goals. He was a back up for John Vanbiesbrouck in the 1998–99 season. The Flyers bowed out in the first round of the playoffs both years.

The Flyers put Hextall on waivers in the summer of 1999, and he was not claimed by any team in the expansion draft (the Atlanta Thrashers joined the league that year.). In September, Hextall announced his retirement. "There's a million things in a bowl that I kind of grinded together, and it all came out pointing to the fact that it was time to move on," he said at the Flyers training camp. "I thought about it all summer. In the end, I felt the right thing to do was call it a career.

"In the next few years, there's going to be a new dimension added to goaltending right around the league. Offense. Ron Hextall is revolutionizing goaltending the way Bobby Orr changed defense. Pretty soon, the young goalies coming up will play the way Hextall does."[25]

Philadelphia Flyers legend
BERNIE PARENT, *in* 1989

"I just told them upstairs that I wanted to play this year. But you know, with my body aging and all the [other] factors, most things pointed to the fact that it was time."[20]

RETIREMENT

Hextall accepted a job offer as a scout for the Flyers and stayed in that position until 2002, when he became director of hockey personnel. The Flyers' success during Hextall's first six seasons in a suit and tie—they advanced to the conference final twice and finished among the top three in conference standings four times—drew the attention of the Los Angeles Kings. When they offered him a job as assistant general manager in 2006, Hextall packed his bags and flew to the City of Angels. "It was a difficult decision considering my history with the Flyers organization, but moving forward with my career I thought it was the best move for myself and my family," he said.[21]

In Los Angeles, he helped general manager Dean Lombardi with contract negotiations and player personnel. He also oversaw development of the club's top prospects. Lombardi, who had worked with Hextall in Philadelphia, also made him general manager of the Kings' affiliate, the Manchester Monarchs of the AHL, to oversee hockey and business operations. Six years later, the Kings won the Stanley Cup and Hextall hoisted hockey's Holy Grail at long last. "It's unbelievable," he said, standing on the ice in a dark suit and tie while Kings supporters crowded the ice and photographers snapped pictures of the players celebrating with family members. "Just being a part of management, a small part of it, it's a phenomenal feeling."[22]

That summer, Hextall took the Cup back to Brandon for a charity event and then to the family cabin in Clear Lake, Manitoba. He spent hours taking pictures with his father and visiting area landmarks before ending the day with a bonfire. Also that day, he stopped at the home of Bobby Clarke, the Flyers senior vice president, hoping to share the moment with the man who had taken a chance on him as a player and as part of management. Clarke wasn't home, so Hextall left a photo for him.

Hextall had paid tribute to Clarke four years earlier, in 2008, when the former goalie was inducted into the Flyers Hall of Fame. At the ceremony, which was held on the ice at the Wachovia Center between periods of a Flyers-Capitals game, former Flyers teammates Howe and Dave Poulin unveiled a plaque commemorating Hextall's career with the Flyers. Hextall, wearing an orange carnation on his lapel, struggled to keep his emotions in check as he posed for pictures with his former teammates. Fans gave him a standing ovation as Diane and the couple's four children, Kristin, Brett, Rebecca and Jeff, looked on, beaming.

That night, a reporter asked Capitals coach Bruce Boudreau, who had once competed against the former goalie in the AHL, to share his memories of Hextall. "He didn't break either of my legs," he said, "but I sure ended up with more than a few bruises standing near the net."[23] "If I was like that off the ice, I would probably be in jail now," Hextall says, looking back. "And if I had been a journalist in those days writing about Ron Hextall, I probably would have said the same thing everybody else did: 'That guy is a maniac!'"

HEXTALL · ALL-TIME RANKING*

REGULAR SEASON			PLAYOFFS		
GAMES	**WINS**	**SO**	**GAMES**	**WINS**	**SO**
608 [39th]	269 [29th]	23 [85th]	93 [18th]	47 [18th]	2 [77th]

* statistics as of July 2, 2013.

> NHL ALL-ROOKIE TEAM **(1ST)**: 1986–87

> NHL ALL-STAR TEAM **(2ND)**: 1986–87

9

THE COCK
OF THE WALK
PATRICK ROY

"He had that walk of confidence.
He was a leader in the dressing room, and every time he
was in the net, you knew you had a chance to win."[1]

Former Colorado Avalanche
teammate **JOE SAKIC**, in 2006

WHEN THE Granby Bisons goalie allowed three goals on
the first four shots of a major junior game against the Hull
Olympiques, a tall, skinny teenager took his place. He faced
more than 80 shots in that game but remained unshaken—
and unbowed. After stopping an Olympiques forward on a
breakaway, he threw the puck back at him and bellowed, "Take
another shot!" The shooter obliged but came up short again. He
skated to his bench wondering who the cocky kid was. A few
years later, he knew. Patrick Roy had become one of the best
goalies in the world—one whose prodigious talent was matched
only by his swagger.

PATRICK ROY was born in Quebec City in October 1965. His
father, Michel, was an insurance executive. His mother, Barbara,
had been a nationally ranked synchronized swimmer. She didn't

expect her eldest son to master the "water wheel" position, but she hoped he would make a splash in the pool. "He learned how to swim when he was one and would sit in his carriage beside the pool while I coached," Barbara once said. "When he was six to nine years old he had some of the top qualifying times in the whole country in his age group [in the 50-meter breaststroke]. I thought he could be a world-class swimmer."[2]

As a boy, Roy trained at a pool near his home in Sainte-Foy, an affluent area west of downtown Quebec City, but his interest lay elsewhere. He was obsessed with hockey. He watched *La Soirée du hockey*, the French-language equivalent to *Hockey Night in Canada*, on Saturday nights. His maternal grandmother, Anna Peacock, was a die-hard fan of the Montreal Canadiens, but Roy cheered for the Quebec Nordiques, who played in the World Hockey Association before joining the NHL. When Roy got his hands on a stick that had once been used by Daniel Bouchard— a Quebec goalie who played for the NHL's Atlanta Flames and then the Nordiques—he didn't let go. Rumor has it that he sometimes took the stick to bed and fell asleep with the sweet scent of fiberglass laminate in his nostrils.

Roy started playing organized hockey as a forward. But he was as drawn to the goalie equipment as he was to the game itself and fashioned a pair of his own pads by strapping pillows to his legs. He made his first save in the hallway of the home he shared with his parents, his brother, Stephane, and his sister, Alexandra. When his team's goalie got hurt, he volunteered to take his place. His coach balked, insisting the seven-year-old was too scrawny to play a position that required him to stand his ground against bigger kids. But Roy wasn't discouraged. He registered as a goalie the following season.

After playing for the Triple-A Sainte-Foy Gouverneurs, Roy set his sights on a professional hockey career. He dropped out of high school and joined the Granby Bisons of the Quebec Major Junior Hockey League (QMJHL) in the fall of 1982. The team was so weak in the first of his three seasons there that Roy often faced 50 or more shots a game. Yet the young goalie's talent was undeniable. In June 1984, the Montreal Canadiens selected Roy in the third round of the NHL Entry Draft. He was the 51st pick overall.

1984-85

At the Habs training camp a few months later, *Le Devoir* reported that Roy showed "confidence without arrogance" and felt he had as good a chance as anyone of becoming the backup to Steve Penney.[3]

The Habs sent Roy back to the Bisons in October, but he returned when Penney got injured in February. Doug Soetaert moved into the top spot, and Roy became his backup. Roy was prepared to sit on the bench while Soetaert played in a home game against Winnipeg on February 23. But after Soetaert allowed four goals on 11 shots, coach Jacques Lemaire tapped Roy to start the third period. The teenager stopped both shots he faced in those 20 minutes, and the Habs won 6–4.

Roy stayed with the team for a few more weeks but didn't play, and he headed back to Granby in March. When the Bisons were eliminated from the playoffs, Roy joined the Sherbrooke Canadiens, Montreal's farm team in the American Hockey League (AHL). He started as a backup to Greg Moffett but was called into action when Moffett left the ice with equipment problems during a game against New Haven. Roy was credited with the win and became the team's starting goaltender in the playoffs. He recorded 10 wins in 13 games as Sherbrooke won the Calder Cup. Moffett faded from view.

WHILE IN SHERBROOKE, Roy benefited from the tutelage of goalie coach Francois Allaire, who cured the young goalie's tendency to drop to the ice again and again, like a marionette whose strings had been cut. (Lemaire once said Roy spent so much time sprawled on the ice, he should have reported for work with a mattress and a pillow.) Under Allaire's guidance, Roy refined the butterfly technique that Glenn Hall had introduced years before.

Whereas Hall was a stand-up goalie who dropped to the ice in a butterfly position only when necessary, Roy played in a variation of the butterfly position at all times. Pushing off his toes, he moved from one side of the net to the other with his knees close together and his legs spread to the sides. His pads formed a barrier across the lower part of the net. Roy used his size—he was six-foot-two—and his lightning-quick glove hand to protect the top of the net.

"Some goalies had used the [butterfly] position before, but Patrick was the first one to use it consistently and with a purpose," says Allaire, whose success with Roy and Jean-Sebastien Giguere made him the éminence grise of goalie coaching. He attributes much of Roy's success to his size and his skating ability. "He was probably one of the best skaters among goalies at the time. That was the foundation of his system. It allowed him to make saves that would have been impossible otherwise," Allaire says.

"His personality was a factor too. He had an open mind. As soon as he saw something that would improve his game, he would adopt it. He was an intelligent athlete," continues Allaire. Roy was acutely aware of his surroundings on the ice, amazing teammates and reporters with his ability to give a detailed account of how a particular play unfolded weeks and months after the fact. He was also supremely confident in his abilities—even when others weren't—and was able to bounce back from a bad goal or game. He thrived on pressure. In time, his mental toughness became legendary.

NHL

1985-86

Fresh off his success in Sherbrooke, Roy reported to training camp feeling sure of himself. If he was nervous to be on the ice with Bob Gainey and Larry Robinson, who had been part of the Habs dynasty of the previous decade, it didn't show. "We had our training camp and Patrick was, again, the best goalie," Jean Perron, who had replaced Lemaire as coach, recalled years later. "Better than [Steve] Penney. Better than Doug Soetaert." Perron urged general manager Serge Savard to add Roy to the roster, but he refused. Savard felt Roy needed more seasoning in the AHL.[4]

However, the issue became moot when Penney got injured just before the regular season started. Roy played in the opener, a road game against the Pittsburgh Penguins, five days after his 20th birthday. The Canadiens notched a 5–3 win. "It was great. I could send Patrick against Mario Lemieux and the Penguins in Pittsburgh for the first game. Can you imagine that?" Perron said. "He was spectacular, and we won."[5]

Roy emerged as the Canadiens' top goalie that season. He played in 47 of their 80 regular-season games, while Penney and Soetaert looked on from the sidelines. Thanks in part to his contribution, the Canadiens finished second in the Adams Division and seventh overall, with 87 points.

Despite this success, some fans viewed him as the team's weak link heading into the playoffs. Roy had no NHL post-season experience, and more troubling, he tended to allow one or two soft goals a game. But their fears proved unfounded. In the opening game of the first round, the division semifinal, Roy stopped the first 10 shots the Boston Bruins (86 points) fired at him. He stopped 25 shots overall as the Habs won 3–1—and he never looked back. Roy was solid in net as Montreal won three games to clinch the series. (At the time, all the division semi-finals were best-of-five.)

They defeated the Hartford Whalers (84 points) in the division final, when Claude Lemieux scored six minutes into overtime of Game 7. "I was very nervous, but very confident," said Roy, who had won a classic goaltenders' duel with the Whalers' Mike Liut. "These guys were very positive in the dressing room before the overtime."[6]

RON TUGNUTT: ◄
SECOND TO NO. 1

DRAFTED BY the Quebec Nordiques in 1986, Ron Tug-nutt spent 16 seasons in the NHL. He's best known for his strong 1998–99 season with the Ottawa Senators, when he posted the NHL's best goals-against average (1.79), and for being in net in one of the longest playoff games in NHL history. Playing for the Pittsburgh Penguins in the 2000 Eastern Conference semifinal, Tugnutt made 70 saves before Philadelphia scored 12 minutes into the fifth overtime of Game 4.

He drew less attention during the 19 months he spent in Montreal as backup to Roy. Tugnutt played just 15 regular-season games during that time—and just one playoff game. But it was a memorable one. With the 1994 conference quarter-final between the Canadiens and the Boston Bruins tied at one game apiece, St. Patrick was hospitalized with appendicitis. Tugnutt replaced him in Game 3 and made 20 saves as the Habs lost 6–3. Roy returned for Game 4 and played the rest of the series.

"Roy was a fierce competitor. The bigger the game, the more he elevated his play. That propelled him to great heights," says Tugnutt. But Roy's ferocity also meant he "wasn't best friends with everyone in the dressing room. He didn't mind calling guys out to the point where guys would argue with him or fight with him. He was that fierce," says Tugnutt. Roy never hesitated to remind Tugnutt of the status quo. "His message was always, 'You do realize, you'll only play when I don't want to play.' I had great respect for him as a goalie, but I wouldn't say he was my favorite goalie partner," says Tugnutt. "It definitely wasn't the most fun I have ever had in hockey."

Robinson had seen great goaltending in his career; he had played with the legendary Ken Dryden. But he was floored by Roy's performance. "Patrick has given us the best goaltending we've had in my 14 years here," he said.[7]

The Canadiens then squared off against the New York Rangers (78 points) in the Prince of Wales Conference final. The Canadiens were leading the series when the teams stepped onto the ice at Madison Square Garden for Game 3. It turned out to be one of the most memorable of Roy's career.

The game went into sudden death overtime with the score tied 3–3. Roy, who had been deemed "technically unsound" by Rangers coaches, made 13 saves in the first nine minutes, most of them spectacular. Lemieux put the puck past Rangers goalie John Vanbiesbrouck 10 minutes into overtime, giving the Canadiens the victory and a 3–0 series lead. Roy left the ice having stopped all but 3 of the 47 shots fired at him—making a fool of Rangers forward Wilf Paiement, who had suggested before the game that 35 shots would be too much for the rookie to handle. "He made a believer out of a lot of us," New York's Don Maloney said afterwards. "Before the game we were climbing a hill, now we're climbing a mountain."[8]

As it turned out, the Rangers couldn't find their footing in the series, and the Habs prevailed four games to one. Montreal then faced off against Calgary (89 points) in the Stanley Cup final. The Flames won the first game, but the Habs won the next three. Game 5 was a nail-biter. Late in the third period, with Montreal leading 4–3, the Flames were given a two-man advantage. Desperate to even the score, Calgary forwards buzzed around Roy like angry hornets, but they couldn't put the puck past him. "He was a skinny kid, and he was moving like crazy," Perron recalled. "Patrick did miracle saves on Al MacInnis, Joey Mullen, Joe Nieuwendyk, Gary Suter, Joel Otto, Lanny McDonald and Hakan Loob. He was just unbelievable."[9]

When the game ended, players leapt over the boards to celebrate the Canadiens' first Stanley Cup in seven years. They surrounded their young goalie and congratulated him as dozens of reporters, cameramen and photographers descended on the ice to capture the moment. When the celebrations subsided, Montreal players started chanting, "Roo-AH! Roo-AH!" in anticipation of the inevitable.

The 20-year-old goaltender was presented with the Conn Smythe Trophy as the most valuable player in the playoffs, becoming the youngest recipient of the award. He had played in every minute of all 20 games, posting an incredible 1.92 goals-against average. "Not too many thought we could do it," he said, beaming, while McDonald broke down in the other dressing room. "I think I have proven myself in the NHL, but I have to start all over next year. Only it will be more difficult. But winning this trophy is something no one will ever be able to take away from me."[10]

The Montreal faithful were as surprised as they were euphoric to see the Habs hoist the Cup in the Saddledome. The Canadiens had started the season without any bona fide stars aside from Mats Naslund, who finished eighth in league scoring with 110 points, and Gainey and Robinson, then in the twilight of their careers. The team had not been expected to achieve much. But no one knew a phenom was in their midst—and in their net. Roy started the season as a talented but unpolished goaltender. He ended it as "St. Patrick."

As much as fans admired Roy's athleticism, they delighted in talking about his idiosyncrasies. While standing at center ice before the start of each game, he turned and looked at his net, growing more confident as it grew smaller in his mind's eye. He also talked to his goal posts, craning his neck as if to make eye contact with them while imploring them to help him keep the puck out of the net. Roy was so averse to having his skate blades touch the lines on the ice that his trip from the bench to the net was as fraught with danger as a walk through a minefield.

After the Canadiens won the Cup, the city of Montreal held a parade in their honor. Throngs of people cheered in the sunshine as the players moved along Saint Catherine Street in top-down convertibles. With fans chanting "Roo-AH! Roo-AH!" a group of young women rushed up to the goalie and ripped off his shirt. Standing on the trunk of a car, Roy broke into a dance later described by one reporter as a "bare-chested boogie."[11]

Roy was an instant celebrity. He was asked to participate in dozens of promotional events and golf tournaments. A bank cast him in a series of television commercials. He received bags of mail from fans, who swarmed him everywhere he went, asking for his autograph. Roy accepted a job as a part-time video jockey on MusiquePlus, the French-language equivalent to MuchMusic, admitting that he loved Madonna—the music, that is, not the Material Girl herself.

The attention was so intense that Roy left his basement apartment in a working-class area of Montreal for the relative tranquility of his parents' home in suburban Quebec City.

Many other aspects of his life changed that summer, but some stayed the same. Roy continued to indulge his appetite for hamburgers, french fries and potato chips—an approach to nutrition he soon changed at the insistence of the Habs' dieticians.

1986-88

The Habs fared well in the next two seasons—they advanced as far as the conference final and the division final respectively—but neither the team nor Roy soared to the heights of their recent Cup-winning season.

Roy shared goaltending duties with Brian Hayward, whom the Habs had acquired from the Winnipeg Jets in exchange for Penney in August 1986. They formed a first-rate goaltending team. In both seasons, Hayward had the best goals-against average among starters (2.81 and 2.86), and Roy finished one spot behind (2.93 and 2.90). Roy played 15 more games than his partner during that span. They twice shared the William M. Jennings Trophy, given annually to the goalie(s) on the team allowing the fewest goals (if more than one of the team's goalies play 25 games or more, the award is shared).

Roy got some pointers from Hayward, who had been in the league since the 1982–83 season. "I was older, more mature and probably more professional at that point. I had to leverage all those things to get playing time," Hayward, now a California-based sportscaster, recalls. "But everyone could see what an incredible athletic talent Pat was... I recognized that he had physical gifts I didn't have, like better size and flexibility." Although they competed for ice time, the men got along well and even roomed together for a while. "I think we had a great relationship... I mean, neither of us would hide our disappointment when the other guy was chosen to start a game, but I don't consider that being nasty. It was just the competitive reality of the situation," says Hayward, who stayed with the Habs until he was traded to Minnesota in November 1990.

"They're like good friends. When you need them, they are there." [31]

PATRICK ROY, *on his goal posts*

"Pat always thought things would go his way, almost to the point of it being laughable," Hayward says, citing one game as an example. "He played an exceptional game, but he also had a few lucky breaks. The other team hit the crossbar and the goal posts a few times. They scored a goal on him late in the game. He was so angry when he came off the ice, he smashed his stick. I asked him what he was mad about. He said, 'I can't get a break! I was so unlucky on that last goal.' Well, I remember thinking to myself, 'Man, you had five or six big breaks in that game.' But that was Pat. He had that expectation that things were *always* going to go his way."

During a scuffle in front of the net during a game against Minnesota in October 1987, Roy slashed forward Warren Babe. The North Stars player limped off the ice with a bruised ankle. Roy later said he had been trying to help a teammate who was being jostled. Minnesota head coach Herb Brooks was incensed

and said he would "make sure Roy [got] his throat cut next time."
Roy was suspended for eight games.[12]

1988-89

The Canadiens returned to top form in the 1988–89 season,
becoming formidable in the second half—especially at home.
They finished first in their division and second overall, with
115 points. Roy was dominant during that time and recorded a
29-game unbeaten streak at the Montreal Forum. He surpassed
Hayward, notching the best goals-against average (2.47) and
save percentage (.908) among NHL starters. He also finished second in wins (33) and shutouts (4). He and Hayward combined
to win another Jennings Trophy.

With star defenseman Chris Chelios, then in his sixth season with the team, and veteran forward Guy Carbonneau, Roy
led the Habs deep into the playoffs. They beat the Whalers (79
points) and the Bruins (88 points) before meeting the Philadelphia Flyers (80 points) in the conference final. With Tim
Kerr and Rick Tocchet up front and star Ron Hextall between
the pipes, the Flyers were a strong team. But the Habs won the
series in six games.

In the final, the Canadiens met the only team that had finished ahead of them in the standings, the Calgary Flames (117
points). Doug Gilmour, Joe Mullen and Joe Nieuwendyk led
a formidable offense. Proving too hot to handle, the Flames
avenged their 1986 loss, eliminating the Habs in six games.
Montreal players stood dejected at the end of the final game as
McDonald hoisted the Cup for the first time in his 16-year career.
"It has no weight at all," the mustachioed veteran said after taking the trophy on a victory lap around the Forum ice. "It's the
most peaceful feeling I've ever had in hockey."[13]

Roy's accomplishments were not overlooked. Two weeks
after the end of the season, he was awarded the Vezina Trophy
as the NHL's top goaltender.

1989-90

In the 1989–90 season, Roy cemented his status as one of the world's best goalies. Among starters, he had the best save percentage (.912) and, along with Liut, the best goals-against average (2.53). He also finished in a three-way tie for most wins (31). He and three other goalies had three shutouts apiece, one less than leader Liut.

The Habs finished fourth overall (93 points), and with forward Stephane Richer firing on all cylinders, they felt confident heading into the playoffs. Even without Chelios, who was sidelined with a knee injury, Montreal eliminated the Buffalo Sabres (98 points) in six games in the division semifinal. But their run ended in the next round, when the Bruins (101 points) defeated them in a five-game series.

In June, *Toronto Star* columnist Damien Cox predicted Roy would win his second Vezina Trophy at the NHL awards ceremony: "Is there anyone better than Patrick Roy? Nope. Goals-against averages of 2.53 in 54 games don't lie. Our condolences to able runners-up Andy Moog (Boston) and Daren Puppa (Buffalo)." Sure enough, Roy won.[14]

1990-92

The Habs were eliminated in the division final in each of the next two seasons. The team didn't make much of an impression, but their goalie turned heads.

In the 1991–92 season, Roy posted the best goals-against average (2.36) and save percentage (.914) among NHL starters and finished in a four-way tie for most shutouts (5). He also recorded 36 wins, the second-best total in the league. He alone claimed the Jennings Trophy. (Since Hayward had been traded in 1990, Montreal's other goalies had assumed spectator status.) And Roy won his third Vezina Trophy.

1992-93

The beginning of the 1992–93 season almost spelled the end for Roy in Montreal. As his goals-against average inflated like the

Hindenburg, Habs fans grew restless. In January 1993, a local newspaper conducted a poll in which a majority of the respondents said Roy should be traded. He closed out the season with a 3.20 goals-against average, his worst in seven years.

With the Canadiens, who had finished third in their division and sixth overall (102 points), about to start the playoffs, columnist Michael Farber fired a shot at the goalie. "Roy-is-the-best-goalie-in-the-world has become a mantra, not a given," he wrote, "and chanting it over and over won't necessarily make it so."[15]

The situation worsened when the Canadiens dropped the first two games of the division semifinal to their bitter rivals, the Quebec Nordiques (104 points). Roy allowed soft goals in both games. "What I want to do is make the saves that keep my team in the game and I didn't do that in the first period," the dejected goalie said after Game 2. "We knew they would come at us hard, but we didn't do enough about it, especially me, and that makes me disappointed."[16]

But Jacques Demers, who had taken over as coach that season, resisted calls to replace the goalie in Game 3. Roy stepped on the ice at the Forum determined to prove his critics wrong.

Roy stopped 34 shots in the game, leading his team to a 2–1 victory. The highlight of his night came in the first period. With the Nordiques ahead, Roy mishandled the puck behind his net. Quebec forward Scott Young took a shot at the empty net and was about to raise his arms in celebration, when Roy dove from outside the post and speared the puck with his glove. From that point on, he was formidable. The Habs won the next three games and advanced to the division final.

With St. Patrick in net, the Habs beat the Buffalo Sabres (86 points) in four straight games and eliminated the New York Islanders (87 points) in a five-game conference final. The Islanders' lone win, in Game 4, ended Montreal's record-tying 11-game playoff winning streak.

On June 1, the puck dropped in Montreal to start the 1993 Stanley Cup final, a showdown between one of the league's top goalies and one of the best forwards in NHL history. Wayne Gretzky notched one goal and three assists in the opening game, leading his team to a 4–1 win.

Later than night, Roy went to Lakeshore Hospital in Montreal to help his wife deliver their daughter. No sooner had little Jana Roy taken her first breath than her father was back in the Habs dressing room, suiting up for battle.

The Canadiens won the next four games and their first Cup in seven years. "I wouldn't be sitting here without him," said Montreal's Paul DiPietro, who had scored two goals for the Canadiens in that night's 4–1 win. "He's the best goalie in the league and he deserves everything he gets. What can I say about him? He put a ring on my finger."[17]

Holding the big silver trophy over his head, Roy skated toward a television camera, peered into its lens and warmed the hearts of Mouseketeers the world over by shouting, "I'm going to Disneyland!" Minutes later, he was awarded his second Conn Smythe Trophy.

"In '86 nothing much mattered," Roy said, referring to his previous Cup win. "We weren't supposed to win anything and everything that happened was a good thing. This year it was different. A first-round loss to Quebec would have made for a real bad summer and Patrick Roy probably would have been traded... The season was a little bit up and down with lots of critics on me, but it was a great feeling to come back and have a great playoffs and win the Stanley Cup."[18]

Not long after, he received his Disneyland citizenship and even let Goofy take a shot on him with an oversized puck. Roy later boasted that the showdown had given him a chance to make yet another save.

THE HABS had set a record by notching 10 overtime victories in the 1993 playoffs—the previous record was six, which had been set by the Islanders in 1980—and of all the dramatic moments in those extra periods, the most memorable was the least athletic.

Late in the overtime period of Game 4, the Kings fired a shot at the Habs net. As Roy made the save, Tomas Sandström lunged forward, looking for a rebound. But there was none. Roy smothered the puck then stood up and winked at the Kings forward as if to say, "Who's your daddy?" Television cameras caught the gesture, and it was beamed into living rooms and bars across the continent. Many hockey fans were disgusted, but Roy and his supporters couldn't have cared less.

"He was always pushing me and always hitting me in the pad," Roy said. "[That time] when I had the puck in my glove, he gave me a shot in the glove. Not that I was cocky. I just wanted to show him I was in control of the situation."[19] A few years later, he changed his tune. "Maybe I *was* cocky," he told hockey broadcaster Dick Irvin Jr., "but you get kind of cocky when you feel that confident."[20]

1993-94

The Habs followed up their Cup victory with a mediocre season. They were eliminated in the Eastern Conference quarter-final by the Bruins. Roy allowed some soft goals in the last two games, both Montreal losses, and ended the series with a whimper. But he was hailed as a hero.

A week before, with the series tied at one game apiece, he had checked into Montreal General Hospital complaining of abdominal pain. Diagnosed with appendicitis, he had been told he might have to undergo surgery that would sideline him for up to two weeks.

He missed the next game, which the Bruins won, but after spending time on an intravenous feed of antibiotics, he returned for Game 4—and played some of the best hockey of his career. He led his team to victory in that game, and the next one, allowing just three goals on 102 shots. "We are all involved in something to tell the grandchildren about," columnist Bob Ryan said breathlessly in the *Boston Globe*. "We are watching a man determine the outcome of a Stanley Cup series all by himself. No power pitcher, no high-scoring basketball player, no pick-'em-apart quarterback can affect a game as much as a goal-tender who breaks hearts continually for 60 minutes a night. Or however long is necessary."[21]

Boston forwards were dumbfounded. "He's never out of position. He never seems to overplay or underplay anything," Ted Donato said after Roy had stonewalled the Bruins in overtime of Game 5. "He takes every shot at face value. He also covers the bottom of the net so well, which is important because guys have a tough time being accurate when they shoot high. That causes a lot of trouble."[22]

1994-96

The following season, Montreal tumbled down the standings. Now without Carbonneau, Denis Savard and some of the other players who had propelled the team to the final two seasons before, the Habs failed to make the playoffs for the first time in 25 years.

The freefall continued in the 1995–96 season. In mid-October, with Montreal languishing at the bottom of the standings, club president Ronald Corey hired Mario Tremblay as head coach and Rejean Houle as general manager. The former players replaced Demers and Serge Savard respectively, both of whom had been fired a few days before.

Tremblay confronted his players like Dirty Harry staring down members of a biker gang. He ordered them to compete with more intensity, all but daring them to make his day. His relationship with Roy, who had once been his roommate, was strained. Whereas Demers had cut Roy slack, Tremblay kept him on a short leash. It didn't help that, in his former role as a radio commentator, Tremblay had often criticized Roy. The conflict came to a head in December, during a game against the powerful Detroit Red Wings.

The Habs allowed five goals in the first period alone. But rather than replace Roy during intermission, Tremblay sent him back on the ice—and the goalie continued to get pummeled. Fans cheered sarcastically whenever he touched the puck, prompting him to raise his arms in mock gratitude. By the 12-minute mark of the second period, he had allowed nine goals on 26 shots.

At that point, Tremblay showed some mercy, pulling Roy from the game and replacing him with Pat Jablonski. Roy stepped off the ice and headed to the end of the bench. He and Tremblay glared at each other. Suddenly, Roy turned around and walked back toward Corey, who was seated behind the bench. Furious, he told the club president he wouldn't play another game in a Habs jersey. The Habs suspended him the next day.

Some of the fans who had idolized Roy turned on him, accusing him of being petulant and childish. At a press conference at a suburban hotel, an emotional Roy apologized to them. "I really wanted it to end differently, not in a stupid way like this. I hope my fans will forgive me for the gesture I made," he said, sobbing. "I was frustrated and humiliated." Still, he ruled out reconciliation with Tremblay, insisting that "what's done is done."

Montreal traded him to the Colorado Avalanche as part of a five-player deal.

THE AVALANCHE (formerly the Quebec Nordiques; they relocated that summer) had advanced to the conference final only twice in the franchise's 16 NHL seasons—and lost both times. But with Joe Sakic and Peter Forsberg leading the attack, and Adam Foote on defense, Colorado was now a strong team with great potential. Coach Marc Crawford hoped that Roy would be the final piece of the puzzle.

When "Le Trade" was announced, NFL star John Elway said he was confused about the goalie's last name. He wondered aloud why he didn't pronounce his last name "Roy," rhyming with *boy*, instead of "Roo-AH." But the Denver Broncos quarterback, and other Colorado sports fans, warmed up to the newcomer soon enough.

While playing cards on a flight in January, Roy turned to Colorado's assistant coach, Joel Quenneville, and said, "You know Joel, we're going to win the Cup this year." Quenneville was shocked. "I looked at him and didn't say another word. He didn't say another word, either. We left it at that."[23]

In early February, the Avalanche played the Canadiens at McNichols Arena in Denver. Roy stopped 37 shots, and the Avalanche notched a 4–2 victory. As Tremblay headed to the dressing room, Roy flipped the puck to his former coach. It fell at Tremblay's feet, and he left it there. "It was maybe a little bit arrogant," Roy conceded later. "But I was happy… It was just for fun. I think the fans enjoyed it just as much as me. My new fans."[24]

Colorado finished second in the Western Conference and in the overall standings, with 104 points. Only the Red Wings (131 points) fared better. The Avalanche started the post-season by eliminating the Vancouver Canucks (79 points) in a six-game conference quarter-final. They then played the Chicago Blackhawks (94 points) in the conference semifinal, a series that featured a clash of titanic egos—Roy and star Blackhawks forward Jeremy Roenick.

The series was tied at one game apiece when the puck dropped in Chicago for the third game. With Colorado leading 3–2 in the third period, Roenick broke in on net alone. He faked out Roy, forcing the goalie to move left while he moved right. Roenick tied up the game, and the Blackhawks ended up winning 4–3 in overtime.

In Game 4, the teams battled to a 2–2 tie at the end of regulation time. In the first overtime period, Roenick had another breakaway. As he bore down on net, he was hooked from behind by Colorado's Sandis Ozolinsh and fell to the ice. The officials failed to award a penalty shot. Sakic later scored in triple overtime, giving the Avalanche a 3–2 win.

Colorado players praised Chicago goalie Ed Belfour, who had stopped 54 shots. Roy, who had stopped 32 shots, admitted his rival had played well but said the game's outcome was never in doubt. "I knew I was going to win," he said. "I got in a very positive frame of mind, and did not let any stupid thoughts in."[25]

Roy also said he would have stopped Roenick even if the Blackhawks player had been awarded a penalty shot. "I like Patrick's quote that he would have stopped me," Roenick responded. "I'd just want to know where he was in Game 3— probably getting his jock out of the rafters in the United Center." The war of words continued. "I can't really hear what Jeremy says," the goalie said, sporting a goatee and a smirk, "because I've got my two Stanley Cup rings plugging my ears."

Colorado won the series in six games.

The Avalanche took on the Red Wings in the conference final. Detroit had won a record 62 games in the regular season and was the odds-on favorite to win the Cup. But with Sakic leading the charge and Roy tending net, the Avalanche overwhelmed the Red Wings and clinched the series in six games.

Colorado took on Florida (92 points) in the Cup final. The third game was arguably the most memorable of the series. The Panthers scored two quick goals in the first period, and in keeping with tradition, jubilant hometown fans showered the ice with rubber rats. Roy refused to duck under his net, as other goalies had, to avoid the faux rodents. He declared there would be "no more rats" on the ice. Sure enough, he didn't allow any more goals in that game, or in the next one, and the Avalanche swept the series.

When Colorado defenseman Uwe Krupp blasted in the winning goal early in the third overtime period of Game 4, Avalanche players poured onto the ice in celebration and gathered around Roy, who had made 63 saves in the 1–0 victory. It was his eighth career playoff shutout.

He had started the season with one Stanley Cup ring in each ear and ended it with a third ring. Where he put that one, only he knows for sure.

1996-2000

Colorado didn't win any Cups in the next four seasons, but the team fared well enough, advancing to the conference final three times.

The Buffalo Sabres' Dominik Hasek was the league's dominant goalie during that span, winning the Vezina Trophy three times, but Roy was no slouch. In the 1996–97 season, he notched the most wins (38) among NHL goalies. In April, he recorded his 89th post-season win, breaking a record set by Billy Smith, who had retired eight years before.

Also that season, Roy took part in a massive on-ice brawl in a game between the Avalanche and the Red Wings. Tension between the teams had been building since the 1996 conference final, when Colorado forward Claude Lemieux had hit Detroit's Kris Draper from behind, sending him off the ice for reconstructive facial surgery. So when Detroit forward Darren McCarty decked Lemieux during a game in March 1997, all hell broke loose. Roy jumped into the fray and exchanged punches with Red Wings goalie Mike Vernon. By the time officials restored order, the ice was covered in patches of blood—some of which had gushed from Roy's head.

ALMOST A YEAR after his face took a beating, Roy's ego suffered the same fate. As Team Canada's starting goalie at the Winter Olympics in Nagano, he was in net for the semifinal against the Czech Republic. The game was tied 1–1 at the end of overtime, so the teams took part in a shootout. Roy shut down all except one of the five Czech shooters, but Hasek stonewalled all the Canadian snipers. The Czechs advanced to the final against Russia and ultimately went home with the gold medal (see pages 251–253). After losing the bronze-medal game to Finland, the Canadians left empty-handed.

2000-01

A few weeks into the 2000–01 season, Roy reached a milestone that cemented his status as one of the all-time greats. In a road game against the Washington Capitals, he recorded win number 448, breaking a record set by the legendary Terry Sawchuk decades before.

In a long ceremony honoring him before a home game on Friday October 20, Avalanche owner Stanley Kroenke presented Roy with a bronze sculpture of the goalie leaning against the net. Guy Lafleur, representing the Canadiens, gave him a silver plate, whose inscription read, "You recognize great athletes with the dimension of their goals. Congratulations Patrick Roy, goaltender with the most victories in the history of hockey." NHL commissioner Gary Bettman and Jerry Sawchuk, Terry Sawchuk's eldest son, presented Roy with a silver stick that was incorporated into a display. In one of the most poignant moments of the night, Sawchuk lifted Roy's arm.

Denver mayor Wellington Webb declared that day Patrick Roy Day, and not to be outdone, Colorado governor Bill Owens declared October 20 to 26 Patrick Roy Week.

Michele Piuze, whom Roy had wed in 1990, gave her husband a personalized golf cart on behalf of her and their three children, Jonathan, Frederick and Jana. By the end of the weekend, she may have wanted to take it back.

THE NIGHT AFTER the ceremony, Denver police were called to the Roy family's suburban home. During an argument with Michele, Roy had lost his temper and ripped two doors off their hinges. He spent six hours in custody on charges of misdemeanor criminal mischief related to domestic violence. Unlike Ed Belfour, who had scuffled with police in a Dallas hotel, Roy was apprehended without a fight. Said lieutenant Stephen Keller: "As far as I know, he was a perfect gentleman." Roy was released on $750 bail and was later cleared of all charges. Roy and his wife divorced a few years later.[26]

HIS BRUSH with the law didn't faze Roy. With help from Sakic and Forsberg, two of the NHL's top scorers, and star defenseman Ray Bourque, who had joined the Avalanche in 2000, Roy led his team to the top of the standings. Colorado finished first overall (118 points).

The Avalanche beat the Vancouver Canucks (90 points) in four games, the L.A. Kings (92 points) in seven and the St. Louis Blues (103 points) in five before squaring off against the New Jersey Devils (111 points) for the Cup.

The defending champions had finished just seven points behind Colorado in the regular season. They had three of the NHL's top scorers in Patrik Elias, Alexander Mogilny and Petr Sykora, and included three of the league's best defensemen— Scott Stevens, Scott Niedermayer and Brian Rafalski.

Their goalie, Martin Brodeur, was also one of the best in the league. Since being named the NHL's top rookie in the 1993–94 season, he had won two Stanley Cups. He had also notched a league-leading 42 wins in the 2000–01 season, two more than Roy. Brodeur had once emulated Roy, a fellow Quebecois. Brodeur's father, Denis, had been the Habs' photographer, so Martin had spent hours at the Forum as a kid. He had met Roy when the Habs goalie was the NHL's hot young thing and Brodeur was a gawky teenager. The meeting had made an impression on Brodeur, but not on Roy. He didn't remember it.

As it turned out, Brodeur didn't impress anyone in the series against Colorado. He mishandled average shots, gave up long rebounds throughout and was outplayed by Roy. The Devils couldn't match Colorado's speed, and the Avalanche clinched the series with a 3–1 victory in Game 7. Fans raised the roof of the Pepsi Center—the Avalanche's home since 1999—when Bourque hoisted the Cup over his head for the first time in his 22-year career. (See page 277)

Roy had notched the most shutouts (4) of his playoff career, the best save percentage (.934) and the best goals-against average (1.70). He had tied his own record for most wins (16), and last but not least, he had won his third Conn Smythe Trophy. A sign in the crowd read, "St. Patrick's Day. June 9, 2001."

2001-03

Roy was 36 years old when the 2001–02 season started, but he was still in fine form. He recorded more shutouts (9) than any of his peers. Among all starters, he posted the best goals-against average (1.94) and the second-best save percentage (.925). He also notched win No. 500 in December, becoming the first goalie to reach that plateau. He won his fifth Jennings Trophy.

But Roy didn't end the season with a flourish. The Red Wings defeated the Avalanche in a seven-game conference final, and to add insult to injury, Detroit annihilated Colorado 7–0 in the final game. Roy was pulled in the second period after allowing six goals. He was outplayed by Hasek, who helped lead his team to a Cup victory two weeks later.

ROY WASN'T a standout the following season, but he did reach another milestone. In January, he became the first NHL goalie to play 1,000 regular-season games. He was in net three months later when the Minnesota Wild upset the Avalanche in a seven-game conference quarter-final.

In May, Roy held a press conference at the Pepsi Center. Surrounded by family members, Avalanche coach Tony Granato and three teammates, he announced his retirement.

"I've had a blast. It's been unbelievable," he said, sitting in front of a large mural of himself. "I've been so fortunate to have lived a dream and have fun for more than 18 years, earning a living by playing a game I love." Years of sliding across the net with his legs splayed had taken a toll on his hips, but Roy said his health had no bearing on his decision. "I really feel like I emptied the tank, and I'm ready to move on," he explained. "I step aside with no regrets."[27]

RETIREMENT

After retiring, Roy headed home to work with the Quebec Remparts, a QMJHL team he co-owned. By 2005, he was general manager and head coach. In his first season behind the bench, his team won the Memorial Cup, awarded to the winner of a tournament featuring the champions of Canada's three major-junior leagues.

In November 2006, Roy was inducted into the Hockey Hall of Fame. "It was a great career," he said at the ceremony in Toronto. "It was fun, every minute of it, and I'm happy to still be involved in hockey today. Hockey is my passion."[28]

HE MADE headlines again two months later when he reportedly exchanged blows with Pierre Cardinal, a co-owner of another team, the Chicoutimi Saguenéens, in front of the Remparts team bus. Cardinal filed an assault complaint with police but dropped it when Roy apologized.

The fun didn't end there.

The Saguenéens had a 7-1 lead in the second game of the 2008 playoffs when the Remparts goalie charged at his counterpart, Bobby Nadeau, and pulverized him. The Remparts goalie then exchanged blows with another Saguenéens player before skating off the ice holding both middle fingers up to the crowd. That goalie was Roy's son Jonathan. He was suspended for seven games and fined $500.

The elder Roy denied encouraging his son to attack the Saguenéens goalie, but television cameras had shown him gesturing to Jonathan, apparently spurring him on. The league suspended Patrick Roy for five games and fined him $4,000. In July 2009, police charged his son with assault. In October, Jonathan, who had quit hockey to pursue a musical career, received an absolute discharge.

Roy's other son also made headlines. During a game in November 2008, Frederick Roy cross-checked an opponent in the head during a stoppage in play. The league suspended the Remparts forward for 15 games.

The next day, the Montreal Canadiens retired Patrick Roy's jersey.

IN THE SPRING of 2012, the Canadiens made Marc Bergevin the team's new general manager. But in the weeks leading up to that appointment, there had been speculation that Roy would move into the position. Roy had said little about the prospect. But when two newspaper polls indicated he was readers' top choice for the job, he couldn't resist. "If I go by the polls," he said grinning, "I guess the Canadiens are going to call me." All the attention, he said, had been "very good" for his ego. After the Habs instead selected Bergevin, Roy faded from view—but not for long.[29]

In May 2013, the Avalanche appointed him head coach and vice president of hockey operations. The club said he would be working with former teammate Sakic, who had been named executive vice president of hockey operations earlier that month. Avalanche fans hoped the men would help turn things around for the team, which had finished last in its conference and second-last in the 30-team league in the 2012–13 season.

"The jury's still out on whether Sakic and Roy can do what they did for the Avalanche a decade ago, from the front office. There's a nostalgia element that's very cool, but may not necessarily turn the franchise around," wrote Yahoo! Sports Canada blogger, Harrison Mooney. "That said, it would be tough for the Avalanche to take a step backwards, and Roy's junior resume speaks for itself. This isn't a hire based on what he did during his days as a player. It's based on what he's done since. Plus, if it's a personality transplant the Avalanche needed, and they did, boy oh boy, did they just get one."[30]

ROY · ALL-TIME RANKING*

REGULAR SEASON			PLAYOFFS		
GAMES	**WINS**	**SO**	**GAMES**	**WINS**	**SO**
1,029 [2nd]	551 [2nd]	66 [14th]	247 [1st]	151 [1st]	23 [2nd]

* statistics as of July 2, 2013.

> NHL ALL-ROOKIE TEAM **(1ST)**: 1985–86

> NHL ALL-STAR TEAM **(1ST)**: 1988–89, 1989–90, 1991–92, 2001–02

> NHL ALL-STAR TEAM **(2ND)**: 1987–88, 1990–91

10

||||||||||||||||||||||||||||||||||||||||||||

THE
FANATIC
ED BELFOUR

||||||||||||||||||||||||||||||||||||||||||||

"I don't think you can talk about Eddie without
talking about his intensity. You just can't."[1]

Former Dallas Stars executive
CRAIG BUTTON, in 2011

ED BELFOUR HEADED into a game against the Montreal
Canadiens in March 1991, hoping to tie a record for most wins
(38) by a Chicago Blackhawks goalie. Instead, the rookie *broke* a
record—a less prestigious one.

Incensed that officials had not called interference on a play
that ended with the puck in his net, Belfour marched into the
officials' dressing room after the game, a Chicago loss; and confronted referee Dan Marouelli. The men exchanged words—the
referee was heard yelling, "You have no right to talk to me like
that!"—and Belfour ended up with a 10-minute penalty for gross
misconduct. That gave him 32 penalty minutes for the season,
6 more than the previous team record for goalies, set by Bob
Sauve five years before. "When I was 12 years old, I used to get
thrown out of games all the time. It was really bad," Belfour later
admitted. "I'm a competitor, and it gets intense out there."[2]

Throughout his career, Belfour was seen as having an intensity that matched his great talent. His dedication to success bordered on pathological. He tinkered endlessly with his equipment, adhered religiously to a game-day stretching routine and lashed out at anyone who stood in his way. He also blew a gasket when things didn't go according to plan and laid waste to more than one dressing room.

ED BELFOUR was born in Carman, Manitoba, a small agricultural community southwest of Winnipeg, in April 1965. He and his younger sister, Patricia, lived in a three-bedroom bungalow with their parents, Henry, a public works employee, and Alma.

Belfour and his friends spent hours chasing a puck on an outdoor rink. When the weather was especially frigid, the boys would take off their skates and have their parents rub their feet until feeling returned to their toes. But that didn't dampen the kids' enthusiasm. "We didn't know any different," Belfour recalled years later. "We just wanted to play."[3]

Belfour watched *Hockey Night in Canada* every Saturday, looking forward most of all to games featuring the Chicago Blackhawks. He idolized the team's all-star goaltender, Tony Esposito. When he was eight years old, Belfour drew a picture of his hero and won first prize in the town fair.

Inspired by the "awesome-looking" masks and acrobatic saves of Esposito and other NHL goalies, Belfour became a netminder. He didn't seem destined for greatness at first. He was cut from his high school team, the Carman Cougars, when he was 15 years old, but he eventually battled his way onto the roster. "He was a six-sport athlete in high school—he played almost every sport there was in the school—and always wanted to be the best there was and the best conditioned there was, so he could never say that he let himself down," his high school coach, Ernie Sutherland, said years later.[4]

Belfour joined the Winkler Flyers of the Manitoba Junior Hockey League in the fall of 1983 and stayed with the Junior A team for three seasons. He was 21 years old when he played his last game there.

Although he was not invited to play in any of the major junior leagues that groom future NHL players, Belfour managed to win a scholarship to the University of North Dakota. As a freshman, he helped the Fighting Sioux win the NCAA championship. He notched 29 wins and just four losses while recording a solid 2.37 goals-against average.

His success caught the attention of professional scouts. The Chicago Blackhawks took a chance on him and signed him as a free agent. No one sounded the trumpets to herald his arrival. The *Chicago Sun-Times* noted simply that Belfour had been "held back by limited competition in his small hometown," and that he had led the Fighting Sioux to a title as "an overaged freshman."[5]

At the start of the 1987–88 season, the Blackhawks sent Belfour to the Saginaw Hawks, their farm team in the International Hockey League. He recorded 32 wins and 25 losses and posted a 3.19 goals-against average in Michigan. He was named the league's best rookie along with forward John Cullen, who went on to play 14 seasons in the NHL.

NHL

1988-90

By the end of September 1988, Darren Pang had been designated the Blackhawks starter, but it wasn't yet clear whether his backup goalie would be Belfour or Jimmy Waite. The answer came soon enough. A day before the start of the regular season, Belfour was sent back to Saginaw. But by mid-October, Chicago coach Mike Keenan was unhappy with the goalies on his roster and decided to give Belfour a chance. He made his NHL debut on October 18, 1988, at Joe Louis Arena in Detroit. He made 45 saves, but the Red Wings won 4–3 when Steve Yzerman scored in overtime. "It's sad. I was a little upset with the loss," said

Belfour. "But you can't let it affect you. There are a lot of games to come."[6]

Belfour started to make an impression. Moving out of his net to cut down angles, crouched low to the ice with his feet wide apart, he dared shooters to put the puck between his legs. When they tried, he foiled them by dropping to the ice with his knees together and his legs spread to the sides. Using the butter-fly technique, Belfour protected the bottom of the net with his pads and used his quick glove hand to keep pucks out of the top of the net.

Belfour played 23 regular-season games for the Blackhawks that season and won four of them. But the Blackhawks, who were eliminated in the Clarence Campbell Conference final, weren't convinced Belfour was ready for prime time, so before the start of the 1989–90 season, he joined the Canadian Olympic development team.

SHARING GOALTENDING duties with Warren Skorodenski, Belfour won 13 of 33 games on the national team. The Blackhawks called him up for the playoffs.

Alternating with Greg Millen and Jacques Cloutier, Belfour played in nine games, recording four wins and two losses. He stopped 31 shots in the fourth game of the Norris Division final against the St. Louis Blues, helping Chicago notch a 3–2 win.

When the Edmonton Oilers eliminated the Blackhawks in the conference final, Belfour headed home uncertain about his standing with the team. Keenan had relied on several goalies that season, rotating them not just between games but often during games. No one knew who would be in net for the start of the 1990–91 season.

1990-91

A handful of goalies attended the Blackhawks training camp in September, each determined to win the top job. Veterans Millen, Cloutier and Pang stepped on the ice, followed by some upstarts, including Belfour and a little-known Czech goalie named Dominik Hasek.

When the Hawks goalie coach put the men through their paces, Belfour paid close attention to his instructions; the coach was Vladislav Tretiak, the Russian goalie who had become a household name in Canada because of his outstanding play in the 1972 Summit Series. Belfour thrived under his tutelage and emerged as a strong contender for the starter's job. Wearing a mask adorned with two menacing eagles, Belfour was his acrobatic best in a 6–4 exhibition game victory over the Blues, stopping nearly a shot a minute in the first half of the game.

Still, Keenan wasn't sold on Belfour. "We don't feel we have a No. 1 goaltender that can compete with other No. 1 goaltenders in the league right now," he said three days before the start of the regular season. "We don't have a Vezina Trophy winner yet."[7]

But despite Keenan's doubts, Chicago won 7 of the 10 October games in which Belfour played, and he finished the month with a 1.92 goals-against average. He was named the NHL's rookie of the month—and he was just getting started.

Belfour brought fans to their feet twice in the first period of a game against the Los Angeles Kings on November 4, 1990. He stopped Wayne Gretzky on a breakaway and on a two-on-one. On the breakaway, Gretzky moved to his forehand then cut right, hoping to put the puck in the net with a low backhand, but Belfour moved with him and stopped him cold. Chicago lost the game 2–0 because none of the Blackhawks' top scorers, including Steve Larmer and Jeremy Roenick, could find the back of the net. But fans left the building buzzing. "Eddie the Eagle" had taken flight.

The Hawks had climbed to the top of the standings by December, thanks to their hard-charging forwards, a solid defense corps anchored by Chris Chelios—and the exploits of their new goalie. "Ed Belfour has been playing unbelievably well. He's a man on a mission, and you can see it in his play," Keenan said. "He's going after everything. He wants to be the best every night."[8]

➤ MAN IN MOTION ◄

BELFOUR WAS as active off the ice as on. Devoted to year-round fitness long before it became de rigueur in professional hockey, Belfour competed in numerous triathlons during his career.

He was almost 40 when he outran a young athlete at a goalie camp in the summer of 2004. After the race, "Eddie walked over to me and puked on my shoes," Steve McKichan, a former NHL goaltender who was running the camp, recalled. "He looked up at me and said, 'That kid will never beat me.'"[24]

Then, as now, Belfour indulged his passion for fishing and hunting. After retiring, he discovered target shooting. "I enjoy guns," he told the *Toronto Star*, perhaps giving some rivals pause for thought. "I feel comfortable around them. Almost everybody in Texas has a gun, so it's the norm there."[25]

||||||||||||||||||||||||||||||||||||||||||||||||||||||||||||||||||

On January 26, 1991, Belfour's parents and 11 other family members and friends were in Chicago Stadium to see the goalie notch his 30th win. The 5–1 victory over the hapless Leafs put him in elite company. Only two Chicago goalies had ever reached the 30-win milestone—Glenn Hall and Esposito.

Belfour won his second rookie-of-the-month honor, cementing his status as the Blackhawks starter, ahead of Hasek and the other contenders.

REPORTERS GATHERED around the talented newcomer in the locker room. Answering their questions, he appeared as comfortable as a man undergoing a prostate exam. Belfour's relationship with media was strained from the beginning—and his relationship with his teammates wasn't a lot better. He kept his distance from most of them and seemed disinterested at best. His attitude shifted from indifferent to aggressive when he felt threatened—and no one got his back up like other goalies vying for the starter's job. On occasion, Belfour even lashed out at his own coaches.

A combative leader, Keenan was often described as a bully and was called "Captain Hook" because he pulled goalies from games as readily as a child plucking crayons from a box. It rankled many of his netminders, none more so than Belfour. When Keenan pulled him during a game against Philadelphia in December 1990, Belfour skated to the bench, slammed his stick against the boards and sat down. When Keenan approached him to explain, Belfour put his palms up and turned away, giving the international signal for "Talk to the hand, because the face ain't listening." Keenan lunged at Belfour, grabbing him by the shirt. It looked like they were going to come to blows, but with the sellout crowd on West Madison Street chanting "Ed-dee! Ed-dee!" Keenan softened. Less than a minute later, he sent Belfour back onto the ice. "I was mad. He yelled at me," Belfour said later. "I yelled back."[9]

THE BLACKHAWKS finished the season at the top of the standings (106 points) and were touted as possible champions, but they were eliminated in the first round of the playoffs, the division semifinal. The lowly Minnesota North Stars (68 points) rolled past them in a six-game series. Chicago was undisciplined and Minnesota goalie Jon Casey outclassed Belfour. The Blackhawks were stunned. Roenick, the team's second-leading scorer in the regular season, was at a loss for words. He said simply, "That wasn't us."[10]

The debacle didn't diminish Belfour's accomplishments. He had played in 74 of 80 regular-season games—more than any other goalie in the NHL—and had led the league in wins (43). He had the best save percentage (.910) and goals-against average (2.47) among starters. He finished in a three-way tie for the second-highest shutout total (4). It was a rookie season par excellence.

At the NHL awards ceremony in Toronto, Belfour won the Calder Memorial Trophy as the league's best rookie, the Vezina Trophy as its best goalie and the William M. Jennings Trophy as the goaltender for the team allowing the fewest goals. He stepped up to the microphone sporting a tuxedo and a mullet. "I can't believe this is happening to me," he said, looking as *verklempt* as a woman at her grandson's bar mitzvah. "When I came to training camp, I just wanted to make the team."[11]

1991-92

Belfour was soon locked in a contract dispute with management, and he was sitting on the sidelines when the puck dropped to start the 1991–92 season. Both sides voiced their indignation in meetings and in the media—Keenan said the team was suffering because of Belfour's intransigence—but they agreed to terms in late October.

By mid-December, Belfour's goals-against average (2.41) was lower than it had been at the end of the previous season. He was as good as ever—and just as volatile. When he was pulled from a game in Detroit that month, he made a beeline for the dressing room, kicking a chair, sticks and various other objects in his path.

After allowing three goals in 39 seconds in a 6–2 loss to Buffalo in March, Belfour leveled Sabres star Pat LaFontaine and sparked a brawl. "Eddie's a heart-and-soul type of player," teammate Steve Smith explained. "He decided we weren't bumping people, so he would."[12]

Belfour was inconsistent in the second half of the season, and many attributed his troubles to his personal life. His mother-in-law became terminally ill that spring, and his wife, Rita, rushed to her bedside in Minnesota, even though she was about to give birth to the couple's second child. (Their son, Dayn, had been born three years earlier.) Rita gave birth to a daughter, Reaghan, in early March, and Rita's mother died two weeks later. Belfour took time off for both events.

The Blackhawks finished second in their division and seventh overall, with 87 points. Despite his personal woes, Belfour was one of four goalies who finished with a league-leading five shutouts. He was in net for the start of the post-season.

The Blackhawks stormed through the first three rounds of the playoffs, beating the St. Louis Blues (83 points) in six games and then eliminating the Detroit Red Wings (98 points) and the Edmonton Oilers (82 points) without losing once. Chicago then took on the Pittsburgh Penguins in the Blackhawks' first Stanley Cup final in 19 years.

They were trailing the Penguins three games to none when the teams met for Game 4 in Chicago. A sign hanging from the upper deck of Chicago Stadium declared, "It's Not Impossible." But it was. Mario Lemieux and Kevin Stevens, who finished first and second in the NHL in scoring that season, proved too much to handle. The Penguins scored two goals on their first four shots, and Belfour was given the hook. Hasek took over and played well—he stopped Lemieux cold on a breakaway—but the Penguins won the game 6–5 to clinch their second straight Cup. Hasek was traded to the Buffalo Sabres two months later.

Scotty Bowman, who had replaced the ailing Bob Johnson as Penguins coach early in the season, spoke to reporters after the game. He made a comment that left reporters and expectant mothers scratching their heads. "I took over on October 1 and it's now June 1," he said. "If I was a lady, I would have had enough time to have a baby, and that's how I feel now."[13]

1992-93

Belfour bounced back. He finished the 1992–93 season first in shutouts (7) and second in wins (41). Among starting goalies, he placed third in save percentage (.906) and second in goals-against average (2.59). Toronto's Felix Potvin had a better goals-against average (2.50), but he played 23 fewer games than Belfour. The Blackhawks goalie played in 71 of 84 games, more than any of his peers.

The Blackhawks didn't score a lot of goals that season, but they allowed very few. With Belfour in net and two of the NHL's best defensemen, Chelios and Bryan Marchment, in front of him, they let in just 230 goals, the fewest in the league. Belfour won his second Jennings Trophy.

Chicago finished first in their division and third in the standings (106 points) and was considered a strong Cup contender, but the team was swept aside by the St. Louis Blues (85 points) in the division semifinal. After the Blues' Craig Janney scored the winning goal 10 minutes into overtime of Game 4, Belfour slammed his stick on the ice. He refused to line up for the postgame handshaking ceremony and stormed off the ice in a rage. He destroyed a coffee pot, a cooling fan and some other items on a table outside the Hawks dressing room.

He had calmed down by the time the NHL awards ceremony was held in Toronto, where he was awarded the Vezina Trophy.

1993-97

The Blackhawks were a middling team for most of the next four years. The 1994–95 season, which started three months late because of a labor dispute, was their best during that span. They advanced to the Western Conference final that season but were eliminated by the Red Wings in a five-game series.

Belfour remained one of the best goalies in the NHL during that period. He and two other goalies had the most shutouts (7) in the 1993–94 season, and he tied one other goalie for most shutouts (5) the following season. Also in the 1994–95 season, he was second in wins (22) and had the second-best goals-against average (.228) among starters, winning his third Jennings Trophy.

In the 1995–96 season, the 30-year-old goalie suffered from back problems and was forced to watch from the sidelines as Jeff Hackett took over in the Blackhawks net. As Hackett emerged as a first-rate goalie, tension between the two men escalated. In December 1996, media reported that Belfour had confronted Hackett and told him he was nothing more than a second-string goalie. Belfour had reportedly warned Hackett to keep his distance and ordered him not to arrive at the rink before the veteran on game days—unless he was scheduled to start. According to reports, Belfour had also told Hackett he was to be seen and not heard on the bench when the veteran was playing.

> "My intensity is what got me here. Why change?"[28]
>
> **ED BELFOUR**

BELFOUR WAS scheduled to become a free agent after the 1996–97 season and wanted the Blackhawks to offer him a lucrative contract to keep him in Chicago. He felt he deserved more than Hasek, who had emerged as an outstanding goalie and was being paid $4.2 million per year. "I think I'm as good or better than Hasek," he said. "In my mind, I'm better."[14] But was he worth the hassle? "Sure, Belfour is still a heck of a goaltender when he wants to be," columnist Tim Sassone wrote in the *Daily Herald*. "But there are those in the organization who will tell you his best days are behind him, he's selfish, he lets in soft goals at critical times and his nagging back problem is a cause of real concern." The columnist suggested a trade. "Thanks for the memories, Eddie, but it's time to move on."[15]

Belfour's mood darkened. When a reporter asked him to do an interview in early January, Belfour, who had recorded six losses and four ties in his previous 10 starts, gave what was described as "an unprintable two-word response."[16]

In January, Chicago traded him to the San Jose Sharks in exchange for three players. Belfour left Chicago in a huff, saying his only regret was not having won a Stanley Cup for Blackhawks fans. He lashed out at Chicago media, accusing reporters of fabricating stories about a confrontation with Hackett. "For guys to start stories and say things they're not sure of... those guys are confused and losers," he said. "They're in total darkness and they're wrong."[17]

In his first game with the Sharks, Belfour allowed the Vancouver Canucks to score three goals on their first nine shots, and San Jose lost 5–2. Belfour played in 13 games for the Sharks that season, recording three wins and nine losses. The team finished second-last in the league (62 points).

The experience prompted Belfour to change his stance. Seven months after saying "Show me the money!" to the Blackhawks, he threw his hands in the air and, in effect, shouted, "Get me outta here!" His agent contacted the Dallas Stars, who had finished second in the conference and tied for second overall with 104 points. Belfour signed a three-year deal worth $10 million—less than what the Sharks had offered.

1997-98

With coach Ken Hitchcock at the helm, the Stars played a grinding, defensive style of hockey with an opportunistic attack. High-scoring forwards Mike Modano and Joe Nieuwendyk spearheaded the offense, and Derian Hatcher and Darryl Sydor anchored the defensive corps.

Belfour made an immediate impression. All elite athletes are mindful of health and nutrition, but Belfour's preparation was meticulous to the nth degree. He was so specific about what he ingested that he drank a specific brand of orange juice before road games. He also sharpened his own skates, sometimes devoting as much time to one pair as the team trainer did to two dozen. He once spent six hours working on his blades to ensure they met his specifications. He insisted on having a high inside edge at the front of the blades. This allowed him to push off his toes and move side to side or come out and challenge shooters. On game days, he followed a strict routine that included sharpening his skates and tinkering with his glove, pads and other pieces of equipment. He also undertook a rigorous stretching routine, transforming himself into a human pretzel before the eyes of his amazed teammates.

"All of these types of things that people can't imagine actually existed," Nieuwendyk said years later. "We lived with it and no one really blinked an eye at it because we knew he was going to be ready and stop the pucks for us."[18]

"He gave everything because he aspired to be the best," says Rick St. Croix, the Stars goalie coach at the time, now with the Toronto Maple Leafs. "He was eccentric in terms of preparation. You can imagine how it might have been hard for the people around him," he adds with a laugh. "He was very competitive." "I'm very picky, especially when it comes to my professional life," Belfour later explained. "Anything I care about is really precise and detailed. I want it to be perfect."[19]

BELFOUR THRIVED in north Texas, posting the best goals-against average (1.88) among the NHL's starting goaltenders in his first season there.

The Stars finished at the top of the standings (109 points) and advanced through the first two rounds of the playoffs, eliminating the Sharks (78 points) and the Oilers (80 points). But the party ended when they met the Detroit Red Wings (103 points) in the conference final. The Stars power play faltered in the series, and although Belfour was phenomenal at some points, he was mediocre at others. He let in some soft goals and came unspooled more than once.

In Game 4, he put his stick between the legs of Martin Lapointe and swung it upwards, nearly castrating the Detroit forward. Lapointe crumpled to the ice. Fox replayed the incident and the announcer—likely haunted by memories of his high school gym class—exclaimed, "Oh no! Ohhh!" Belfour's penalty gave the Red Wings, who were already on a power play, a two-man advantage. They scored and recorded a 3–2 victory and went on to win the series in six games.

Many people felt the Stars should unload the volatile goaltender, but general manager Bob Gainey had faith in him. He managed to persuade the goalie to chill out. "I think Gainey really understood that level of competitiveness," said Craig Button, former director of scouting for the Stars.[20]

1998-99

Sniper Brett Hull joined Dallas for the 1998–99 season, adding considerable firepower to the team's offense. He finished second in team scoring that season, behind Modano. The Stars finished first overall, with 114 points.

Belfour finished second in wins (35) among all NHL goalies and, among starters, tied for third in goals-against average (1.99). His success didn't surprise fans—he had posted great numbers before—but his poise did. Belfour managed to keep his composure throughout the season, disappointing reporters who had delighted in writing stories with words such as "berserk" and "castration." But could his team depend on him in the playoffs? In previous seasons, he had soared to great heights, only to stumble when the chips were down. The answer came soon enough.

In the first two rounds, the Stars swept aside the Edmonton Oilers (78 points) in four games and beat the St. Louis Blues (87 points) in a six-game series. Dallas then took on the Colorado Avalanche (98 points) in the conference final.

That series pitted Belfour against Patrick Roy, who had twice been awarded the Conn Smythe Trophy as the most valuable player in the playoffs and had won the Vezina Trophy three times. Roy was the more accomplished goalie, but Belfour prevailed in this series. He finished with a 2.05 goals-against average and a .926 save percentage, whereas Roy posted a 3.15 average and .902 save percentage. Dallas won the series in seven games.

Avalanche fans leapt to their netminder's defense, reminding anyone who would listen that St. Patrick had faced 45 more shots than Belfour—but few people were listening. Dallas had scored four goals in the final game, and Roy had been out of position on every one. Belfour had allowed just one goal.

When the Stars and the Buffalo Sabres (91 points) lined up for the start of the 1999 Stanley Cup final, Belfour stood across from the man who had once been his backup. Since the Blackhawks had traded Hasek to the Sabres in 1992, he had emerged as an outstanding goaltender. He had won the Vezina Trophy in four of the previous five seasons. In each of the previous two seasons, he had taken home the Hart

"Looks like he's combed his hair with a pork chop."[27]

Dallas Stars teammate **MIKE KEANE**, *on Belfour's sartorial splendor, in 1999*

Memorial Trophy as the NHL's most valuable player. Both men brought spectators to their feet with spectacular saves throughout the series and made it the lowest-scoring Stanley Cup final in more than 40 years. The story unfolded according to script, with the drama reaching a climax in the final game.

The Stars were leading three games to two when the teams squared off at Marine Midland Arena in Buffalo. It was a heated battle from the moment the puck dropped. The game was tied 1–1 late in the third overtime period when Hull—who had suffered a torn medial collateral ligament and a pulled groin—banged the puck into the net past Hasek, who was lying facedown on the ice with his arms and legs spread apart. Dallas players sprang from the bench and jumped over the boards to celebrate the franchise's first Stanley Cup. They crowded around

Belfour, whose performance had been so sensational that even heartbroken Sabres fans saluted him by chanting, "Ed-dee! Ed-dee!"

Replays showed that Hull's left skate had been in the crease when he scored, which could have nullified the goal according to league rules. NHL officials insisted the goal should have counted because Hull had possession of the puck when his foot entered the crease. Buffalo coaches and players disagreed. (See page 255) There was no consensus on that point, but there was agreement on another—the series had featured a goaltending duel for the ages.

Belfour had made 53 saves in the final game, 3 more than Hasek. Both goalies finished the post-season with goals-against averages under 2.00.

At the NHL awards ceremony in Toronto the following week, Hasek won his fifth Vezina Trophy. Belfour claimed his fourth Jennings Trophy, sharing it with backup Roman Turek, who had played 26 games that season.

1999–2000

After finishing third in the conference and sixth overall in the 1999–2000 regular season (102 points), the Stars sailed through the first two rounds of the playoffs. They eliminated the Oilers (88 points) and the Sharks (87 points) in five games each. Belfour, who had notched the best save percentage (.919) among the league's goalies that season, battled the flu during the series against the Sharks but managed to make 32 saves in the final game, a 4–1 Dallas victory.

The conference final was a rematch with Colorado (96 points). For the second straight year, the Stars beat the Avalanche in seven games, and Belfour outshone Roy. The Avalanche had scored an average of 2.84 goals a game during the regular season. But Belfour shut them down in this series, never allowing more than two goals in a game. Dallas fans were sure which goalie had the upper hand. In the final game they chanted, "Eddie's better! Eddie's better!"

"The Dallas Stars' sensational goaltender continually frustrated a team that features the goal-scoring likes of Peter Forsberg and Joe Sakic," said one game report. "If Dallas goes on to beat the New Jersey Devils in the Stanley Cup final, Belfour should be a slam dunk for the Conn Smythe Trophy."[21]

The final against the Devils (103 points) turned out to be another dramatic showdown. Belfour notched his fourth shutout of the playoffs in Game 5, which the Stars won in triple overtime. The next game also stretched well into the night, with Belfour and Devils goalie Martin Brodeur "breaking hearts and busting bedtimes" as action swung from end to end. Devils forward Jason Arnott put the puck past Belfour midway through the second overtime period to clinch a 2–1 win and the second Stanley Cup in franchise history. Jubilant New Jersey players crowded around their goalie, exchanging high fives and hugs. (See pages 274–275)[22]

2000-02

The Stars and their top goaltender floundered in the next two seasons. They finished fifth overall (106 points) in the 2000–01 campaign, and the St. Louis Blues (103 points) swept them aside in the conference semifinal. Dallas tumbled down the standings the following season, landing in 17th place (90 points) with a resounding thud. The Stars missed the playoffs altogether.

MEANWHILE, THE NEW and improved Ed Belfour, who had garnered headlines during the team's championship season, had crawled back into the Tickle Trunk and popped out as "Crazy Eddie."

One night in March 2000, he stumbled into an upscale hotel and security personnel escorted him to his room. A short time later, a woman who was with Belfour told hotel security she was

➤ BETTER THAN ◄ TWEETY BIRD

BELFOUR WAS identified with his distinctive mask. It sported his team's colors and had an eagle painted on either side. With its eyes narrowed and its beak open, each bird seemed poised to snatch an opposing forward off the ice with a swipe of its talons. Belfour said he chose the eagle rather than, say, Tweety Bird in part because he admired the bird's hunting abilities and aggression. The design of the mask spoke not just to Belfour's temperament but also to some of his interests.

The chin of his masks featured the image of a wishbone, the logo for the Make-A-Wish Foundation, which grants wishes to children with life-threatening medical conditions. Belfour got involved with the non-profit organization when he played in Chicago.

The plate that covered the back of Belfour's head during games sported an etching of a vintage car (a 1941 Willys) along with the words "Carman Racing," the name of Belfour's car customization and restoration shop in Freeland, Michigan. Belfour's business venture confused some fans, but it made perfect sense to people who knew him well. Belfour had been a muscle car and hot rod enthusiast since he was a teenager and had long indulged in drag racing. During his playing career, he collected a small fleet of cars.

afraid of him and left in a cab. When the goaltender attempted to leave his hotel room, a guard tried to subdue him. According to police reports, Belfour slammed the guard against the wall and put him in a headlock. Police subdued him with pepper spray—but the story didn't end there.

Once in the squad car, he offered the officers $100,000 to let him go. When they declined his generous offer, he upped the amount to $1 *billion*. That didn't work either. Belfour later pleaded guilty to resisting arrest and was placed on two years' probation, fined $3,000 and ordered to visit two high schools to warn teenagers about alcohol abuse. He also was enrolled in the NHL's substance-abuse program.

Ten months after running afoul of the law, Belfour came up against his coach. When Hitchcock announced that backup goaltender Marty Turco would play one night against the Boston Bruins, Belfour refused to take part in a morning skate or an off-ice workout. He stormed out of the arena. The club suspended him. Belfour missed three games and lost $134,000 in salary. (Turco posted his first shutout, in a 4–0 Dallas victory.)

When the coach pulled him from a game in Vancouver in February 2002, Belfour headed to the visitors' dressing room and proceeded to break two televisions, a VCR and a clock. The Canucks sent him a bill for $5,000.

2002-06

Unhappy with his performance and confident in the abilities of Turco, the Stars traded Belfour's rights to the Nashville Predators. He became an unrestricted free agent in July 2002 and signed with the Toronto Maple Leafs.

At a press conference in Toronto, he pulled on a Leafs jersey and said his goal was to bring the Stanley Cup to Toronto. No one laughed. The Leafs (100 points) had finished second in the Eastern Conference and third overall in the previous season. They had advanced as far as the conference final, and even though they had fallen to the Carolina Hurricanes in a six-game series, the Cup seemed within their grasp.

Belfour's predecessor, Curtis Joseph, had been popular before leaving for Detroit, so Belfour didn't receive a warm welcome when he first touched down in Toronto. But Leaf Nation soon took him to its ample bosom, where high-scoring captain Mats Sundin had long been nestled. Belfour notched 37 wins in the 2002–03 season. It was the third-best record in the league and the most wins ever by a Leafs goalie. He was the team's backbone that season and sparkled in the conference quarterfinal against the Philadelphia Flyers. In Game 4, he made 72 saves before Mark Recchi put a shot between his legs late in the third overtime period. The Flyers went on to win the series in seven games, but no one blamed Belfour.

> "I was fortunate to be around Eddie in Dallas and watch how he played. To me, he was the best in the world at that time."
>
> *Former Dallas Stars goalie coach*
> **RICK ST. CROIX**

OFF THE ICE, he was as meticulous as ever about preparing for games. "You had to do a lot for him," recalls the Leafs' long-time equipment manager, Brian Papineau. "He had to show me how he liked his skates sharpened. We put a lot of time into that. It was like a training session. Sometimes he would rip his equipment apart. In fact, I've heard stories from people on other teams he was with—that he would tear apart his catch glove to see what kind of materials were in there. Then the glove would have to be put back together." Whether it was equipment, nutrition or fitness, Belfour "prepared like no other," according to Papineau. "That's what made him successful."

Belfour was unmatched in dedication. "I remember standing in a room across from the Leafs dressing room an hour before a game in Washington," recalls Toronto sports broadcaster Greg Ross. "I had a plate with some cookies on it. One of the Leafs goalies walked up to me and said, 'Whose cookies are these?' and he started eating them. Meanwhile, Belfour was 20 or 30 feet away, doing his game-day routine, stretching and working with a trainer. I said to the guy, 'This is crazy. Belfour is over there going through these meticulous preparations and you're here eating cookies with me.' He just laughed."

Ross remembers seeing Belfour outside the New Jersey Devils' arena the morning of a game day. "He looked like he had slept in his suit, rolled out of bed and come to the rink. His suit was wrinkled, his hair was a disheveled mess and he had four or five days' growth on his face. Yet when I saw him inside a little while later, he was going through his usual routine with a trainer. I don't know what he did the night before, but he didn't let it affect him when he was at the rink. He never did. He was just militant about his routine."

BACK PROBLEMS forced Belfour to miss 11 games in the 2003–04 season, but he stood out in the conference quarter-final against the Ottawa Senators, posting three shutouts as the Leafs defeated the Senators in a seven-game series. (Toronto fell to Philadelphia in the next round.)

Belfour was 40 years old when the next season started in the fall of 2005—the 2004–05 season had been canceled because of a labor dispute—so few people were surprised when injuries forced him to the sidelines. He played just 49 games in the 2005–06 season, and the Leafs missed the playoffs.

2006-07

The Leafs released Belfour when he became a free agent in July 2006. He signed a one-year deal with the Florida Panthers later that month. He didn't make much of an impact that season— but he did make headlines.

He was charged with disorderly intoxication and resisting arrest after an incident at a South Beach bar. According to police reports, Belfour walked toward an officer "in a fighting stance" and pushed him. Belfour grabbed the officer's shirt, fell to the ground and put his hands under his stomach to avoid being handcuffed. Police subdued him with a stun gun. His drinking buddy, teammate Ville Peltonen, was charged with criminal mischief after laying siege to a nearby fire truck. Police released the men when they posted bond the next day. They later agreed to a plea bargain.

A few months after the Panthers missed the playoffs for the sixth straight season, Belfour became a free agent once again. This time, he wasn't signed by another NHL team.

2007-08

The 42-year-old netminder headed to Sweden and suited up for Leksands IF, a team in the country's second-best league. Belfour led his team to a 4–1 victory in his debut. Journalists reported that he had been buoyed by a recent hunting trip during which he and a member of the club's board of directors had bagged a moose. The team hoped Belfour would help them earn a spot in the Swedish Elite League. But that didn't happen—and Belfour headed back across the Atlantic Ocean.

RETIREMENT

The St. Louis Blues hired Belfour as a goaltending coach in August 2009, but that job lasted as long as Dennis Rodman's marriage to Carmen Electra. He quit after five months, claiming he wanted to travel less and spend more time at home in Dallas with Ashli, his second wife, and their two-year-old son, Adler. (The couple had wed in 2002.)

In October 2010, Belfour was inducted into the University of North Dakota Athletics Hall of Fame—Ed Belfour bobblehead dolls lined the shelves of a campus store that month—and the following June, he found out he was to be inducted into the Hockey Hall of Fame with Joe Nieuwendyk, Doug Gilmour and Mark Howe.

At the induction ceremony in Toronto five months later, Belfour stepped up to the microphone wearing a black suit, crisp white shirt and silver tie. He looked much the same as when he had accepted his first NHL award 20 years before, but his mullet was noticeably absent—a disappointment to the five Billy Ray Cyrus fans in Toronto.

He thanked Tretiak, Chelios, family members and even the Ruler of the Universe. "Last but not least I want to thank God for giving me this life and blessing me with all these wonderful people and experiences," he said. "Thank you all, and God bless."

Earlier that day, Belfour had spoken about his life at the time. He said he was still adjusting to retirement. He also said he was playing two or three nights a week in a men's hockey league near his home in Dallas. He was a defenseman. Why wasn't he playing the position he loved most? "First of all," he explained, "it takes about an hour and a half to get ready to play goal."[23]

BELFOUR · ALL-TIME RANKING*

REGULAR SEASON			PLAYOFFS		
GAMES	WINS	SO	GAMES	WINS	SO
963 [4th]	484 [3rd]	76 [9th]	161 [3rd]	88 [4th]	14 [5th]

* statistics as of July 2, 2013.

> NHL ALL-ROOKIE TEAM **(1ST)**: 1990–91

> NHL ALL-STAR TEAM **(1ST)**: 1990–91, 1992–93

> NHL ALL-STAR TEAM **(2ND)**: 1994–95

11

|||||||||||||||||||||||||||||||||||||||||||

THE
ENIGMA
DOMINIK HASEK

|||||||||||||||||||||||||||||||||||||||||||

"The Dominator may be temperamental,
unpredictable and at times exasperating, but when he
is on the ice and in good health he promotes the
[Buffalo] Sabres to the hockey stratosphere."[1]
Columnist **LARRY FELSER**, in 2000

DOMINIK HASEK AND a writer are chatting over hamburgers and light beer when their conversation is interrupted. Having kept a respectful distance for 10 minutes, a fan has succumbed to the gravitational pull of celebrity. "Holy shit! You're Dominik Hasek!" The response is succinct. "Yes, I am."

The middle-aged man crouches beside his hero to pose for a photo. His wife fumbles with the smartphone, but despite her best intentions, can't operate it. They giggle as they switch places and the fan takes a picture of his wife with the lanky Czech athlete. Widening his stance to maintain his balance, the fan lists Hasek's many accomplishments—then asks the goalie to play in a weekend beer league. The former NHL star politely declines and the couple zigzags back to the bar.

It would make sense for Hasek's conversation with the writer to turn to hockey at that point, but it doesn't. Instead,

Hasek veers off into politics, talking about the late Czech states-man Vaclav Havel, the Czech economy and the pros and cons of membership in the European Union. The writer is surprised, but she shouldn't be. The "Dominator" can be unpredictable. From the time he arrived in Chicago as an unknown European import to his fourth retirement announcement almost two decades later, Hasek's exploits left people gasping in astonishment—and scratching their heads in confusion.

DOMINIK HASEK was born in January 1965 in Pardubice, an industrial city in Czechoslovakia. Almost from the moment he could walk, he was playing hockey. He and his younger brother, Martin, squared off in the living room of his grandfather's apart-ment, using tiny sticks and a table tennis ball. "He would put me in front of a small goal and he would stand in front of a big one to compensate for the difference in our size," Martin remem-bers. "The small goal was a single living room door. The big goal was the double doors. Actually, Dominik always started our games and competitions with a handicap, but it was never so big that he would end up losing. He gave me that handicap so that the game would be exciting right up to the end—but he would always end up winning."

The boys' grandfather was an important figure in their lives. They spent time with him at his cottage in the summer, and in the winter, he took them to hockey games. Sitting in the stands of a cold arena, they cheered for Tesla Pardubice, a local team in the Czechoslovak First Ice Hockey League.

Dominik's father worked in a mine that was a two-hour drive from Pardubice, so he was only home on weekends. On one of their few days together, he took Hasek to a tryout for a local hockey team. The six-year-old didn't have a pair of real skates—just shoes with blades screwed into the soles—but he made an impression. He ended up on a team of boys three years older than him.

He made a beeline for the net. "Even when I was three years old, I never tried to kick the [soccer] ball and score a goal, or grab a stick and try to score one," Hasek says. "When I played in the apartment, I put my shoes around me, or a basket or a garbage can, and made them my posts. I told my grandfather or my father to shoot at me. In the earliest pictures of me, I'm in net."

Hasek also played competitive soccer—his brother went on to become a professional player—and tennis, but his heart was set on hockey.

HASEK ROSE through the ranks quickly and turned professional when he was just 16 years old. He spent eight seasons with Tesla Pardubice, leading the squad to two championships, and one season with another team in the Czechoslovak First Ice Hockey League.

Hasek also played for the junior national and national teams, winning a bushel of medals at world championships in the 1980s and earning a reputation as the best goalie in Europe. His performance in those competitions, and in two Canada Cup tournaments, aroused interest among NHL scouts.

NHL teams were hesitant to draft players from Communist countries, because most of those athletes couldn't leave home without defecting. But the Chicago Blackhawks selected Hasek in the tenth round of the 1983 entry draft. The Iron Curtain was closed so tightly that Hasek didn't find out until months later.

Blackhawks general manager Bob Pulford met with the goalie in 1987 and offered him a contract. Hasek turned it down;

"I saw him practice once in Buffalo, and you couldn't even beat him in practice. He was doing drills that I couldn't believe a goalie would do. His teammates were taking turns blasting shots at him from close range, maybe just 15 feet away. He never flinched."

New Jersey Devils goalie coach
JACQUES CARON

he wanted to finish his university degree in history and the Czech language. But when Communism collapsed in Czechoslovakia two years later, Hasek was ready to pursue a hockey career.

NHL

1990-92

Hasek reported to the Blackhawks training camp for the 1990–91 season and fared well there, but coach Mike Keenan was more impressed by Ed Belfour, who had played for Chicago in nine playoff games the previous season. When the season started, Belfour was on the Blackhawks roster, and Hasek was cooling his heels in the U.S. Midwest, playing for the Indianapolis Ice of the International Hockey League.

"Hasek, who showed as much as any goalie in training camp, was confused and disappointed by being abruptly shipped out," wrote one reporter. "A few encouraging words from Keenan might have helped Hasek's confidence. After all, Keenan may want Hasek to play for him someday soon. But they weren't forthcoming. Welcome to the U.S., kid."[2] Hasek was so discouraged that he considered returning to Pardubice.

But the Blackhawks called him up in November. In his NHL debut, he made 28 saves in a 1–1 tie with the Hartford Whalers. He played some more games for the Blackhawks but didn't make headlines—until the 1992 Stanley Cup final.

The Blackhawks (87 points), who had finished second in the Norris Division and seventh overall, were trailing the Pittsburgh Penguins (87 points) three games to none when the puck dropped for Game 4 at Chicago Stadium. The Penguins scored two goals on their first four shots against Belfour. Keenan pulled him and sent Hasek out to take his place. Hasek kept the team alive with some acrobatic saves and even stopped Mario Lemieux, the league's top scorer, on a breakaway. But the Penguins had the upper hand and won the game 6–5 to clinch their second straight Cup.

||||||||||||||||||||||||||||||||||||||||||||||||||||||||||||||||||||||||

➤ HASEK'S HEROES ◄

IN 2001, Hasek contributed $1 million to establish the Dominik Hasek Youth Hockey League. It helps kids from low-to-moderate-income families in Buffalo play organized hockey. The organization established a program called Hasek's Heroes, which teaches kids basic skating and hockey skills after school and on the weekends.

||||||||||||||||||||||||||||||||||||||||||||||||||||||||||||||||||||||||

"Mario Lemieux was the attacker I feared most," Hasek says today. "Any time I played against him, I said to one of my teammates, 'Stay on him even if another player is open. Stay on him all the time.' Lemieux was everything. He was a playmaker and a goal-scorer. He could shoot the puck ... he could find openings. I think, in his prime, he was the best."

Despite his solid play, Hasek couldn't push "Eddie the Eagle" from his perch at the top of the Blackhawks goaltending ladder. In August 1992, Chicago traded Hasek to the Buffalo Sabres.

1992-93

Hasek arrived in Buffalo determined to make his mark, but he ended up sharing the workload with three other goalies in the 1992–93 season, including Grant Fuhr, who had been a mainstay of the Edmonton Oilers dynasty in the 1980s. Hasek played in just 28 games. The Sabres chose not to protect him in the expansion draft. Neither of the new teams, the Florida Panthers or and the Mighty Ducks of Anaheim, picked him up.

"That situation helped me become a strong person," Hasek said later. "I was about to give up. [Fuhr] had been on five Stanley Cup champions. I had been on none. I didn't think I'd ever be a No. 1 goalie in the NHL. But we say in Czech that 'everything bad is good for something.' I remember what happened in Chicago and I said, 'Now I am down, and something good will happen.'"[3]

1993-94

Hasek remained in the shadows until midway through the 1993–94 season, when Fuhr injured his knee. Hasek bounded onto center stage and stayed there. He played 58 games that season, notching the best goals-against average (1.95) and save percentage (.930) among the NHL's starting goaltenders. He also finished in a three-way tie for most shutouts (7).

HIS SUCCESS led coaches, players and fans to examine his technique, but they could only scratch their heads. His style was as difficult to make out as his broken English. Hasek had quicker hands and feet than most of his peers and was more flexible than all of them. He dropped to the ice on most shots and contorted his body into impossible positions, stopping the puck with his limbs, his torso and even his head. He made saves while sprawled on his front and on his back. He often dropped his stick to cover the puck with his blocker hand.

Hasek had emerged from an unknown world to spread panic and chaos at every turn—the NHL's Creature from the Black Lagoon. Yet some people saw method in his madness. "Dom's unorthodox style was based on sound principles," says Jim Corsi, who was the Sabres goalie coach when Hasek was on the team. "He would put the paddle down to force the attacker away from the net and give him less open space to shoot at. The attacker would be forced to go around Hasek, who would lean back, rotate his body in the air and come down on the other side to make the save. People didn't recognize Dom's style because it didn't fit into any of the boxes."

Hasek himself couldn't agree more. "I developed my style through my whole life, through my hockey career. I don't believe you can be a great goaltender without a particular style," he says. "You have to be a great athlete, but you need to have a style."

If Hasek's style was unlike anything seen in the NHL before, it was because he hadn't seen NHL hockey until he was in his teens. Unlike other goalies of his generation, he didn't grow up emulating Ken Dryden, Tony Esposito and other top goalies of the 1970s. "When I was a young kid I never could see the NHL players. I saw them a little bit at the very end of the 1970s, in international competition... but even when I could see a little bit of the NHL goalies, I didn't know so much about them," he explains. Instead, Hasek took his cues from Jiri Holecek, who played for the Czechoslovak national team in the 1960s and 1970s and whose success brought him recognition as one of the best goalies in international hockey. He was known for his acrobatic style of play and for having quick hands and feet.

> "I never agreed with people who said Hasek had no particular style. We watched a lot of tape of him when we were playing against the Sabres. It was clear that he was very athletic, very smart and knew exactly what he was doing."
>
> *Former Dallas Stars goalie coach*
> **RICK ST. CROIX**

Holecek trained Hasek when the young goalie played for the junior national team. "We would advise the boys and correct their mistakes," Holecek says. "But we always gave them freedom regarding their style. We never told them to do things in a particular way, like the Swedish do nowadays when they teach goalies to remain on their knees. We never wanted that. We would tell them, 'Once you understand the basic principles of goaltending, you can choose to play however you want. Dominik studied the game and came up with his own style. He is flexible and he has a slender body with long limbs. His body is ideal for a goaltender." Holecek continues: "Of course his style developed in a certain way because he could not watch NHL goalies when he was a kid—and he was lucky in that way. If had taken his cues from them, he would not have been Hasek!"

AFTER FINISHING sixth in the Eastern Conference and tenth overall with 95 points, Buffalo met the New Jersey Devils (106 points) in the 1994 conference quarter-final. The Sabres were trailing the Devils three games to two when the teams squared off at Memorial Auditorium in Buffalo for Game 6.

Moments before the teams stepped on the ice, an audio clip from the movie *Animal House* blared over the loudspeaker in Buffalo Memorial Auditorium. "Over? Did you say over? Nothing is over until we decide it is!" Six hours later, spectators sat slumped in their seats wondering if the game would ever end. Hasek and Devils goaltender Martin Brodeur took turns bringing spectators to their feet, making one incredible save after another. At one point, Hasek dove across his net to stop a shot with his elbow. The game extended late into the night—through regulation time and three overtime periods, neither team could score.

Then, a few minutes before 2 a.m., Sabres forward Dave Hannan picked up a rebound in the Devils end and sent a backhand shot past a sprawling Brodeur. Sabres fans suddenly sprang to life, jumping up and down and exchanging high fives.

"Dave Hannan is mobbed by his teammates!" yelled Sabres Hockey Network broadcaster Rick Jeanneret as Hannan slid across the ice on his knees with his arms spread in jubilation.

"Dave Hannan finally put away the backhand, and this series is going to where Jimmy Hoffa is… back to the Meadowlands in New Jersey!"

The reference baffled those fans who were unaware that the body of the former Teamsters union leader may (or may not) have been dumped somewhere in East Rutherford, New Jersey, but that hardly mattered. The party was well underway in bars and rec rooms across Buffalo.

The Devils won the next game 2-1 to end the Sabres' season, but the team's early exit didn't diminish the accomplishments of its prized European import. In June, Hasek and Fuhr together won the William M. Jennings Trophy, given to the goalie(s) on the team allowing the fewest goals in the regular season.

Hasek also won the Vezina Trophy as the best goalie of the season. He was pleased but admitted to having his eye on a bigger prize—the Hart Memorial Trophy, given to the NHL's most valuable player as determined by the league's general managers. "I think some day a goalie can win it," Hasek said. "For myself, I'd like to think that maybe some day in the future. I think I would have to have another year like last year. I don't think the people who vote these things would want to give it to someone who had just one good year. If I can have another year like last year… well maybe."[4]

1994-96

The 1994-95 NHL season started late because of a labor dispute, but Hasek didn't miss a step. He played in all but 7 of the team's 48 games, recording the best goals-against average (2.11) and save percentage (.930) among starters. He also tied Belfour for most shutouts (5). His emergence as an elite goaltender spelled the end for Fuhr, who was traded to Los Angeles in February.

After placing 6th in their conference and 11th overall with 51 points in the regular season, the Sabres were eliminated when the Philadelphia Flyers (60 points) beat them four games to one in the conference quarter-final. Hasek recorded a 3.50 goals-against average in that series, but that disappointment didn't overshadow his accomplishments during the regular season. At the NHL awards ceremony, he won his second Vezina Trophy.

Buffalo sent sniper Alexander Mogilny to the Vancouver Canucks a month later. The Sabres seemed to miss his scoring touch in the 1995–96 season, when they failed to make the play-offs. Hasek led NHL starters in save percentage (.920), but not in any other category.

1996-97

The Sabres' first season in Marine Midland Arena unfolded like an episode of *The Young and the Restless*, replete with family feuds, mysterious disappearances and dramatic outbursts.

Pat LaFontaine, the Sabres' leading scorer from the previous season, suffered a concussion just two weeks into the 1996–97 campaign and watched from the sidelines as the "lunch pail" team struggled to find the back of the net.

Twelve teams scored more goals than Buffalo that season, but only five teams allowed fewer goals. Hasek deserved most of the credit for the strong defensive showing. He was in net for all but 3 of his team's 40 victories, and the Sabres were out-shot in many of those games. Hasek and Brodeur tied for second-most wins (37), one less than Patrick Roy of the Colorado Avalanche, and the Czech goalie had the best save percentage (.930) in the league. He also had the third-best goals-against average (2.27) among starters.

But Hasek's ride through the season was bumpy. He and coach Ted Nolan had an uneasy relationship that grew more strained as the season progressed. During a practice in Boston on April 9, 1997, Nolan ordered his players to take part in a shooting drill. Hasek bolted from the ice then burst into the dressing room and began throwing pieces of equipment in every direction. Nolan followed his goalie into the dressing room. "I asked Dom twice if I had said or done anything to upset him," the coach said. "Both times he said, 'No.' Actually, the second time he really didn't say [that]. Dominik's a real quiet man, and he didn't respond. So I told him that if I had done anything, I apologized for it, but it was the last time I ever would, because I'm not going to apologize for something I don't know about."[5]

THE SABRES finished third in their conference and sixth overall, with 92 points, and met the Ottawa Senators (77 points) in the conference quarter-final. With the series tied, the teams headed to Ottawa for Game 3. In the second period, after Ottawa scored its first goal, Hasek skated to the Sabres bench and walked to the dressing room. Steve Shields took over in net, and the Sabres won 3–2. Hasek watched the third period in his street clothes. Afterwards, the team doctor said Hasek had suffered a mild knee sprain, and he declared the goalie's status as day-to-day.

"You have to be a really strong person to be a goalie—or at least, the position makes you a mentally strong individual. That's because you are the only one. The others, they depend on their teammates. You depend only on yourself. You're the one who can save the game or lose the game. So the position is very special. You have to have a strong mentality to become a great goalie."

DOMINIK HASEK

Columnist Jim Kelley filed a story that appeared in the *Buffalo News* the next day. "Hasek said he isn't in any pain but that he 'wouldn't be back this week,'" he wrote. "Pressed on the subject, he then said, 'My feeling is I won't be back until the end of this series.' He then sprinted out of the Corel Centre. Literally sprinted."

Kelley reported that Hasek had skipped an optional skate the morning of that game and had missed a team meeting. Also, Hasek had "nearly [gone] wild after missing several shots in succession" in the pre-game warm-up. "After one particularly galling miss, he spun around and attempted to smash his goalie stick against the goal post. The sold-out crowd in the Corel Centre saw it and immediately began chanting his name in a mocking fashion. Twice after that Hasek interrupted the shoot-around by skating out of the crease, apparently in disgust. On the second occasion, several Sabres players were seen talking to him, apparently urging him to calm down, all the while steering him back into the crease."

Kelley felt that something was "horribly amiss. I don't for a moment believe that Dominik Hasek intentionally bailed out on his coach and his teammates Monday night, but I do believe the pressure of having to be unbeatable may well be more than even he can bear… If that's the case, there may be more than a slightly sprained knee to worry about."[6]

Hasek read the article. Four days later, the Sabres lost a game at home and fell behind, three games to two. In a corridor outside the dressing room, Hasek confronted Kelley, calling him a liar and "the worst person in the world." He then lunged at the reporter, grabbing him by the collar and ripping his shirt. Several people, including teammate Jason Dawe, had to intervene.[7]

With Shields in net, the Sabres won the series in seven games and advanced to the conference semifinal against the Flyers.

People wondered what accounted for Hasek's unusual behavior. Did he have a drinking problem? Was he upset about the ongoing conflict between Nolan and Sabres general manager John Muckler? Hasek dismissed both possibilities.

The NHL suspended him for three games for his attack on Kelley, and he sat on the sidelines as the Sabres lost the first three games of the series against Philadelphia (103 points). He was set to return for Game 4, but after a pre-game skate, he said his knee was bothering him and declared himself unfit to play. Shields took over and the Sabres notched a 5–4 overtime victory. Shields played in the next game too, after Hasek declared himself unfit a second time, but the Sabres lost that one 6–3 and were eliminated.

IN JUNE, Hasek headed to Toronto for the NHL awards ceremony. He won his third Vezina Trophy as well as the Lester B. Pearson Award, given to the most valuable player as determined by his peers. He also won the Hart Trophy, becoming the first goalie to win it since Jacques Plante, in 1962, and the first player ever to win all three awards in one season. "This is something I can't describe in words," said Hasek, wearing a tuxedo. "It is the biggest individual honor or award for a hockey player to win this trophy. It is a fantastic honor for me."

Nolan won the Jack Adams Award as coach of the year, and Sabres forward Mike Peca picked up the Frank J. Selke Trophy as best defensive forward. The coach and his award-winning players smiled for photographers, but the picture wasn't worth a thousand words. It wasn't even worth the newsprint it appeared on. "I don't respect him," Hasek said about Nolan. "These feelings are here for half a year, maybe more. I kept my mouth shut and didn't tell anybody. I didn't want to bother my teammates," he said, setting the record straight. "But now I feel much better." Then he wished upon a star—that his coach would be gone when training camp resumed.[8]

During the summer, the Sabres offered Nolan a one-year contract extension. He asked for a better offer and the team refused. His days in Buffalo had come to an end. He told the media he was "really hurt and disillusioned by the whole thing."[9]

1997-98

Some Sabres players were furious about Hasek's comments. Forward Matthew Barnaby said he was disgusted, and he vowed to attack the goalie during training camp. Hasek expressed his earnest desire not to be pummeled by his teammate, and said he intended to "put everything behind [him]."[10]

|||||||||||||||||||||||||||||||||||||||||||||||||||||||||||||||||||

➤ FOR THE LOVE OF PASTA ◄

DURING A team dinner at an Italian restaurant in Dallas, Hasek commented that his dish, pasta fagioli, was excellent. Sabres goalie coach Jim Corsi insisted that his mother's version was better. When Hasek tried Adriana Corsi's pasta fagioli, he agreed. In fact, he liked it so much that whenever the Sabres played in Montreal, she prepared the dish and had it delivered to Hasek in a Tupperware container.

Once, when Sabres trainers left a container of the pasta on a plane after landing in Buffalo, Hasek asked them to go back to the airport to retrieve it. Years later, Corsi received a phone call from Hasek, who was in Toronto for an NHL awards banquet. "I picked up the phone and I heard, 'Jim, it's Daamaneek. How are you? I was at a restaurant yesterday and I ordered pasta fagioli. I still think your mother's is the best!'"

|||||||||||||||||||||||||||||||||||||||||||||||||||||||||||||||||||

Barnaby had a change of heart—at management's request, apparently—but fans weren't quite as forgiving. They showered Hasek with a chorus of boos for the first month of the 1997–98 season. The din subsided as Hasek turned in one great performance after another. In December alone, he recorded six shutouts.

By the end of January, a healthy LaFontaine was playing well and new coach Lindy Ruff was managing to keep the team on track, despite some upheaval in the front office when the Sabres switched ownership. Hasek was also playing well when the season stopped for the 1998 Winter Olympics.

THE CANADIAN, American and Russian teams were brimming with NHL talent and were considered the strongest contenders for the gold medal at the Olympics in Nagano, Japan. The Czech squad was barely considered at all. It consisted mostly of second-rate NHL players and players from Extraliga, the elite Czech league. In terms of the crème de la crème, the team had only Hasek and forward Jaromir Jagr, who had won two Cups with the Pittsburgh Penguins and had once picked up the Art Ross Trophy as the NHL's top scorer. But that turned out to be more than enough.

The Czechs beat Finland 3–0 and trounced Kazakhstan 8–2 in the first round of the competition. They then met the Americans in the quarter-final. The Americans launched a full frontal assault on the Czech net in the first period, but Hasek held the fort. At one point, he turned aside five shots in rapid succession. Onlookers were convinced he was playing on instinct, because he didn't appear to see the puck. The Americans out-shot the Czechs 39–20. The Czechs won 4–1.

Hasek's teammates were awestruck. "You never know what Dominik does. One time his left leg goes out like this," Vladimir Ruzicka said, putting his left leg straight out, "and one time his left leg goes up like that... then his arm goes up, one arm goes up like this, and then Dominik puts the other arm over here. You never can say what Dominik will do, but only you can say the puck does not go in."[11]

Reporters asked Hasek how people in Buffalo would respond to the outcome of the game. "I don't know. My son is at home and he goes to school today so I guess I'll find out," he said. "I hope they'll understand my job is to win the game."[12]

Two days later, the Czechs and Canadians met in the semi-final. The game remained scoreless until Jiri Slegr gave the Czechs a 1–0 lead in the third period. With just 63 seconds left,

Canadian Trevor Linden fired a shot that hit a Czech defenseman's stick and ricocheted into the Czech net. Neither team scored in the 10-minute overtime, so a shootout was called. Hasek would face five Canadian shooters while five of his teammates would take on Roy, who had won the Vezina Trophy three times and had twice won the Conn Smythe Trophy as the best player in the NHL post-season.

Czech Robert Reichel was the first shooter. He bore down on the Canadian net on the right side and then twisted his body left and fired the puck. It caromed off the post and into the net. Roy stopped all the other Czech shooters. He was great. But Hasek was better.

Theo Fleury tried to put the puck up high, but Hasek got his right shoulder in front of it. Ray Bourque missed the net entirely. When Joe Nieuwendyk tried to deke Hasek right, the goalie slid across the net and forced him to shoot wide. Eric Lindros sped up the ice and, just in front of the Czech net, moved suddenly to his left and tried to flip a backhand past Hasek. The goalie slid across the ice on his back, throwing up his arm and letting go of his stick. The puck deflected off his glove—or the post, depending whom you ask—and away from the net. Finally, it was Brendan Shanahan's turn. He gathered the puck on his stick and steamed toward the Czech net, bearing the weight of a nation on his shoulders. He skated in too deep and never had a chance. It was over.

> "I don't understand why people in the NHL are so concerned with the goalie's style rather than his success. Why is it important that a goalie look good in a goal? Why is it so important that he doesn't fall to the ice that often? Because he needs to look good in photographs? They're stupid, those Canadians. Lumberjacks!"
>
> *Former Czech goalie and Hasek's mentor*
> **JIRI HOLECEK**

Hasek leapt in the air. His teammates jumped on him, and the men fell to the ice, forming a giant mass in the middle of the rink. The Canadian players looked on in stunned silence. Wayne Gretzky sat stone-faced on the bench. He may have been wondering, as millions of fans were, why he had not been chosen to take part in the shootout.

"This will go down in history as a classic hockey game with two great goaltending performances," Canadian coach Marc Crawford said. "I just wish we could have been on the other end of the score. But we couldn't beat Hasek when we had to. It's getting to the point where no one beats Hasek."[13]

Two days later, the Czechs and Russians met in the final. Pavel Bure, who had scored five goals in a semifinal game against Finland, and his teammates had as much luck against Hasek as the Canadians had. The Czechs notched a 1–0 victory to win the gold medal. Hasek had allowed just six goals in the tournament and finished with a 0.97 goals-against average. He and his teammates received a rapturous welcome in Prague, where thousands gathered in the city's historic center, chanting, "Hasek is God! Hasek is God!"

WHEN HASEK returned to Buffalo, hundreds of fans greeted him at the airport and at his home in Amherst, New York. His neighbors had replaced their American flags with Czech colors and they cheered when Hasek donned his national team jersey and showed them his gold medal. City officials later honored him in a ceremony at Marine Midland Arena.

Then Hasek got down to business. He continued to play well and ended the season having played more games (72) than any other goalie. He notched the best save percentage (.932) among starters and the most shutouts (13) overall. He also finished third in wins (33).

The Sabres finished sixth in their conference and tenth overall, with 89 points. They advanced through the first two rounds of the playoffs, beating the Flyers (95 points) and the Montreal

Canadiens (87 points) before being eliminated by the Washington Capitals (92 points) in a six-game conference final.

For the second straight season, Hasek won the Vezina Trophy and the Pearson Award. He also won the Hart Trophy again, making him the only goalie ever to win that award more than once.

1998-99

Hasek suffered a groin injury in the 1998–99 season and was sidelined from mid-February to mid-March. Nonetheless, his numbers were impressive. Among starters, he recorded the best save percentage (.937) and the second-best goals-against average (1.87). Only Ron Tugnutt of the Senators, who played 21 fewer games than Hasek, had a better goals-against average (1.79). Hasek also finished second in shutouts (9).

With the Dominator in net and a strong defense corps, the Sabres allowed fewer goals (175) than every team but the Dallas Stars (168) in the 1998–99 season. Buffalo finished sixth in the conference and ninth overall (91 points) and advanced through the first three rounds of the playoffs by eliminating the Senators (103 points), the Bruins (91 points) and the Leafs (97 points).

The Sabres met the top-ranked Stars (114 points) in the final, a series that pitted Hasek against his former teammate. Since he and Belfour had first met at a Blackhawks training camp, Belfour had emerged as a world-class goaltender. He had been named the NHL's top rookie and had won the Vezina Trophy twice. During contract negotiations with the Blackhawks in 1996, Belfour had said he was a better goalie than Hasek. Fans expected the rivals to put on a great show, and they weren't disappointed.

Dallas was leading the low-scoring series three games to two when the teams squared off for Game 6 in Buffalo. With the scored tied 1–1 at the end of regulation time, the players returned to the ice for sudden death overtime. The teams remained locked in mortal combat until 14 minutes and 51 seconds into the third overtime period, when Brett Hull put the puck past Hasek, who was sprawled facedown on the ice. Dallas players jumped in the air and crowded around Belfour. Family members, friends and others flooded onto the ice to join the celebration.

Replays showed that Hull's left skate had been in the crease when he scored. That could have discounted the goal according to NHL rules, but game officials allowed it, saying Hull had possession of the puck when his foot entered the crease. The Sabres were furious. (See page 228)

"His foot was in the crease when he scored the goal," Ruff said afterwards. "You can't explain that to me. That was the worst nightmare right there." The indignant coach continued, "They have 200 people on the ice [celebrating]. The [officials] are not going to review it. I just wanted an explanation." "I still cannot believe it. It's really a shame," Hasek said. "I don't know what the video judge was doing."[14]

It was the end of one of the longest playoff games in NHL history. Belfour had made 53 saves, 3 more than Hasek. Both goalies had finished the post-season with goals-against averages under 2.00. Hasek won the Vezina Trophy for the fifth time.

Hasek was famous. He was wealthy. He was at the peak of his powers—and he was done. In July 1999, he held a press conference in Prague to announce that he would retire at the end of the following season. He said he and his wife, Alena, whom he had been with since high school, wanted to raise their children, Michal and Dominika, in the Czech Republic. He also said he was tired of living in the limelight. "The attention I've received is overwhelming. It's something I don't enjoy at all. It's time to step back," he said. He added that he would not change his mind. "Once I take off my equipment for the last time, that's going to be forever."[15]

1999-2000

In a game against the Florida Panthers early in the 1999–2000 season, Hasek went down to stop a shot and didn't get up. He had torn a groin muscle, and the injury would keep him out of the lineup for three months.

The team proceeded to tumble down the standings. The Sabres finished 16th overall, with 85 points. Hasek returned to the lineup in February, and was in net for the playoffs—but it hardly mattered. The Flyers eliminated the Sabres four games to one in the first round.

Hasek changed his mind about retiring.

2000-01

Hasek returned to form in the 2000–01 season, recording the most shutouts (11) in the NHL and, along with two other goalies, the third-most wins (37). Among starters, he had the second-best goals-against average (2.11) and, along with one other goalie, the third-best save percentage (.921).

Buffalo allowed the fewest goals in the league (184), giving Hasek another Jennings Award. The Sabres finished fourth in their conference and eighth overall with 98 points. They beat the Flyers (100 points) in the conference quarter-final before being eliminated by the Pittsburgh Penguins (96 points) in the next round.

Hasek won his sixth Vezina Trophy.

A few weeks later, Buffalo traded him to Detroit. It was revealed that Hasek had told the team he wanted to leave Buffalo, to play for a Cup contender. "He's been driving the [Interstate] 90 to work on a daily basis, he's kind of memorized the trees, he knows how to spell 'Tonawanda' now as he goes by the water tower. It was time for a different challenge," Hasek's agent, Ritch Winter, said. "This was never about the money. It was about trying to find a compromise that would work for everybody."[16]

"I personally have never seen a goaltender like this person," said Darcy Regier, who had replaced Muckler as Sabres general manager in 1997. "I think that people here will reflect back on the time that Dom was here and really appreciate his greatness. We wish him only the best."[17]

2001-02

The Red Wings had finished second in the league the previous season, thanks to the efforts of star defenseman Nicklas Lidstrom and top forwards Steve Yzerman, Brendan Shanahan and Sergei Fedorov. General manager Ken Holland felt the summer acquisition of Hasek and two of the NHL's best snipers, Hull and Luc Robitaille, would push the team to the top—and he was right. The Red Wings finished first overall with 116 points, 15 more than the second-place Boston Bruins, and Hasek played a pivotal role in that success. He led NHL goaltenders with 41 wins.

> "I think many people who are the best in something, who are almost genius, can sometimes make an impression of having a screw loose. Dominik was not just good, he was genius."
>
> *Hasek's brother,* **MARTIN HASEK**

In the playoffs, Detroit eliminated the Vancouver Canucks (94 points), the St. Louis Blues (98 points) and the Colorado Avalanche (99 points) and then took on the Carolina Hurricanes (91 points) in the final.

Carolina won the first game, but Detroit stormed back to win the next four, the second of which was decided in triple overtime. In Game 5, Shanahan scored two goals and Hasek made 16 saves as the Red Wings posted a 3–1 victory. When Shanahan scored late in the third period to all but guarantee victory, Hasek bolted out of his net and skated to the blue line, where he jumped in the air with his arms raised. He celebrated with his teammates for a moment and then headed back to his net to play out the game. Less than a minute later, the horn sounded and the Red Wings won their third Cup in six years—and Hasek's first ever. When it was his turn to hold the 35-pound trophy, he lifted it high over his head and performed a few over-head presses with it. "There's no better feeling than to raise the Stanley Cup," he said beaming. "It's fantastic. It's heavier than I thought."[18]

Eleven days later, Hasek retired. He headed back to the Czech Republic and met with media to discuss the end of his career. He spent a week celebrating his Cup victory—and then announced he was disappearing from public life. "The next four, five months, no more media, no reporters, no TV, just very quiet," he said. "I am keeping myself very quiet. No invitations. I have said no to everything. This is what I was waiting for 20 years for, and now I want to do it this way."[19]

HASEK DIDN'T keep a low profile for long. He was back in the news less than a year later. While playing defense in an inline hockey game, he reportedly cross-checked an opponent in the back, sat on him and, for good measure, clubbed him several times in the neck with his stick. The player was sent to the hospital with a broken nose, a concussion and two chipped teeth. "I have never seen such unbelievable short-circuited behavior in my 15-year career," the referee said. "On top of that I wouldn't expect it from someone of Dominik Hasek's caliber. I still can't believe it."[20] Hasek was charged with assault and faced two years in jail.

While authorities were deciding whether to prosecute, Hasek announced he was returning to the NHL. "My primary moti-vation is exactly to get back to the game and compete again," Hasek said. "When I retired I feel like I'm not hungry. I feel like my fire is back. I want to play. I want to compete."[21] His decision put the Red Wings in a bind. At the time, they had an elite goalie in Curtis Joseph, whom they had signed the previous summer to a lucrative three-year contract with a no-trade clause. They also had a capable goalie in Manny Legace. It was an embarrass-ment of goaltending riches.

2003-04

Hasek was named the Red Wings starter, but his return to the NHL wasn't quite as successful as the Who's first farewell tour. He injured his groin just 14 games into the season and sat on the sidelines for months. Then, on February 11, 2004, he skated onto the ice at Joe Louis Arena to warm up for a game against the San Jose Sharks. He faced a few shots then headed to the dressing room. He said his groin was still bothering him and declared that his was season over.

Joseph, who had spent much of the season on the trading block and in the minors, reclaimed the starter's position. Legace was his backup. The Red Wings finished first overall that season with 109 points but were eliminated in the second round of the playoffs by the Calgary Flames (94 points).

Hasek headed home but wasn't arrested when he landed at Ruzyne International Airport in Prague; Czech prosecutors had reduced his assault charge to a misdemeanor. A free man, Hasek spent time with his family, played squash, went cycling and promoted his clothing line—but he felt something was missing.

When he became an unrestricted free agent in July, he signed a one-year contract with Ottawa. The 39-year-old goalie was looking forward to stepping onto the ice in a Senators jersey, but that didn't happen as soon as he expected. A protracted labor dispute forced the cancellation of the entire 2004–05 NHL season.

2004-05

In December, Hasek joined a team of almost two dozen NHL players that played 10 exhibition games in European cities. When he skated onto the ice in Pilsen, a two-hour drive from his hometown, the crowd roared its approval. Half the 8,000 fans in the sold-out arena were on their feet for the entire game. Hasek allowed all three goals in his team's 8–3 victory over an Extraliga squad, but that didn't dampen his fans' ardor. Hundreds of them surrounded the NHL players' bus after the game, hoping to get his autograph. "It was a nice feeling to play in the Czech Republic for the first time in 10 years," Hasek said. "It was a very special game for me and it was obvious the people liked it."[22]

2005-06

When Hasek arrived in Ottawa for the start of the 2005–06 season, he was joining one of the strongest teams in the league. Forwards Daniel Alfredsson and Martin Havlat were among the league's top scorers and had helped the Senators (102 points) finish fourth in the Eastern Conference and sixth overall in the previous NHL season. Forward Dany Heatley, the NHL's top rookie in 2002, had recently been acquired in a trade and promised to add some firepower to the Senators offense.

Sure enough, the Senators burst out of the gate, winning 21 of their first 25 games. Ottawa had one of the best records in the NHL when the season broke for the 2006 Winter Games in Torino.

> "When Hasek was on the national team, the players used to play chess. Antonin Stavjana and Jiri Kralik used to beat Dominik regularly, so he started to study the game thoroughly. He studied every aspect of it. Then he started to beat the others."
>
> *Czech reporter* **ROBERT ZARUBA**

This Olympic experience was anything but magical for Hasek. He arrived in Italy without his equipment and missed several Czech team practices waiting for it to arrive. Just nine minutes into the team's first game, against Germany, he injured his adductor muscle while making a save. He headed home a few days later, intending to finish the season in the Senators net. But his injury sidelined him for the rest of the season.

The Senators finished first in their conference and second overall, with 113 points, but were eliminated by the Sabres (110 points) in the second round of the playoffs. At the end of the season, Ottawa chose not to keep Hasek.

2006-08

Hasek was down but not out. Detroit was looking for a starter—Joseph had gone to the Phoenix Coyotes in 2005—and decided to take a chance on their former netminder. They signed Hasek to a one-year contract. "Dom seems very committed and very excited about an opportunity to come back to Detroit and try to help our team win a Stanley Cup," Holland said. "We really see Dom coming into training camp as our No. 1 goaltender. Bringing Dom back is a real positive for our team and is very exciting."[23]

In the 2006–07 season, Hasek recorded the best goals-against average (2.05) among starters and the second-most shutouts (8) in the NHL. The Red Wings finished first overall, with 113 points. But their season ended when they were eliminated by the Anaheim Ducks (110 points) in the Western Conference final. (The Ducks then beat the Senators to win their first Cup in franchise history.)

Hasek contemplated retirement in the summer—then changed his mind. He told the Red Wings he wanted to play another year, and after weeks of negotiations, he signed a one-year contract.

HASEK SHARED the workload with veteran Chris Osgood in the 2007–08 season. Detroit allowed the fewest goals in the league (184), earning Osgood his second Jennings Award and Hasek his third.

With Pavel Datsyuk, Henrik Zetterberg and Lidstrom on the attack, the Red Wings finished first overall with 115 points and were considered strong Cup contenders heading into the playoffs.

Hasek played the first three games of the opening round against the Nashville Predators (91 points), two of which Detroit won. But in Game 4, he gave up three goals on 14 shots and was replaced by Osgood. The younger goalie stayed in net for the rest of the playoffs.

After eliminating the Predators in six games, the Red Wings swept aside the Colorado Avalanche (95 points) and then dispatched the Stars (97 points). Detroit met the Penguins (102 points) in the final and managed to hold off budding superstar Sidney Crosby and his supporting cast. The Red Wings won the series in six games.

Standing in the dressing room after the game, surrounded by piles of sweat-drenched equipment and opened champagne bottles, Hasek confessed to having mixed emotions. "Obviously, it's not the same if you're not in net," he said. "But overall, it was a great experience and winning a Cup is why I came back and signed with the Red Wings."[24]

He retired a few days later.

It may have been the least restful retirement in recorded history. He soon signed a one-year contract with Pardubice, the club he had first joined almost 30 years before. He played 33 games in the 2009–10 season, posting a .922 save percentage and a 2.26 goals against average. He led his team to the Extraliga title—then he turned northeast.

In June 2010, he signed a one-year deal with Spartak Moscow of the Kontinental Hockey League (KHL). Hasek turned 46 in the middle of the 2010–11 season and played the same number of games. He posted a .915 save percentage and a 2.48 goals-against average.

"Dominik sometimes gives the impression he's a little flaky," says Czech journalist Robert Zaruba, who has written extensively about Hasek. "He retires, comes back, retires, comes back, etc. But it's just that he hates idleness. He hates doing nothing, having no goal. He always needs something big to shoot for."

A year after that season, Czech media reported that Hasek was planning to go cycling in Russia and South America—then return to the ice. His agent approached several NHL clubs to see if they were interested in hiring the 47-year-old. None were.

"You know, I'm ready. I've been preparing for eight months nearly every day, and over the last two months, I was on the ice, so I'm well prepared. Right now, my equipment is in the garage. But let me put it this way: If someone calls tomorrow, I'm going the next day."[25] He was asked about his plans for the future. "That's a good question and I wish I knew what I'm going to do every day, but I don't. I don't see myself as a coach or a manager or an agent so I will look around and see. But right now, I don't have an answer for you."[26]

HASEK · ALL-TIME RANKING*

REGULAR SEASON			PLAYOFFS		
GAMES	**WINS**	**SO**	**GAMES**	**WINS**	**SO**
735 [21st]	389 [11th]	81 [6th]	119 [10th]	65 [11th]	14 [5th]

* statistics as of July 2, 2013.

> NHL ALL-ROOKIE TEAM **(1ST)**: 1991–92

> NHL ALL-STAR TEAM **(1ST)**: 1993–94, 1994–95, 1996–97, 1997–98, 1998–99, 2000–2001

➤ 12 ◄

THE COOL
CUSTOMER
MARTIN BRODEUR

"He's a laid-back kind of guy.
Nothing bothers him, and that goes a long way for
any hockey player, but especially a goalie."[1]

New Jersey Devils teammate
BRIAN ROLSTON, in 2009

THE NEW JERSEY Devils are battling to make the 2012
playoffs. Their star goalie is coming back from a mediocre performance in the first half of the season, and rumors about his
possible retirement have been swirling around him for months.
His father had brain surgery four days ago. But standing in the
visitors' dressing room at the Air Canada Centre wearing a dark
blue suit, Martin Brodeur looks relaxed. If he wasn't talking
about the game that just ended, you might think he had spent
the last few hours on the dock at his summer home in the Lau-
rentians. Gathered around him like a group of ring-tailed lemurs
facing the sun, reporters ask him questions about the Devils'
4–3 victory over the Toronto Maple Leafs.

Did you hear that shot hit the crossbar?

"I think everyone in the building heard it. It was pretty loud."
Brodeur shrugs and runs his hand through his hair, which is still
damp from the shower. "We got a little fortunate there."

What lies ahead for the team?

"I don't think there will be any easy games for the rest of the year. We just have to play hard. We're a team that makes our own life difficult at times," Brodeur says, smiling. "We play well and then fumble a little."

A team official declares the interview over. "Thanks, guys," Brodeur says, nodding at the reporters. "Next time."

According to conventional wisdom, the greatest goalies are the most temperamental. But Martin Brodeur is an exception to the rule—and that makes his laid-back nature as incredible as his long and storied career.

THE DAY AFTER the Montreal Canadiens' Ken Dryden was named the NHL's top rookie, another great goalie made a grand entrance. Martin Brodeur was born in May 1972 in St. Leonard, Quebec, in the east end of Montreal. He was connected to the NHL even then, two decades before he would play his first NHL game. His father was the official photographer for the Montreal Canadiens. Denis Brodeur often brought Martin, the youngest of five children, to the Forum to watch players such as Larry Robinson and Bob Gainey put through their paces. One of Martin's earliest memories is of attending a Habs Christmas party. He was three years old at the time and didn't protest when his father lifted him up, placed him on top of the net and snapped a picture.

Martin was a forward when he started playing organized hockey, but when he was six years old, he started moonlighting as a goalie on an older boys' team and took to the position like a puppy to an old tennis ball. Denis had been an excellent goalie as a young man and had helped the Canadian team win a bronze medal at the 1956 Winter Olympics. But when Martin took up the position, Denis refused to create his son in his own image. He advised him on the dos and don'ts of moving out from the goal crease, but for the most part, he kept his distance. He had been a small goalie who had caught with his right hand, whereas his son was a big goalie (and still growing) who caught with his left. "For him it was not about me making it," Martin recalled years later. "It was about me having fun, making sure I did everything I could to make it but really enjoying myself."[2]

As a teenager, Brodeur looked up to another Quebec goalie. Patrick Roy led the underdog Canadiens to a Stanley Cup victory in his rookie season of 1985–86, and was heralded for his athleticism and mental toughness. "I idolized him because he came in [to the NHL] so young and he showed he could do the job," Brodeur said about Roy, who is seven years older. "He made me see the possibility of doing it myself."[3]

When Brodeur was cut from his Bantam team in 1986, the 14-year-old goalie considered quitting hockey, but his brother Claude talked him out of it.

Brodeur played in the Quebec Major Junior Hockey League in the 1989–90 season, suiting up for the Saint-Hyacinthe Laser, whose arena was a 40-minute drive from Montreal. He made steady progress and impressed the New Jersey Devils. The NHL team selected him 20th overall in the 1990 draft, making him one of just two goalies taken in the first round that year. (The other was Trevor Kidd, who became a journeyman in the NHL.)

NHL

1991-93

When New Jersey lost two goalies, Chris Terreri and Craig Billington, to injury late in the 1991–92 season, the Devils summoned Brodeur. The teenager stepped on the ice for a home game against the Boston Bruins on March 26.

"I was 19, and I couldn't stop a puck in warm-up," he remembered. "The coaches came up to me and said, 'Don't worry, kid. Just go out there and have fun.' So I did."[4] Brodeur played well throughout—he had to make 3 of his 24 saves during one hectic minute in the second period—and allowed just two goals in the third period. The Devils clinched a playoff berth with a 4–2 win. "Playing in his first game in the National Hockey League, exhibition or otherwise, the 19-year-old Brodeur provided the most inspiring goaltending the Devils have had in quite a while," the *New York Times* reported. "Brodeur, a native of Montreal, showed plenty of signs that justified his selection as the team's first choice in the draft two years ago. Judging by tonight's performance, he could solve some problems for the Devils."[5]

Brodeur played three more games during the regular season and then replaced Terreri in the middle of the fifth game of the Patrick Division semifinal. The Devils were trailing the New York Rangers 5–0 when Terreri left the ice at Madison Square Garden. The Devils scored five goals with Brodeur in net but were no match for the Rangers, who peppered the young goalie and beat the Devils 8–5. The Rangers won the series in seven games, and the Devils were eliminated in the first round of the playoffs for the third straight season. They assigned Brodeur to the Utica Devils, their farm team in the American Hockey League (AHL), and he stayed there for the 1992–93 season.

1993-94

Brodeur showed up at the Devils training camp in September 1993 and, like all newcomers, faced the prospect of being sent back to the farm team. But he was unfazed. "It's not a shame at all; for a goalie that's just the way it is," he said with a shrug. "You have to be very ready before you go there [to the NHL]. If it takes me another year to be ready, it takes me another year."[6]

As it turned out, Brodeur made a good impression. "He wasn't a typical rookie," says Jacques Caron, who became the Devils goalie coach that season. "I could see a lot of confidence in him. He smiled a lot, and you could see he was happy to be there."

Caron recalls that Brodeur was "a typical Quebec goalten-der" at the time, frequently going down in the butterfly posi-tion, often for no good reason. "You could see he had some real potential, but he had to play with more control," says Caron, who is still working with the team's goalies. "I said, 'Marty, if you want to have a long, successful NHL career, you'll have to change a few things.' He just said, 'Let's do it!' There was no resistance."

With Caron's guidance, Brodeur became more mobile. He learned to keep his balance and skate, not slide, across the crease. This allowed him to follow the play and stay square to the puck at all times. He learned to control the puck and give up fewer rebounds. He went down in a butterfly position when necessary but not often enough to put a lot of strain on his knees, which had already been surgically repaired. He was becoming a solid all-around goalie.

He showed enough poise to earn a spot on the team's roster. He and Terreri shared duties at first, but two months into the season, Terreri went through a bad stretch and coach Jacques Lemaire began giving Brodeur more starts. Brodeur rose to the challenge. He won 27 of the 47 games in which he played that regular season. He also had a 2.40 goals-against average, second among starting goalies.

With the solid rookie in net and star defenseman Scott Ste-vens coordinating the attack, the Devils finished with 106 points, good enough for second in the Eastern Conference and overall. When Lemaire announced that Brodeur would start in the con-ference quarter-final against the Buffalo Sabres (95 points), the 21-year-old goalie appeared nonchalant. "I don't get nervous about the playoffs. I just get a little anxious," he told reporters. "I'm that kind of guy."[7]

"Big games or off days for me are the same," Brodeur says almost two decades later. "I try not to get too high or too low… I think, at a young age, I learned quickly that if I was going to be one of the top goalies, I needed to be really even-keeled in any kind of situation."

THE DEVILS-SABRES series was a dramatic one, featuring a duel between Brodeur and Sabres star Dominik Hasek, the only netminder who had posted a better goals-against average (1.95) than Brodeur in the regular season. Both goalies played spectacularly through the first five games, with the Devils winning three. Game 6 was a marathon contest in Buffalo (see page 244). Hasek and Brodeur were stellar, neither of them allowing a single goal until the fourth overtime, when the Sabres' David Hannan ended the game. (Hannan later admitted that all he wanted to do after the goal was lie down.[8]) Brodeur fished the puck out of his net and fired it at the sideboards in disgust. He dropped his head and skated off the ice. He had made 49 saves that night. Hasek had made 70.

The Devils rebounded and notched a 2–1 victory in the deciding game. They advanced to the conference semifinal and beat the Boston Bruins (97 points). Then they took on the league-leading New York Rangers (112 points).

With Brodeur in one net and Mike Richter—one of the best American goalies in NHL history—in the other, the conference final was a low-scoring affair. It stretched to seven games, three of which went into double overtime. It ended when Stephane Matteau put the puck past Brodeur in the second overtime period of the deciding game. No one blamed Brodeur. He had faced 48 shots that night and stopped all but 2.

By the end of his season, Brodeur had played in 17 playoff games and won 8 of them. He had recorded one shutout and posted a .928 save percentage and a 1.95 goals-against average. He was awarded the Calder Memorial Trophy as the league's best rookie.

1994-95

Brodeur was anxious to return to the ice and prove his success had not been a fluke, but he had to wait longer than expected for the 1994–95 season to start. Team owners locked out the players during heated contract negotiations, putting the entire season in jeopardy. The dispute was settled, and a 48-game season started in January.

Brodeur had worked on his game with Devils goalie coach Caron during the lockout, so he started the season looking better than ever. He turned heads not just with his success at keeping the puck out of the net but also with his ability to move it. Brodeur proved to be a great stickhandler, often moving out of his net to clear the puck or pass it to a teammate streaking up the ice.

"Marty made our job that much easier," recalls Ken Daneyko, a defenseman with the Devils for 20 years before retiring in 2003. "He could get the puck to a teammate by making a direct pass or chipping it off the boards. We always knew he could make that outlet pass. Besides stopping the puck, that is what made him so special. He had a great glove hand too. He would sometimes leave part of the net open and dare the attacker to shoot there. And then, in an instant, he would just take [that space] away. You don't teach that stuff. It's athletic ability and instinct."

The Devils had an unspectacular regular season, finishing sixth in the conference and tenth overall, with 52 points, but the post-season was a different matter. In the first three rounds of the playoffs, they upset the Bruins (57 points), the Pittsburgh Penguins (61 points) and the Philadelphia Flyers (60 points). Brodeur posted three shutouts in a five-game series against Boston and allowed just eight goals in five games against Pittsburgh. In that series, he stood his ground against Jaromir Jagr, who had led the NHL in scoring that season. The Czech, whose mullet was as mind-blowing as his speed and strength, managed to score just three goals. Flyers captain Eric Lindros, who had shared the scoring title with Jagr, notched just two goals as Philadelphia was eliminated in six games.

Impressive as the Devils had been in the post-season, few people expected them to beat the Detroit Red Wings (70 points) in the Stanley Cup final. Paul Coffey, Sergei Fedorov and Steve Yzerman had led a strong Detroit team to the top of the NHL standings. But the Devils had two things working in their favor—an effective neutral zone trap and Brodeur. When Detroit snipers managed to break through the Devils' defensive wall at mid-ice, they came face to face with the hottest goalie in the NHL. Detroit fans taunted Brodeur and even pelted him with octopuses, but the discarded mollusks didn't faze him. He allowed just seven goals as the Devils swept the Red Wings aside in four games. More than 19,000 spectators at the Brendan Byrne Arena in East Rutherford, New Jersey, leapt from their seats when the Devils beat the Red Wings 5–2 in the last game, winning the first Cup in franchise history.

Brodeur, who later described the last minute of that game as the best 60 seconds of his life, had no interest in false modesty. "We own the place," he said after the game, chomping on a cigar. "We couldn't say anything during the playoffs because we wanted to keep the low profile all the time. But now we won it, so, we're the best."[9]

1995–99

The Devils weren't nearly as successful in the next four years. In the 1995–96 season, the defending champions missed the playoffs entirely. In the three seasons after that, they never advanced farther than the conference final.

But during that span, their goalie emerged as a star. In the 1996–97 season, he led the league in shutouts (10). Among starters, he had the best goals-against average (1.88) and the second-best save percentage (.927). He also posted 37 wins, second only to Roy (38). That season, Brodeur and backup goalie Mike Dunham shared the Jennings Trophy, which is awarded annually to the goalie(s) on the team allowing the fewest goals in the regular season.

The 1996–97 season also featured one of the most memorable games of Brodeur's career. The Devils were leading the Montreal Canadiens by two goals late in the first game of the conference quarter-final when the Canadiens, in a desperate bid to score, pulled their goalie in favor of an extra attacker. The Habs dumped the puck in the Devils end, to the right of the net. Brodeur lofted the puck in the air and it landed near center ice. As it skidded into the empty Montreal net, the jubilant goalie sprang into the air with his arms spread wide. He had sealed a 5–2 victory and become just the second goalie in NHL history to score in the post-season. (Ron Hextall had done it in 1989—see page 175)

"This is the greatest thing that has happened to me, personally," Brodeur said after the game. "I take a lot of pride in playing the puck. I always looked up to Ron Hextall and the way he did it. I saw him score goals. It's something that's pretty hard to do for a goalie... I wanted to get one myself."[10] The Devils goalie coach assured reporters the goal was no fluke. Caron told them Brodeur had been practicing that shot two or three times a week before practice.

Brodeur finished the 1997–98 season with the most wins (43) among goalies and the second-most shutouts (10). He also had the second-best goals-against average (1.89) among starters. He won the Jennings Trophy again but didn't have to share it this time; he played in 70 of the 82 regular-season games. He played the same number of games the next season and again finished with more wins (39) than any other goalie.

1999-2000

The Devils returned to form in the 1999–2000 season. They finished second in the conference and fourth overall, with 103 points—and much of the credit went to their goaltender. Brodeur led the league in wins (43) yet again, and he notched another goal—this one in a regular-season game against Philadelphia in February. When the Flyers goalie left the ice in favor of an extra attacker, Philadelphia forward Daymond Langkow tried to set up an attack. But when Devils forward Sergei Brylin jammed him along the boards, the puck rolled straight back into the empty Flyers net. Brodeur had been the last New Jersey player to touch the puck, so he was awarded the goal. It put the Devils ahead 3–1, and they went on to win the game 4–2. Brodeur was less enthusiastic about his second NHL goal. "My first game-winner… and it had to be like that?" he said with a grin. "Wow."[11]

THE DEVILS marched through the post-season, downing one opponent after another. Brodeur led the charge. He allowed just six goals in four games as the Devils swept aside the Florida Panthers (98 points) in the conference quarter-final. New Jersey then won the conference semifinal against Toronto, beating the Maple Leafs (100 points) four games to two. Brodeur recorded two shutouts in that series. The Devils were unstoppable in the final game. The top line of Patrik Elias, Petr Sykora and Jason Arnott scored two goals in the 3–0 victory, and Brodeur faced just six shots.

The conference final against the Flyers (105 points) was more challenging. Philadelphia won three of the first four games, pushing the Devils to the brink of elimination. "We were pretty demoralized at that point, but Marty stepped up and said, 'Hey, it's not over yet.' He had that quiet confidence and that calm demeanor," recalls Daneyko. "It made us feel good to see he had it under control." Brodeur gave up just one goal in each of the next three games, and the Devils won the series four games to three. "Marty is one of the biggest reasons, if not the biggest reason, we were so consistently good," Daneyko says.

Four days after eliminating the Flyers, the Devils launched a full frontal assault on the defending Stanley Cup champions, the Dallas Stars (102 points). In the first game of the final, the Devils scored six goals on Ed Belfour and one on Manny

Fernandez, who stepped into the line of fire in the third period and stood there for 17 whole minutes. Brodeur allowed three goals. He made 15 saves overall, including two spectacular stops a split second apart on top snipers Mike Modano and Brett Hull, and the Devils won 7–3.

Belfour attributed his poor performance to the decongestant he had been taking to battle a cold. Reporters asked him when he had identified the problem. "After six goals," he replied.[12]

The Devils were leading three games to one when the teams squared off for Game 5. New Jersey hoped to wrap up the series at home that night, but Belfour wouldn't cooperate. He matched Brodeur save for save, and the game remained scoreless until six minutes into the third overtime period, when Modano tipped in Hull's shot from the point to give the Stars a 1–0 win. It was almost 1:30 a.m. when the teams skated off the ice.

Soon afterwards, the bleary-eyed Devils boarded a flight to Dallas. Their plane had to be diverted to Tulsa, Oklahoma, because of bad weather, so they didn't arrive at their destination until 8 p.m. Less than 24 hours later, the teams skated onto the ice at Reunion Arena for Game 6. The game was a fierce battle featuring the "rock 'em, sock 'em" style of play that sends superlatives shooting out of Don Cherry's mouth like pulp from an over-ripe tomato. The game ended eight minutes into the second overtime period, when Arnott ripped a shot past Belfour to clinch a 2–1 victory—and the Devils' second Stanley Cup. After the game, reporters found Brodeur sitting in the visitors' dressing room with a cigar in his left hand and his right arm wrapped around his wife, Melanie, with whom he had three sons. (They had a daughter two years later.) "There

> "Marty has so much confidence in what he's going to do on the ice, he has no anxiety, no fear, before a game. I have never seen anyone like him."
>
> *New Jersey Devils goalie coach*
> **JACQUES CARON**

were some bumps along the way, but I'm so happy it's over and I'm glad we're on the good side of it," he said. "Winning the Cup every five years is not so bad."[13]

Brodeur asked Caron to stick around until the commotion died down. Hours later, when a janitor was about the only other person left in the building, teacher and student walked to center ice. They stood in the darkened arena and reflected on their accomplishments. "We just stood there and took in the moment," Caron recalls. "Marty was happy and filled with joy that night."

IN KEEPING with NHL tradition, each player on the winning team had the Cup for a day that summer. When it was Brodeur's turn, he organized a road hockey game near the home where he once lived with his parents, Denis and Mireille, and four siblings. Two teams of his boyhood friends competed for the grand prize. Reporters and photographers descended on the area. Mike Bolt, the official keeper of the Cup, was also on hand.

"I remember sitting in Marty's parents' yard with him after the game," says the man who protects Lord Stanley's Cup as earnestly as a Secret Service agent looks after the U.S. president. "He talked about how police had shut down the street for that game. He compared that to what it was like when he was a kid and police would order him and his friends to stop playing there," he says. "Marty has a great appreciation for the game— and for the Cup." Quite a compliment coming from a man who might take a bullet for hockey's grand prize.

2000-01

The Devils' results were even better in the 2000–01 regular season. They placed first in their conference and third overall, with III points. Brodeur posted 42 wins, giving him the most victories among NHL goaltenders for the fourth straight season.

The Devils steamed through the playoffs. They eliminated the Carolina Hurricanes (88 points), the Leafs (90 points) and the Penguins (96 points) and then took on the Colorado Avalanche in the final. Colorado, which had finished first overall with 118 points, was brimming with talent. The roster included three of the NHL's top scorers—Joe Sakic, Peter Forsberg and Milan Hejduk—and one of its best defensemen, Ray Bourque. Better yet, the roster included one of the best goalies in history. Roy was nearing the end of an outstanding career but was still formidable.

The Avalanche won the first game 5–0 and went on to win the series in seven games. With Colorado fans roaring in approval, Bourque lifted the Stanley Cup for the first time in his storied NHL career. (See page 208)

Roy had outshone Brodeur. The veteran had allowed just 11 goals in seven games while Brodeur had let in 19. Roy had posted two shutouts—two more than his rival. Media were unforgiving. "And when the finger pointing starts, don't forget to look in Martin Brodeur's direction," one reporter railed. "This was supposed to be the series in which Brodeur stood up and made a difference, but he was nothing more than ordinary."[14]

2001-02

The Devils' fortunes faded the following season. They plummeted in the standings and finished twelfth overall with 95 points. They were eliminated in the conference quarter-final by the Hurricanes (91 points). Brodeur played well, giving up just nine goals in six games, but not well enough.

YET THE SEASON wasn't a complete wash, at least not for Brodeur. In February, he had been part of the team representing Canada at the 2002 Winter Olympics. He arrived in Salt Lake City uncertain of seeing any ice time. But when Leafs star Curtis Joseph imploded in the first game, a 5–2 loss to Sweden, Brodeur took over and played the remaining five games.

His confidence grew with each one, and he was excellent in the final against the United States. With less than five minutes remaining and the Canadians clinging to a 3–2 lead, Brodeur slid to his right and kicked out a leg to make a toe save on Hull. Canada won the game 5–2, and the gold medal. Brodeur and his teammates congratulated each other while his father, who had won a bronze medal almost 50 years before, captured the moment through his camera lens.

"As an athlete, you want to be part of great things for your country, but you've also got the motivation of family," said Brodeur, who had spent the 1998 Nagano Games on the bench as Roy's back up. "We did a lot of great things today, and I can't imagine anything better."[15]

2002-03

Once again, the Devils bounced back from a bad season. They moved up the standings to finish second in their conference and fourth overall, with 108 points, in the 2002–03 season and clinched a playoff berth in the second-to-last game of the regular season. Brodeur finished first among goalies in wins (41) and shutouts (9). He also won the Jennings Trophy again, sharing it with the Flyers' Roman Cechmanek and Robert Esche.

The Devils beat the Bruins (87 points) and the Tampa Bay Lightning (93 points) before squeaking past the league-leading Ottawa Senators (113 points) in a seven-game conference final.

Four days later, the Devils squared off against the Mighty Ducks of Anaheim (95 points). The plucky Ducks pushed the Devils to seven games. In the final one, Brodeur posted his seventh shutout of the playoffs, and the Devils won the game 3–0. The crowd at Continental Arena—formerly Brendan Byrne Arena—erupted when the final buzzer sounded, and the Devils celebrated the third Stanley Cup in franchise history.

When the noise in the arena subsided to a dull roar, NHL officials prepared to present the Conn Smythe Trophy to the most valuable player of the playoffs. Devils fans got set to salute their goalie. But the trophy was awarded to rookie Ducks goaltender

Jean-Sebastien Giguere. Devils fans groaned in disappointment, but Brodeur couldn't have cared less. He was pumping his fists in the air as he anticipated laying his sweaty palms on hockey's Holy Grail once again.

The next night, he appeared on a talk show. Brodeur, "who flashes a smile so often it seems perpetual, continued celebrating the New Jersey Devils' latest championship by carrying the Stanley Cup onto the stage of the CBS Late Show with David Letterman," a wire service reported. Asked if there was anything left for him to achieve, Brodeur replied: "Winning never gets old."[16]

At the NHL awards ceremony, Brodeur won the coveted Vezina Trophy as the best goalie of the season. Like a kid who has just broken the piñata on his tenth whack, Brodeur was elated. He took a few bows. "I've had some great seasons; it's nice to get it off my back," he said. "Everybody always said, 'I can't believe you don't have the Vezina.'"[17]

2003-04

Once again, the Devils reached the peak of the mountain only to lose their footing. In the 2003-04 season, they tumbled to sixth in their conference and ninth overall, with 100 points, and were eliminated by the Philadelphia Flyers (101 points) in the conference quarter-final.

But Brodeur finished with more wins (38) and shutouts (11) than any of his peers, winning his fourth Jennings Trophy and second Vezina Trophy. "I've got to hold onto these two [Vezinas]," he said, "because it's going to be hard to win any more with all the good young goalies coming up."[18]

2004-05

The 2004-05 season was canceled when the league and its players failed to come to terms on a new collective bargaining agreement. The NHL had the dubious distinction of becoming

"ALIMONY DEMANDED FROM YOUR WIFE: $9 MILLION"

DURING A game in the 2003 playoffs, a fan held up a handwritten sign that read, "Tickets to a Stanley Cup playoff game: $95. Alimony demanded from your wife: $9 million. Sex with your sister-in-law: Priceless." The message, a cheeky nod to a popular TV commercial, poked fun at Brodeur's marital woes. His wife, Melanie DuBois, had just filed for divorce; Brodeur had been having an affair with her brother's wife, who had been helping Martin and Melanie take care of the couple's four young children—Anthony, William, Jeremy and Annabelle.

Brodeur didn't let the tumult in his personal life affect his work. He led the Devils to a Stanley Cup victory.

In March 2009, a court ordered Brodeur to pay his ex-wife $500,000 a year in alimony until 2020 and $132,000 annually in child support. In addition, DuBois was awarded $9 million in assets. Today, Brodeur is married to his former sister-in-law, Genevieve Nault, with whom he has a son, Maxime.

Brodeur has admitted to seeing that sign back in 2003. "During the Devils' first-round series against Boston, and in the second round against Tampa Bay, fans in both cities had taunted me with chants and signs," he wrote in his autobiography, "some of which were vicious and some of which were pretty creative, I have to admit."[28]

the first professional sports league in North America to lose an entire season because of a labor dispute.

When the dispute was settled in the summer of 2005, the league introduced new rules intended to generate more offense. Passes would be allowed to cross two lines, the offensive zone would be enlarged and obstruction would be minimized. Also, behind the goal line goaltenders would no longer be allowed to play the puck outside a designated area in back of the net. The so-called trapezoid was delineated by two diagonal lines that started at the goal line just outside each post and ran diagonally out to the boards. It was good news for forwards but not for goalies like Brodeur and the Stars' Marty Turco who excelled at handling the puck and wandered far from the net. Brodeur cried foul, insisting the rule had been introduced by general managers of teams that didn't have good puck-handling goalies. He was sure it had been an attempt to level the playing field. "If they had 30 Martin Brodeurs out there, that rule wouldn't be there," he said. "Nobody would have voted for it."[19]

With goalies no longer able to handle the puck along the back boards and defensemen less able to hold up attacking forwards—because of the crackdown on obstruction—defensemen were being splattered against the boards like snowballs on a windowpane. At a meeting in 2009, general managers considered eliminating the so-called Brodeur rule to cut down on the number of serious injuries to defensemen—but the proposal was rejected.

2005-06

In February 2006, Brodeur was solid in net for Team Canada at the Winter Olympics, especially in a 3–2 win over the Czech Republic. But the team failed to win a medal in Torino.

When the NHL season resumed, Brodeur faced more disappointment. Although he recorded more wins (43) than any other goalie, the Devils (101 points) were eliminated in the conference semifinal by the Hurricanes (112 points).

2006-07

The Devils continued to underwhelm their fans in the 2006–07 season. They finished second in their conference and sixth overall, with 107 points, but were eliminated in the conference semifinal once again, this time by the Senators (105 points).

But Brodeur had an exceptional campaign, recording more wins (48) and shutouts (12) than any of his peers. Among starters, he finished third in save percentage (.922) and goals-against average (2.18). He won his third Vezina Trophy just a few weeks after his 35th birthday, edging out upstart Vancouver Canucks goalie Roberto Luongo. "I'm hanging in there with the young guy so it's good," a smiling Brodeur said about his 28-year-old rival. "I love playing this game and I try to play as hard as I can every game and every year."[20]

2007-08

Brodeur thumbed his nose at critics who said he was too long in the tooth to keep up the pace. He played in all but five of the Devils' 82 regular season games in the 2007–08 season and had the second-most wins (44) in the league.

The Devils finished third in their conference and sixth overall in the standings (99 points) and clashed with the Rangers (97 points) in the conference quarter-final. It was a memorable series—in a most peculiar way. During a Rangers power play in Game 3, forward Sean Avery skated to the front of the Devils net and, facing Brodeur, began dancing side to side and waving his stick in the air, looking like a majorette on speed. Brodeur juked and jived trying to keep his eye on the puck and then, when he reached his breaking point, he raised his hands and gave Avery a little shove.

If the Rangers' renowned pest had pulled that stunt in front of Belfour, odds are he would have ended up in hospital. If he had done that in front of Hextall, he may have ended up in a morgue. But Brodeur is nothing if not even-tempered. "What

[Avery] did wasn't what hockey is all about, and we'll leave it at that," the goalie said with a shrug.[21]

Devils coaches were irate, and even some of Avery's teammates were disgusted by his behavior. "It's not in the spirit of the game," Rangers goalie Steve Valiquette said. "It worked and it's effective, but it's a gentleman's game, much like golf. I wouldn't have been happy if it had happened to me. I probably would have reacted a little differently. Sean would have been picking his teeth up off the ice if it was me."[22]

The NHL promptly revised its unsportsmanlike conduct rule.

> "Playing goal could make you crazy. I think that's what the position could do to you after a while because it's such a mental game."
>
> **MARTIN BRODEUR**

The Devils won that game, 4–3, but it was their only victory of the series. New York dispatched the Devils in five games and advanced to the conference semifinal. The Devils headed to the golf course.

Brodeur dropped in at the NHL awards ceremony in Toronto that June to collect his fourth Vezina Trophy. Appearing as "gracious as always," he suggested that Vezina might be his last. "It's a great honor. The older you get, you see all these young guys coming up and dominating the nets," he said. "It's always nice to be able to compete with these guys... I know every year I say, 'Maybe this will be the last,' but maybe this is the last."[23]

2008-11

If a year in a dog's life is the equivalent to seven in the life of a human, it could be said that one year in an NHL player's career is equivalent to 1.7 years in the career of another professional—which means that, in hockey years, Brodeur was 61 years old when he fastened his goalie pads to start the 2008–09 season. His age finally became a factor on the ice.

During a game in November 2008, he skated off the ice with an injury. He dismissed it as a bruised elbow, but it turned out to be a torn biceps tendon. "I drove myself to the hospital," he recalled. "I was changing the gears with the stick shift with one hand. It didn't seem to be a big deal. But when I saw the guy's face [at the hospital], I knew it wasn't good. It definitely was a shock."[24] Brodeur underwent surgery on November 6 and sat on the sidelines for almost four months. He played just 38 games in the 2008–09 season, including the playoffs. Until then, he had missed just 15 NHL games for health reasons.

A year later, he competed in another Winter Olympics. But he didn't play a pivotal role this time. He was in Team Canada's net for a 3–2 shootout victory over Switzerland, but after his second game in Vancouver, a 5–3 loss to the United States, Luongo took over as the starter and helped the Canadians win the gold medal.

> "Brodeur is probably the most well-adjusted, happiest-seeming person I have ever met, so normal that's it's a little eerie."[29]
>
> Reporter **CHARLES MCGRATH**

Yet Brodeur kept on truckin'—and the more games he added to his career total, the more records he set. During a game against the Chicago Blackhawks in March 2009, he broke the record in wins (551), which had been set by Roy. When the game ended in a 3–2 win for the Devils, Brodeur leapt into the air and pumped his right fist, as the sellout crowd chanted, "Mart-ee! Mart-ee!" His teammates congratulated him and helped him cut down the net, which he kept as a souvenir. Nine months later, he broke the regular-season shutout record (103) in a 4–0 win over the Pittsburgh Penguins. The old record had been set by Terry Sawchuk, who had posted his last shutout in February 1970, just a few months before his death.

Brodeur ended the 2009–10 season with more wins (45) and shutouts (9) than any of his peers. He also had the third-best goals-against average (2.24) among starters and won his fifth Jennings Trophy.

After being eliminated in the conference quarter-final in two straight seasons, the Devils saw their fortunes turn from bad to worse in the 2010–11 campaign. They tumbled down the standings and, despite a strong second half, missed the playoffs for the first time in 15 years. "What we did in the second half, I think as a fan, as a player, you have to be really pleased," Brodeur said, looking on the bright side. "There are positive things that can get translated to next year. I know I'm excited."[25]

2011-12

The Devils managed to regain their equilibrium the following season, finishing fourth in their conference and eighth overall, with 102 points. They beat the Florida Panthers (94 points) and the Flyers (103 points) before taking on the Rangers (109 points) in the conference final. It was a tough series—and one that included a first for Brodeur.

With the Devils leading the fourth game 3–0, Rangers forward Mike Rupp leapt in the air and slammed into the Devils' Peter Harrold behind the Devils net. A penalty was called. On his way to the box, Rupp skated past the Devils net and shoved his glove into Brodeur's face. The surprised goalie fell backwards into the crossbar and then stood impassively as opposing players pushed and shoved each other for a few minutes.

After the game, a Devils victory, Brodeur appeared at a televised press conference with Devils captain Zach Parise. When a reporter asked the goalie if he had been hurt on the play, Brodeur was quick to respond. "Mark," he said, grinning at the reporter, "I'm a tough guy." But he admitted he had been caught off guard. "I just didn't expect it. It was the first time in my career… It surprised me more than anything," he said. "But now I know I can take a punch."

The Devils won the series in six games and then faced off against the Los Angeles Kings (95 points) in the Cup final. New

Jersey lost the first three games, two of them in overtime, but clawed their way back into the series by winning the next two. Bolstered by their hot young goalie, Jonathan Quick, the Kings defeated the Devils 6-1 in Game 6—and won the first Cup in franchise history.

It was a heartbreaking loss for the Devils, who had hoped to make one of the biggest comebacks in finals history, but Brodeur didn't get his knickers in a twist. When asked what Quick had said to him when the two shook hands at the end of the series, Brodeur replied: "He wanted to make sure I don't retire," he said, laughing. "I guess he likes beating me."[26]

2012-13

Brodeur had just turned 40, but he wasn't ready to hang up his skates. He signed a two-year contract with the Devils and was back in net for the 2012–13 season, which didn't start until January because of another labor dispute.

In February, he pinched a nerve in his upper back and sat on the sidelines for a month. But he reached another plateau in his first game back. Carolina Hurricanes forward Jordan Staal was in the Devils end during a delayed penalty when he banged the puck off the boards, intending to send it back to a teammate on the blue line. Instead, the puck slid all the way down the ice and into the Hurricanes net, which their goalie had vacated to get an extra attacker on the ice. Because Brodeur was the last Devils player to have touched the puck, he was credited with the goal, becoming the only NHL goalie to score three.

> "I have my own quirky habits… but not for people to know about."
>
> **MARTIN BRODEUR**

"When the puck went in the net, I was like, 'Whoa, what happened there?'" said Brodeur. "I didn't even know we had a delayed penalty or anything," he said, beaming. "So it was a little surprising, and then [Ilya Kovalchuk] said, 'You scored the goal!'"[27]

No one was happier for Brodeur than Daneyko. "You know, some goalies are kind of quirky, but not Marty. He's just a fun guy to be around," he says. "He's a special player and a special person, no question."

BRODEUR · ALL-TIME RANKING*

REGULAR SEASON			PLAYOFFS		
GAMES	WINS	SO	GAMES	WINS	SO
1,220 [1st]	669 [1st]	121 [1st]	205 [2nd]	113 [2nd]	24 [1st]

* statistics as of July 2, 2013.

> NHL ALL-ROOKIE TEAM **(1ST)**: 1993–94

> NHL ALL-STAR TEAM **(1ST)**: 2002–03, 2003–04, 2006–07

> NHL ALL-STAR TEAM **(2ND)**: 1996–97, 1997–98, 2005–06, 2007–08

||||||||||||||||||||||||||||||||||||||||||

NOTES

||||||||||||||||||||||||||||||||||||||||||

CHAPTER 1

The Tortured Soul: Terry Sawchuk

1 At the time, the Chicago Blackhawks were known as the "Black Hawks"; the one-word name was officially adopted in 1986. For consistency, however, the one-word name is used throughout this book.

2 Dink Carroll, Playing the Field, *Gazette* (Montreal), October 10, 1950.

3 Milt Dunnell, Speaking on Sport, *Toronto Daily Star*, March 28, 1952.

4 Associated Press, "Red Wings Win Stanley Cup on Leswick's Overtime Goal," April 17, 1954.

5 David Dupuis, *Sawchuk: The Troubles and Triumphs of the World's Greatest Goalie* (Toronto: Stoddart, 1998), 96.

6 Associated Press, "Sawchuk Facing Life Suspension," January 17, 1957.

7 Associated Press, "Sawchuk 'Mad'; Threatens Suit of Four Papers," January 18, 1957.

8 Dupuis, *Sawchuk*, 119.

9 Associated Press, "Sawchuk Returns to Detroit Nets," June 11, 1957.

10 Milt Dunnell, "Available and Uncomfortable," *Toronto Daily Star*, May 2, 1967.

11 Jim Coleman, World of Sport, *Calgary Herald*, April 17, 1967.

12 "Leafs Topple Hawks in Chicago: Who Said No Place like Home?" *Vancouver Sun*, April 17, 1967.

13 Red Burnett, "Tired Terry Sawchuk Says, 'It Has to Be the Greatest Thrill,'" *Toronto Daily Star*, May 3, 1967.

14 Gump Worsley and Tim Moriarty, *They Call Me Gump* (New York: Dodd, Mead, 1975), 85

15 Ken Campbell, "Comparing the New and Former Shutout Kings," *Hockey News* blog, December 21, 2009, http://www.thehockeynews.com/articles/29948-THNcom-Blog-Comparing-the-new-and-former-shutout-kings.html.

CHAPTER 2
The Trooper: Glenn Hall

1 Jim Proudfoot, "Mr. Goalie, Sports Hall, Perfect Mesh," *Toronto Star*, October 29, 1993.

2 Gord Fisher, "Glenn Hall Insists Retirement for Real," *Edmonton Journal*, September 21, 1966.

3 Glenn Hall, "Painting the Barn: Glenn Hall," *Legends of Hockey*, season 2, episode 1, directed by Derik Murray (Vancouver: Network Entertainment, 2000), DVD.

4 Ibid.

5 Tom Adrahtas, *The Man They Call Mr. Goalie: Glenn Hall* (Kingston, RI: Albion Press, 2003), 88.

6 Mark Lukens, Mark Lukens' Sports, *Reading Eagle* (Reading, PA), January 15, 1989.

7 Douglas Hunter, *A Breed Apart: An Illustrated History of Goaltending* (Toronto: Penguin, 1995), 114.

8 Associated Press, "Hawks Down Loop Champs; Reach Finals," April 5, 1961.

9 Canadian Press, "Hawks Found Goals Scarce in Montreal," May 3, 1965.

10 Brian McFarlane, *Brian McFarlane's Original Six: The Blackhawks* (Toronto: Stoddart, 2000), 100.

11 E.M. Swift, "Iron Man of the Ice," *Sports Illustrated*, October 27, 1992.

12 Dan Moulton, *Chicago's American*, November 8, 1962.

13 Jim Barber, *Great Goaltenders: Stars of Hockey's Golden Age* (Canmore, AB: Altitude, 2006), 100

14 Brian McFarlane, *Brian McFarlane's Original Six: The Red Wings* (Toronto: Stoddart, 2000), 57.

15 Brian McFarlane, *Brian McFarlane's Original Six: The Blackhawks* (Toronto: Stoddart, 2000), 84.

16 Fisher, "Hall Insists Retirement for Real."

17 Canadian Press, "Glenn Hall: How Glad?" June 8, 1967.

18 Associated Press, "Farmer Hall Most Valuable Hockey Player," May 14, 1968.

19 Hal Walker, World Of Sport, *Calgary Herald*, May 8, 1968.

20 "St. Louis Goalie Hall Is Retiring, Coach Says," *Miami News*, June 7, 1969.

21 "A Trip Down Memory Lane with Glenn Hall," *Calgary Herald*, May 6, 1986.

22 Jim Coleman, *Windsor Star*, April 13, 1973.

23 Canadian Press, "Hall Won't Sue Bookie," April 16, 1973.

24 "A Trip Down Memory Lane," *Calgary Herald*.

25 David Haugh, "Blackhawks' 'Mr. Goalie' on NHL Today: 'It's a Goon Game,'" *Chicago Tribune*, May 21, 2009.

CHAPTER 3
The Maverick: Jacques Plante

1 Pat Curran, "Hodge Available if Plante's Asthma Acts Up," *Gazette* (Montreal), March 28, 1963.

2 United Press International, "Bisons Find Star in Amazing Goalie," January 12, 1953.

3 Canadian Press, "No Changes by Hawks or Canucks," April 7, 1953.

4 Ibid.

5 Ibid.

6 Canadian Press, "Mazur Flashy in Canadien Win," April 8, 1953.

7 Canadian Press, "Gerry McNeil Decides to Retire From Hockey," September 28, 1954.

8 Milt Dunnell, Speaking on Sport, *Toronto Daily Star*, April 11, 1956.

9 Canadian Press, "Canadiens Retain Grip on Stanley Cup," April 17, 1957.

10 Dunnell, Speaking on Sport, April 18, 1957.

11 "Blake Praises Both Teams," *Calgary Herald*, April 21, 1958.

12 "Masked Plante Makes History," *Vancouver Sun*, November 2, 1959.

13 Associated Press, "Jacques Plante Dons Mask as Canadiens Top Rangers," November 2, 1959.

14 Ibid.

15 Ibid.

16 "Punch at Referee Cost Blake $2,000," *Milwaukee Journal*, March 28, 1961.

17 Ibid.

18 Canadian Press, "Canadien Goalie Not Disappointed," June 5, 1963.

19 United Press International, "Life Begins at Forty: Plante Makes Comeback," June 25, 1968.

20 Canadian Press, "Plante, Plager Missing as Cup Action Resumes," May 5, 1970.

21 Ibid.

22 Associated Press, "St. Louis Blues Trade Plante," May 26, 1970.

23 Dan Proudfoot, "Jacques Plante: Alone into the Twilight," *Winnipeg Free Press Weekend Magazine*, March 15, 1975.

24 Ibid.

25 Canadian Press, "Hockey Mourns Loss of Legend," February 28, 1986.

26 Proudfoot, "Jacques Plante: Alone into the Twilight."

27 Tim Burke, "Ex-Mates Remember Plante as a Loner Who Did Things His Way," *Gazette* (Montreal), February 28, 1986.

CHAPTER 4
The Joker: Gump Worsley

1 Dave Stubbs, "Worsley Remembered as a Top Goalie with a Ready Wit," *Gazette* (Montreal), January 30, 2007.

2 Associated Press, "Hall of Fame Goalie 'Gump' Worsley Dies," January 29, 2007.

3 Jim Coleman, "The One and Only: Gump Worsley," *Legends of Hockey*, season 2, episode 1, directed by Derik Murray (Vancouver: Network Entertainment, 2000), DVD.

4 Worsley and Moriarty, *They Call Me Gump*, 29 (see chap. 1, n. 14).

5 Ibid., 36.

6 Ibid., 40.

7 Ibid., 39.

8 Stan Fischler, "The One and Only: Gump Worsley."

9 William J. Briordy, "Goalie Hit by Disk in 5–2 Game Here," *New York Times*, February 6, 1961.

10 Stan Fischler with Chico Resch, *Hot Goalies* (Toronto: Warwick, 1997), 201.

11 Canadian Press, "'Missed Too Many Chances,' Says Toe," April 23, 1965.

12 Worsley and Moriarty, *They Call Me Gump*, 71.

13 Ibid., 73.

14 Jim Coleman, World of Sport, *Calgary Herald*, May 6, 1966.

15 Stevie Cameron, ed., *Hockey Hall of Fame Book of Goalies* (Richmond Hill, ON: Firefly, 2010), 90.

16 "Canadiens Take Hockey Cup; Blues Beaten," *New York Times*, May 12, 1968.

17 Worsley and Moriarty, *They Call Me Gump*, 86.

18 Jim Souhan, "Lorne (Gump) Worsley; 1929-2007; 'My Face Is My Mask,'" *Star Tribune* (Minneapolis, MN), January 29, 2007.

19 Ibid.

20 Jim Proudfoot, "An Old Goalie Explains How You Find One," *Toronto Star*, February 22, 1981.

21 Associated Press, "Goalies Selected for HOF Honours," June 11, 1980.

22 Canadian Press, "Four Added to Hall," September 9, 1980.

23 Associated Press, "Hall of Fame Goalie Worsley Dies," January 28, 2007.

24 Souhan, "Worsley; 'My Face Is My Mask.'"

CHAPTER 5

The Gentleman: Johnny Bower

1 "Bower Named to Hall of Fame," *Toronto Star*, June 9, 1976.

2 Johnny Bower and Bob Duff, *The China Wall: The Timeless Legend of Johnny Bower* (Bolton, ON: Fenn, 2008), 13.

3 Associated Press, "'Never Gave Me a Chance' says Bower of Phil Watson," October 28, 1958.

4 Milt Dunnell, Speaking on Sport, *Toronto Daily Star*, December 1, 1960.

5 Canadian Press, "Leafs Headed for Cup—Imlach," April 8, 1959.

6 Red Burnett, "Punch Leaves Decision to Players," *Toronto Daily Star*, April 20, 1959.

7 Jim Proudfoot, "Wings Must Find Antidote for Kelly-Mahovlich Poison," *Toronto Daily Star*, March 29, 1960.

8 Red Burnett, "Leafs Call Up McNamara to Replace Injured Bower," *Toronto Daily Star*, February 13, 1961.

9 Red Burnett, "Bower's First Move Is to Greet Gump," *Toronto Daily Star*, April 6, 1962.

10 Ibid.

11 United Press International, "Imlach Attributes Success to Centres," April 23, 1962.

12 Red Burnett, "Forget the Score, Bower Big Story as Habs Subside," *Toronto Daily Star*, April 5, 1963.

13 Ibid.

14 Canadian Press, "Bower Loses Fight over Fallen Foes," January 11, 1964.

15 Ibid.

16 Bower and Duff, *The China Wall*, 96.

17 Dave Perkins, "Old Leafs Salute Johnny Bower," *Toronto Star*, June 4, 2009.

18 Bower and Duff, *The China Wall*, 97.

19 Ibid., 111.

20 Canadian Press, "Leafs Come Through in Clutch as High-Flying Hawks Stumble," April 19, 1967.

21 Milt Dunnell, "The Goalies are Bellsheep," *Toronto Daily Star*, April 24, 1967.

22 Jim Proudfoot, "'Bower Is the World's Greatest,' Says Genial Punch after 3–2 Win," *Toronto Daily Star*, April 26, 1967.

23 Associated Press, "Leafs Call On Terry; Rivals Make Merry," April 28, 1967.

24 Milt Dunnell, "The Sentimental Side of Punch," *Toronto Daily Star*, May 3, 1967.

25 Red Burnett, "Punch's Tribute to Bower," *Toronto Daily Star*, May 3, 1967.

26 Red Burnett, "Imlach Fired—Clancy, Bower, Horton May Quit," *Toronto Daily Star*, April 7, 1969.

27 Ibid.

28 Red Burnett, "Roof Falls In to Ruin Bower's Finest Hour," *Toronto Daily Star*, December 11, 1969.

29 Canadian Press, "Bower Retires," March 20, 1970.

30 Jim Proudfoot, "Bower's Haste to Aid Ferguson Caused Trouble," *Toronto Star*, June 10, 1976.

31 Canadian Press, "Here's Johnny, Again!" January 9, 1980.

32 Ibid.

33 Tristan Hopper, "Vintage Leaf Legend Puts His Name on Line of Wine," *National Post* (Toronto), June 1, 2011.

34 Dave Stubbs, "Bower's Flattered by Recognition," *Gazette* (Montreal), March 29, 2011.

35 Red Burnett, "Hull Is Fastest NHL Shooter," *Toronto Daily Star*, November 12, 1960.

36 Red Burnett, "Leaf Goalie Is a 'Cracked Bass,'" *Toronto Daily Star*, November 20, 1965.

37 Bower and Duff, *The China Wall*, 117.

38 Ibid., 118.

CHAPTER 6
The Bon Vivant: Bernie Parent

1 Bill Bennett, "Parent Keeps Bombers Hopes Alive," *Gazette* (Montreal), March 25, 1963.

2 Bill Warwick, "Three Stars," *Edmonton Journal*, May 15, 1965.

3 Associated Press, "Hull Too Much for Boston," December 2, 1965.

4 Kevin Allen and Bob Duff, *Without Fear: Hockey's 50 Greatest Goaltenders* (Chicago: Triumph Books, 2002), 194.

5 Evan Weiner, "Has the NHL Ever Recovered From The WHA's Formation?" *NewJerseyNewsroom.com*, October 11, 2012, http://ns1.newjerseynewsroom.com/professional/has-the-nhl-ever-recovered-from-the-whas-formation.

6 "Goalie Parent Bolts Blazers," *Milwaukee Journal*, April 9, 1973.

7 Bernie Parent and Stan Hochman, *Unmasked: Bernie Parent and the Broad Street Bullies* (Chicago: Triumph Books, 2012), 90.

8 Allen and Duff, *Without Fear*, 196.

9 Jay Greenberg, "Where Are They Now?: Bernie Parent," *PhillyBurbs. com*, December 22, 2011, http://phillyburbs.csnphilly.com/12/25/11/ Where-Are-They-Now-Bernie-Parent/phillyburbs_landing_flyers. html?blockID=618610.

10 "Spotlight: Pinnacle," Hockey Hall of Fame website, http://www.hhof. com/htmlSpotlight/spot_pinnaclep198403.shtml.

11 Jim Proudfoot, "Canadiens Win Not All Finesse but It Did Help," *Toronto Star*, May 18, 1976.

12 United Press International, "Eye Injury Forces Flyer Goalie Parent to Retire," June 1, 1979.

13 Associated Press, "Parent's Eye Injury Forces His Retirement," June 1, 1979.

14 Associated Press, "Parent to Coach Flyers Goalies," September 5, 1979.

15 Associated Press, "Parent Kicks Liquor Habit," June 28, 1980.

16 United Press International, "Parent, Esposito into Hockey's Hall," June 6, 1984.

17 Dick Irvin, *In the Crease: Goaltenders Look at Life in the NHL* (Toronto: McClelland & Stewart, 1996), 100.

18 Michael Vitez, "Flyers to Honor Kate Smith with Statue," *Philly.com*, June 6, 1987, http://articles.philly.com/1987-06-06/news/26185230_1_kate-smith-flyers-president-jay-snider-flyers-first.

19 Frank Seravalli, "After 41 Years, Goalie Mask of Flyers Legend Parent Turns Up," *Philly.com*, June 7, 2012, http://articles.philly.com/2012-06-07/sports/32079855_1_mask-jacques-plante-private-collector.

20 Knight Ridder Newspapers, "Pelle, Like All Goalies, Was 'a Different Breed,'" November 12, 1985.

CHAPTER 7

The Scholar: Ken Dryden

1 Jim McKay, "He Made Believers," *Windsor Star*, May 18, 1976.

2 Jack Olsen, "Banned in Boston, Knighted in Montreal," *Sports Illustrated*, October 18, 1971.

3 Canadian Press, "Canadiens Lose Dryden to Nats," July 16, 1969.

4 Maurice Smith, "Time Out," *Winnipeg Free Press*, July 17, 1969.

5 Jim Coleman, *Calgary Herald*, December 10, 1969.

6 Harold Kaese, "Ashley Let Game Get out of Hand," *Boston Globe*, April 8, 1971.

7 "Goalkeeping Saves Bostonians," *Vancouver Sun*, April 8, 1971.

8 Jim Coleman, World of Sport, *Calgary Herald*, April 12, 1971.

9 Ken Dryden, "Honour Role: Ken Dryden," *Legends of Hockey*, season 2, episode 2, directed by Derik Murray (Vancouver: Network Entertainment, 2000), DVD.

10 Ibid.

11 Canadian Press, "While Ed Was Laughing, Ken Cried," April 14, 1972.

12 Canadian Press, "Ken, Brian Don't Underestimate Soviets," August 30, 1972.

13 Gerald Eskenazi, "Soviet Sextet Downs Canada, 7–3," *New York Times*, September 3, 1972.

14 Tim Burke, "They Beat Us Almost Everywhere—Sinden," *Gazette* (Montreal), September 4, 1972.

15 Jack Dulmage, "Fans' Boos Compound Dreadful Spectacle," *Windsor Star*, September 9, 1972.

16 Frank Orr, "Players Blast Critical Fans, Press," *Toronto Star*, September 9, 1972.

17 "Russ Coach Expects Stronger Opposition," *Calgary Herald*, September 21, 1972.

18 Canadian Press, "Trudeau, Stanfield, Sharp Praise Team," September 29, 1972.

19 Ken Dryden, "Honour Role: Ken Dryden."

20 Associated Press, "Stanley Cup Is Returned to Montreal Where All Loyal Canadiens Insist It Rightly Belongs," May 11, 1973.

21 Canadian Press, "Dryden Rejects Habs for Return to Law," September 15, 1973.

22 Tim Burke, "'System' Hockey in Future Is Coach Bowman's View," *Gazette* (Montreal), May 9, 1975.

23 Al Strachan, "Now That's How You Play Hockey, Comrade!" *Gazette* (Montreal), January 2, 1976.

24 Tim Burke, "A Night of Nights for the Canadiens," *Gazette* (Montreal), January 2, 1976.

25 "Ken Dryden Leads Montreal's March," *Christian Science Monitor*, May 16, 1976.

26 Ken Dryden, "Honour Role: Ken Dryden."

27 United Press International, "The End: Dryden Quits Hockey," July 10, 1979.

28 Hubert Bauch, "Ken Dryden: The Problems of Being a Political Activist," *Gazette* (Montreal), January 13, 1979.

29 Dave Stubbs, "Lach, Bouchard Join Other Habs Greats in Arena Rafters," *Gazette* (Montreal), December 5, 2009.

30 Allen and Duff, *Without Fear*, 136.
31 Hubert Bauch, "Ken Dryden: The Problems of Being a Political Activist," *Gazette* (Montreal), January 13, 1979.
32 Jack Olsen, "Banned in Boston, Knighted in Montreal," *Sports Illustrated*, October 18, 1971.

CHAPTER 8
The Warrior: Ron Hextall

1 Christine Brennan, "Hextall Wields Big Stick; Flyers Goalie Is Fierce P rotector of His Domain," *Washington Post*, April 6, 1988.
2 "Whalers Irate over Turgeon Arm Injury," *Record-Journal* (Meriden, CT), August 13, 1987.
3 Bob Kravitz, "Old Block, Quite a Chip," *Sports Illustrated*, December 1, 1986.
4 Jay Greenberg, "What Makes Ron Hextall Tick…Tick…Tick," *Sports Illustrated*, November 13, 1989.
5 Associated Press, "Flyers' Keenan Turns Off Oilers," October 10, 1986.
6 "Violence Persists as League Fails to Take Action," *Washington Post*, January 27, 1987.
7 Jeff Jacobs, "Meanwhile, Flyers Have Montreal on Edge," *Hartford Courant*, May 12, 1987.
8 "Oiler Seeks Suspension for Hextall Two-Hander," *Toronto Star*, May 25, 1987.
9 "NHL Playoffs: Flyers Feisty under Pressure," *New York Times*, May 26, 1987.
10 Associated Press, "Flyers Finally Even with Oilers in Series," May 30, 1987.
11 Chuck Finder, "Hextall Wins Spot in History," *Pittsburgh Post-Gazette*, June 2, 1987.
12 Ibid.
13 Kravitz, "Old Block, Quite A Chip."
14 Alex Yannis, "NHL Notebook; Flyer Goalie's Goal: 'A Matter of When,'" *New York Times*, December 10, 1987.
15 Bill Modoono, "Hextall Soaks Up Fans' Abuse, but He Isn't Throwing in Towel," *Pittsburgh Press*, April 26, 1989.
16 Francis Rosa, "Flyers Took Parting Shot," *Boston Globe*, May 13, 1989.
17 Irvin, *In the Crease*, 250 (see chap. 6, n. 17).
18 Associated Press, "Pride Pushes Habs to Limit in Series Win," June 3, 1993.
19 Les Bowen, "Hextall Holds Back Temper and Tampa," *Philadelphia Daily News*, April 26, 1996.
20 Associated Press, "No More Games in Goal for Flyers' Ron Hextall," September 7, 1999.
21 Sports Network, "Kings Hire Hextall as Assistant GM," June 13, 2006.

22 Dan Rosen, "Hextall Finally Gets Pleasure of Winning the Cup," NHL website, June 12, 2012, http://www.nhl.com/ice/news.htm?id=634429.

23 David W. Unkle, "Flyers Honoree Hextall Grateful to Clarke," SLAM *Sports*, February 6, 2008, http://slam.canoe.ca/Slam/Hockey/NHL/Philadel-phia/2008/02/06/pf-4831486.html.

24 Andy Lytle, "Cup Hopes Shattered by 'Pest' Trio in Overtime," *Toronto Daily Star*, April 15, 1940.

25 "Flyers Have Gotten New Life," *Boston Globe*, May 11, 1989.

26 The official site of the Hockey Hall of Fame; the website of the Hockey Hall of Fame; "Spotlight: One on One With Billy Smith"; http://www.hhof.com/htmlSpotlight/spot_oneononep199304.shtml.

CHAPTER 9
The Cock of the Walk: Patrick Roy

1 Rick Sadowski, "Roy Ready to Deck the Hall; Ex-Avalanche Goalie Will Receive Honor in First Year Possible," *Rocky Mountain News* (Denver, CO), November 13, 2006.

2 Woody Paige, "Roy Could Have Made Another Big Splash as Swimmer," *DenverPost.com*, October 18, 2000, http://extras.denverpost.com/scolumns/paige1018.htm.

3 Guy Robillard, "Patrick Roy et Moffett devant la cage du Canadien," *Le Devoir* (Montreal), September 21, 1984.

4 Joe O'Connor, "Patrick Roy: Former Canadiens Coach Jean Perron Looks Back," National Post, November 14, 2006.

5 Ibid.

6 "Canadiens Win in Overtime," *Reading Eagle* (Reading, PA), April 30, 1986.

7 Tim Burke, "Series Finale a Real Thriller," *Gazette* (Montreal), April 29, 1986.

8 United Press International, "Overtime Goal Lifts Montreal," May 6, 1986.

9 O'Connor, "Patrick Roy."

10 Tom Casey, "Roy's Selection as Playoff MVP Tickles Perron," *Ottawa Citizen*, May 26, 1986.

11 Bob Kravitz, "King of the Kiddie Corps," *Sports Illustrated*, October 13, 1986.

12 Associated Press, "The Record Book," October 22, 1987.

13 Francis Rosa, "Flames Savor Cup," *Boston Globe*, May 27, 1989.

14 Damien Cox, "The Year Gretzky Wasn't MVP," *Toronto Star*, June 6, 1990.

15 E.M. Swift, "Saving Grace," *Sports Illustrated*, June 21, 1993.

16 Frank Orr, "Nordiques Use a Quick Start and Maturity to Defeat Habs," *Toronto Star*, April 21, 1993.

17 Jennifer Frey, "Only Thing Roy Can't Stop Is Praise for His Goaltending," *New York Times*, June 10, 1993.

18 Jim Kelley, "Roy Was Difference in Habs and Hab-Nots," *Buffalo News*, June 10, 1993.

19 Robyn Norwood, "Montreal Feels Impact of Stanley Cup," *Los Angeles Times*, June 10, 1993.

20 Irvin, *In the Crease*, 272 (see chap. 6, n. 17).

21 Bob Ryan, "Masterpiece in Stop-Action," *Boston Globe*, April 27, 1994.

22 Ibid.

23 Adam Kimelman, "Roy Reigns as NHL's Greatest Goalie," NHL website, November 16, 2008, http://www.nhl.com/ice/news.htm?id=392419.

24 "Roy Does a Flip for Tremblay," *Buffalo News*, February 6, 1996.

25 Dan Bickley, "Avalanche Wouldn't Get Snowed Under," *Chicago Sun-Times*, May 9, 1996.

26 Jeff Kass and Holly Kurtz, "Hockey Star Arrested: Patrick Roy Spends Six Hours in Jail after Dispute with Wife Brought In Police," *Rocky Mountain News* (Denver, CO) October 23, 2000.

27 Associated Press, "Roy Has No Regrets about Decision To Retire," May 29, 2003.

28 Associated Press, "Hockey Hall of Fame Welcomes Roy, Brooks," November 14, 2006.

29 Postmedia News, "Canadiens Haven't Contacted Patrick Roy about Potential Coaching Job," April 20, 2012.

30 Harrison Mooney, "Avalanche Officially Name Patrick Roy Head Coach, as well as VP of Hockey Operations," *Puck Daddy* (blog), Yahoo Sports, May 23, 2013, http://sports.yahoo.com/blogs/nhl-puck-daddy/avalanche-officially-name-patrick-roy-head-coach-well-212844194.html.

31 Tom Casey, "Roy's Selection as Playoff MVP Tickles Perron," *Ottawa Citizen*, May 26, 1986.

CHAPTER 10
The Fanatic: Ed Belfour

1 Scott Burnside, "Ed Belfour's Manic Dedication," ESPN website, November 11, 2011, http://espn.go.com/dallas/nhl/story/_/id/7213314/2011-hockey-hall-fame-look-inductee-ed-belfour.

2 Mike Kiley, "Hawks' Belfour Hasn't Outgrown Feisty Manner," *Chicago Tribune*, March 8, 1991.

3 Doug Harrison, "Sweden Feels Like Home to Belfour," CBC Sports website, January 29, 2008, http://www.cbc.ca/sports/indepth/feature-hockey-belfourqa.html.

4 QMI Agency, "Carman's Ed Belfour to Be Part of Hockey Hall Of Fame," June 29, 2011, http://slam.canoe.ca/Slam/Hockey/ nhl/2011/06/29/18349476.html.

5 Mike Perricone. "Mason Eager to Take On Job as Hawks' Top Goalie," *Chicago Sun-Times*, June 19, 1987.

6 Mike Perricone, "Can Belfour Stand Out in Hawk Crowd?" *Chicago Sun-Times*, October 20, 1988.

7 Herb Gould, "Hawks Flunk Final Tuneup: Goalie Picture Remains Unclear," *Chicago Sun-Times*, October 1, 1990.

8 Herb Gould, "Belfour Sparking Hawks," *Chicago Sun-Times*, December 8, 1990.

9 Herb Gould, "Hawks, Belfour Get Hook: Yanking Ticks Off Goalie; He Faces Off With Keenan," *Chicago Sun-Times*, December 10, 1990.

10 Associated Press, "Early Exit Leaves Blackhawks with Bad Taste," April 16, 1991.

11 Herb Gould, "Belfour's 1st Year Is Rich in Rewards: Goalie Earns Vezina and Calder Trophies." *Chicago Sun-Times*, June 6, 1991.

12 Herb Gould, "Sabres Humble Brawling Hawks," *Chicago Sun-Times*, March 23, 1992.

13 Dave Sell, "Determined Penguins Sweep Up 2nd Straight Cup," *Washington Post*, June 2, 1992.

14 Tim Sassone, "The Eagle Speaks Out: Belfour Takes His Shots at Hawks Bosses over Contract," *Daily Herald* (Arlington Heights, IL), December 28, 1996.

15 Tim Sassone, "Time Is Right For Hawks to Deal Belfour," *Daily Herald* (Arlington Heights, IL), December 31, 1996.

16 Brian Hanley, "Negatives in the Net: Goaltender Belfour Growing Gloomy during Slump," *Chicago Sun-Times*, January 8, 1997.

17 Brian Hanley, "Belfour Fires Back; Accuses Hawks of Spreading Stories to Justify Deal," *Chicago Sun-Times*, February 4, 1997.

18 Sean Fitz-Gerald, "He Was Demanding but Belfour Always Delivered," *National Post*, November 14, 2011.

19 Fischler with Resch, Hot Goalies, 52 (see chap. 4, n. 10).

20 Burnside, "Ed Belfour's Manic Dedication."

21 Randy Holz, "Belfour Proves He Is Best by Shutting Down Avalanche," *Rocky Mountain News* (Denver, CO), May 28, 2000.

22 Adrian Wojnarowski, "Fantastic Finish to a Vicious Battle," *The Record* (Bergen County, NJ), June 11, 2000.

23 Dave Feschuk, "Now a Hall of Famer, Eddie Belfour Still Doing It His Way," *Toronto Star*, November 14, 2011.

24 Burnside, "Ed Belfour's Manic Dedication."

25 Feschuk, "Belfour Still Doing It His Way."

26 Herb Gould, "Belfour Gets Court Date after Traffic Violations," *Chicago Sun-Times*, December 19, 1991.

27 Bob Kravitz, "Belfour, Big Games Not a Good Mix," *Rocky Mountain News* (Denver, CO), May 22, 1999.

28 Ibid.

CHAPTER 11
The Enigma: Dominik Hasek

1 Larry Felser, "To Find a Winner, Show Me the Money Goalie," *Buffalo News*, October 5, 2000.

2 Herb Gould, "Better Defense Means Fewer Goals, More Wins," *Chicago Sun-Times*, October 3, 1990.

3 Stan Fischler, *Detroit Red Wings: Greatest Moments and Players* (New York: Sports Publishing, 2002), 136.

4 Jim Kelley, "Higher Hopes for Hasek: Vezina Nice, Hart Would Be Nicer," *Buffalo News*, June 17, 1994.

5 Michael Farber, "Headed For Trouble?" *Sports Illustrated*, May 5, 1997.

6 Jim Kelley, "Knee Sprain May Not Be the Only Thing Bothering Hasek," *Buffalo News*, April 22, 1997.

7 Farber, "Headed For Trouble?"

8 Associated Press, "Hasek Wants Nolan Fired," June 25, 1997.

9 Budd Bailey, "Nolan Stung by Cut as Contract Expires, Sabres Coach Is Told He Won't Be Retained," *Buffalo News*, July 1, 1997.

10 Jim Kelley, "Hasek Talks Peace with Sabre Teammates," *Buffalo News*, September 8, 1997.

11 Michael Madden, "Hasek Made the U.S. His Dominion," *Boston Globe*, February 19, 1998.

12 Jim Kelley, "Hasek Has It, while U.S. Team Comes Away Empty," *Buffalo News*, February 19, 1998.

13 Jay Mariotti, "World Domination in Hasek's Hands," *Chicago Sun-Times*, February 21, 1998.

14 Associated Press, "Sabres Lose Cup but Gain Respect," June 20, 1999.

15 "Hasek to Retire after Next Season; Buffalo Goalie Wants to Return to Czech Republic," *Washington Post*, July 30, 1999.

16 Melissa Geschwind, "Hasek Left the Sabres No Choice; Star Goalie Made It Clear He Wanted to Move On," *Buffalo News*, July 2, 2001.

17 Allen Wilson, "Hasek Trade Looks Like Good One for Everyone," *Buffalo News*, July 2, 2001.

18 Bob Dicesare, "Hasek Takes Driver Seat in Cup Win," *Buffalo News*, June 14, 2002.

19 Knight Ridder/Tribune News Service, "President Dominator? Hasek Popular in Homeland," August 19, 2002.

20 Tim Graham, "Competitive Fire Pulls Hasek Back to the Ice," *Buffalo News*, July 9, 2003.

21 Ibid.

22 Terry Jones, "Overpaid, Over There," *Slam Sports*, December 14, 2004, http://slam.canoe.ca/Slam/Columnists/Jones/2004/12/14/782193-sun.html.

23 Associated Press, "The Dominator Is Back in Hockeytown," August 1, 2006.

24 Associated Press, "Hasek Expected to Retire," June 9, 2008.

25 Jan Richter, "Hockey Legend Dominik Hašek Announces Retirement," Radio Praha website, October 9, 2012, http://www.radio.cz/en/section/curraffrs/hockey-legend-dominik-hasek-announces-retirement.

26 Ibid.

CHAPTER 12
The Cool Customer: Martin Brodeur

1 Michael Russo, "Winning Sets Brodeur Apart," *Star Tribune* (Minneapolis, MN), March 22, 2009.

2 "NHL Goalie Martin Brodeur Enjoys Playing, and Driving," *Wheels.ca*, February 9, 2012, http://www.wheels.ca/nhl-goalie-martin-brodeur-enjoys-playing-and-driving.

3 "NHL Player Search: Martin Pierre Brodeur," Hockey Hall of Fame website, http://www.legendsofhockey.net/LegendsOfHockey/jsp/SearchPlayer.jsp?player=18223.

4 Ibid.

5 Alex Yannis, "Kids Help Devils Clinch Playoff Berth," *New York Times*, March 27, 1992.

6 "Rats or Devils? Brodeur's Patient," *Albany Times Union* (Albany, NY), September 15, 1993.

7 Alex Yannis, "Devils Put Grown-Up Pressure on the Kid," *New York Times*, April 17, 1994.

8 "Four OTs, But It Ain't Over; Sabres Force 7th Game with 1-0 Win over Devils in 6-Plus Hours," *Washington Post*, April 29, 1994.

9 Barry Meisel, "Night the Devils Reign after Going through Hell, Heaven Is a Sip From Cup," *New York Daily News*, June 25, 1995.

10 Associated Press, "Brodeur Becomes Second Goalie to Score in Playoffs," April 19, 1997.

11 Ralph Vacchiano, "Brodeur Goal-den for Devs; Rare Tally Keeps Flyers Grounded," *New York Daily News*, February 16, 2000.

12 Dave Anderson, "2 Butterflies: One Soars; One Falters," *New York Times*, May 31, 2000.

13 Alex Yannis, "Brodeur Saved His Best for Finals," *New York Times*, June 12, 2000.

14 Mark J. Czerwinksi, "Devils Feeling Empty—Penalties Led to Downfall," *The Record* (Bergen County, NJ), June 11, 2001.

15 Associated Press, "Brodeur again Proves He's a Big-Time Goalie," February 24, 2002.

16 Canadian Press, "Brodeur Wins Vezina to Cap Perfect Season," June 13, 2003.

17 Joe Lapointe, "Brodeur Is Named League's Top Goalie," *New York Times*, June 13, 2003.

18 Associated Press, "Bolts Add to Awards," June 11, 2004.

19 Jason Diamos, "Brodeur Feels Defanged by NHL's New Rule," *New York Times*, September 16, 2005.

20 Canadian Press, "Sidney Crosby Completes Rare Triple in Winning All the Major NHL Awards," June 15, 2007.

21 Dave Caldwell, "Avery's Strategy Draws Ire of Devils," *New York Times*, April 15, 2008.

22 Associated Press, "Rangers Look Past Avery and Focus Again on Devils," April 16, 2008.

23 Richard Chere, "Brodeur Wins Vezina Trophy," *Star-Ledger* (Newark, NJ), June 12, 2008.

24 Mike Zeisberger, "Brodeur Not Thinking Records," *Toronto Sun*, February 26, 2009.

25 Associated Press, "Devils Ending an Unfamiliar One," April 11, 2011.

26 Associated Press, "Kings Goalie Jonathan Quick Is Playoff MVP," June 12, 2012.

27 Associated Press, "Devils Goaltender Martin Brodeur Scores Third Career Goal: 'It Was a Little Surprising,'" March 21, 2013.

28 Martin Brodeur and Damien Cox, *Brodeur: Beyond the Crease* (Mississauga, ON: John Wiley & Sons, 2006), 163.

29 Charles McGrath, "How Come Martin Brodeur Is Still So Good?" *New York Times*, February 21, 2013.

ACKNOWLEDGMENTS

||||||||||||||||||||||||||||||||||||||||

JUST AS IT takes a village to raise a child, it takes an entire community to produce a book. If I paid tribute to every person who contributed in some way to the creation of *Between the Pipes*, the acknowledgments section would be the length of a chapter. To save space, I am listing only those who have devoted hours of their time to the project.

Kirt Berry, Tyler Edwards, Michal Petrak and Tom Sandford helped me with research and interviews. Kirt also provided contact information for some former players, and Tom did a lot of fact checking—no small feat for a book with as many statistics as this one.

Some friends and relatives read one or two chapters each and gave me valuable feedback. They are: Ken Dodd, Howard Gilmore, Victor Gomez, Greg Meyer, Randy Potash, Emmett Shane and Irv Vinsky. Harry Schwartz and Lionel Wild deserve special thanks because they read all the chapters.

Rob Sanders has been a pleasure to work with from the outset. Everyone else at Greystone was professional and, thankfully, patient with me while working on this project. Shirarose Wilensky did an excellent job editing the manuscript—and learned more about save percentages than she thought possible—while

Peter Norman (copy editor) and Jessica Sullivan (art director) also did great work.

Hilary McMahon at Westwood Creative Artists has been incredible, not just as an agent but also as a sounding board, cheerleader and even therapist. (I'm exaggerating on that last point, but only a little.)

I could not have written this book without information gleaned from many sources, including some great books and www.hockey-reference.com, a superb source of statistical information.

I'm thankful to the dozens of NHL coaches, players, equipment managers and others who answered my many questions. Finally, I salute the goalies profiled in this book. They are not just great athletes but also compelling people. I connected with most of them and enjoyed interviewing them. To sum up the experience, I refer to the phrase Bernie Parent often used to greet reporters after his many victories: "Some fun, eh?"

PHOTO CREDITS

RANDI DRUZIN is an author and journalist. Her work has been published in the *New York Times*, *Time* magazine and the *Globe and Mail*. Druzin is the author of *The Complete Idiot's Guide to Women in Sports*, a book that traces the history of women's sports from antiquity to the present. She lives in Toronto.